STAGING SOVEREIGNTY

INSURRECTIONS: CRITICAL STUDIES IN
RELIGION, POLITICS, AND CULTURE

INSURRECTIONS: CRITICAL STUDIES IN RELIGION, POLITICS, AND CULTURE

SLAVOJ ŽIŽEK, CLAYTON CROCKETT, CRESTON DAVIS, JEFFREY W. ROBBINS, EDITORS

The intersection of religion, politics, and culture is one of the most discussed areas in theory today. It also has the deepest and most wide-ranging impact on the world. Insurrections: Critical Studies in Religion, Politics, and Culture will bring the tools of philosophy and critical theory to the political implications of the religious turn. The series will address a range of religious traditions and political viewpoints in the United States, Europe, and other parts of the world. Without advocating any specific religious or theological stance, the series aims nonetheless to be faithful to the radical emancipatory potential of religion.

Infinite Greed: The Inhuman Selfishness of Capital, Adrian Johnston

Energy and Change: A New Materialist Cosmotheology, Clayton Crockett

Accidental Agents: Ecological Politics Beyond the Human, Martin Crowley

Unbearable Life: A Genealogy of Political Erasure, Arthur Bradley

There's No Such Thing as a Sexual Relationship: Two Lessons on Lacan, Alain Badiou and Barbara Cassin, translated by Susan Spitzer and Kenneth Reinhard

Sociophobia: Political Change in the Digital Utopia, César Rendueles, translated by Heather Cleary

The Work of Art: Rethinking the Elementary Forms of Religious Life, Michael Jackson

Heidegger: His Life and His Philosophy, Alain Badiou and Barbara Cassin, translated by Susan Spitzer

The Intimate Universal: The Hidden Porosity Among Religion, Art, Philosophy, and Politics, William Desmond

An Insurrectionist Manifesto: Four New Gospels for a Radical Politics, Ward Blanton, Clayton Crockett, Jeffrey W. Robbins, and Noëlle Vahanian

For a complete list of series titles, please see the Columbia University Press website.

STAGING SOVEREIGNTY

THEORY, THEATER, THAUMATURGY

ARTHUR BRADLEY

Columbia University Press *New York*

Columbia University Press
Publishers Since 1893
New York   Chichester, West Sussex
Copyright © 2025 Arthur Bradley
All rights reserved

Library of Congress Cataloging-in-Publication Data
Names: Bradley, Arthur, author.
Title: Staging sovereignty : theory, theater, thaumaturgy / Arthur Bradley.
Description: New York : Columbia University Press, 2024. |
Series: Insurrections: critical studies in religion, politics, and culture |
Includes bibliographical references and index.
Identifiers: LCCN 2024023472 (print) | LCCN 2024023473 (ebook) | ISBN 9780231217330 (hardback) | ISBN 9780231217347 (trade paperback) | ISBN 9780231561693 (ebook)
Subjects: LCSH: Sovereignty—Philosophy. | Theater—Political aspects. | Theater and society. | Theurgy.
Classification: LCC JC327 .B72 2024 (print) | LCC JC327 (ebook) | DDC 320.1/5—dc23/eng/20240729

Cover design: Chang Jae Lee
Cover image: © Shutterstock

CONTENTS

Preface: Camera Obscura vii

Introduction: In the Theater of Sovereignty 1

1 In the Chair: Shakespeare, Kant, Ionesco, Bacon 27

2 Anointed with Oil: Shakespeare, Milton, Melville 57

3 Behind the Curtain: Hobbes, Benjamin, Derrida, Deleuze 83

4 In the Antechamber: Schiller, Kafka, Benjamin, Schmitt 113

5 Under the Clothes: Montaigne, Kafka, Genet, Agamben 139

6 Inside the Puppet Theater: Cervantes, Hobbes, Benjamin, Derrida 169

7 In the Crowd: Jarry, Le Bon, Kelsen, Foucault 195

Conclusion: In the Empty Space 225

Notes 237
Bibliography 279
Index 301

PREFACE
Camera Obscura

I started writing this book alone, mostly at night, staring at a computer screen in a darkened room during the global lockdown of 2020–2021. It took me a while to realize that it was a really a book about another camera obscura: theater. All my life, I have loved "going to the theater"—which is to say the simple, childlike experience of sitting in the dark and staring at some brightly lit stage or spectacle where people pretend to be something they are not—almost irrespective of whatever play I happen to be watching. Yet it took the political and economic prohibition of that particular dark room called "the theater" during the COVID-19 pandemic to make me want to write about it for the first time. To be more precise, this book is about the—mutually antagonistic but also, I shall argue, mutually constitutive—relationship between theory and theater, or, better, between the two rival forms of political vision or seeing (*thea*) they represent. If the global pandemic produced the first closure of London theaters since the Blitz of 1940 in the name of a very real state of emergency, for instance, it paradoxically also presided over something close to the mass theatricalization of everyday life. For Antonin Artaud, theater should famously be like a plague, but here was a plague that was like a theater: our freedom of movement was "blocked" (in both the normal and the theatrical sense of the word), our gestures were choreographed (wash your hands, keep a safe distance) and everyone was, of course, compelled to wear masks. In the book that follows, I seek to think through the simultaneously suspect, disavowed, prohibited, desired and privileged place of "theater" within our modern political imaginary. What if everything we have learned to call "political theory," the allegedly rational, disinterested, view from nowhere that is supposedly the opposite of theatrical spectatorship, is itself a form of theater?

To be honest, though, I should confess that my own personal theater, like every theater, was also a deeply communal experience because one of the few pleasures of the almost total isolation of lockdown was the renewed sense of solidarity it brought with many other friends and comrades sitting out there, somewhere, in their own dark rooms around the world staring at their screens. So, I want to thank the many people who contributed in large ways or small to the work presented here and whose (real or virtual) presence have made it a better book: Ian Almond; Bernard Beatty, Andrew Benjamin; Agata Bielik-Robson; Brian Black; Ward Blanton; Peter Boxall; Mladen Dolar; Michael Dillon; Ziad Elmarsafy; Charlie Gere; Niall Gildea; Michael Greaney; Montserrat Herrero; Peter Klepec, Christiane Mossin; Boštjan Nedoh; Carl Raschke; John Schad; Mike Shapiro; Yvonne Sherwood; Elettra Stimilli, and Miguel Vatter. In particular, I want to thank Antonio Cerella for his personal and intellectual friendship over the years. Finally, I must thank (real and virtual) audiences at the following institutions for their generous feedback on my work in progress before, during, and after the pandemic: Columbia Global Centre, Paris; Copenhagen Business School; University of Denver; University of Rome La Sapienza; University of Ljubljana; University of Newcastle;

St John's College, University of Oxford, Institute of Philosophy in the Research Centre of the Slovenian Academy of Sciences and Arts; and the University of Vienna.

If this book began life in a camera obscura, it was brought into the light by Wendy Lochner at Columbia University Press. I am incredibly grateful to Wendy for her support of my work over the years. I also want to thank the editors of the Insurrections: Critical Studies in Religion, Politics, and Culture series, Slavoj Žižek, Clayton Crockett, Creston Davis and Jeffrey Robbins. My gratitude also goes to the two anonymous reviewers of the book manuscript for sympathetic readings that enabled me to see my work with fresh eyes and to bring it into sharper focus. Finally, I also want to extend my huge thanks to Alyssa Napier, Susan Pensak, Emily Shelton, and the editorial team at Columbia who oversaw the book through production.

In addition, I am reproducing some material that has been published before in different forms: "In the Sovereign Machine: Sovereignty, Governmentality, Automaticity." *Journal for Cultural Research* 22, no. 3 (2018): 209–23; "Za zaveso: od Hobbesa do Deleuza," *Problemi*, 9–10 (2021): 5–28; and "In the Antechamber of Power: Sovereign Divisibility from Schiller to Schmitt," *Political Theology* 24, no. 1 (2023): 98–114. I am grateful to Taylor and Francis for permission to include my work here: https://www.tandfonline.com/.

Finally, and as always, my love and gratitude go to my wife, Abir, and our daughter, Aya, for keeping me company in the dark.

INTRODUCTION
In the Theater of Sovereignty

Picture men dwelling in a sort of subterranean cavern with a long entrance open to the light on its entire width. Conceive them as having their legs and necks fettered from childhood, so that they remain in the same spot, able to look forward only, and prevented by the fetters from turning their heads. Picture further the light from a fire burning higher up and at a distance behind them, and between the fire and the prisoners and above them a road along which a low wall has been built, as the exhibitors of puppet shows have partitions before the men themselves above, above which they show the puppets.
—Plato, *Republic*

In Plato's cave, we enter what is arguably the original theater (from the Greek *theatron*, a "place for viewing," from *thea* "a view, a seeing" + *tron*, suffix denoting place) of sovereignty. To be sure, the Greek philosopher's celebrated allegory in book 7 of the *Republic*—which has provoked countless epistemological, ethical, and political readings over the centuries—may be the single most overinterpreted episode in the history of

Western thought, but it is rarely observed that his cave is both figuratively and literally a kind of "theater."[1] If Socrates's dramatis personae are famously said to be prisoners in a "subterranean cavern" (*katageiō oikēsei spēlaiōdei*), for example, they are also a crowd of spectators who are compelled to sit in a darkened room and watch an elaborate "puppet show" (*thaumata*), complete with son et lumière special effects, which has been choreographed for them by mysterious hidden actors to mimic or imitate the experience of truth itself.[2] In this sense, Plato's captives are also, and quite literally, a captive *audience*: "such prisoners," Socrates tells Glaucon, "would deem reality to be nothing else than the shadows of the artificial objects."[3]

To be clear—and what is at stake in this allegory if not clarity of vision?—Socrates is inviting Glaucon to renounce abandon theatrical spectatorship in favor of a very different way of seeing the world that will, for better or worse, come to be known as "theory" (from the Greek *theōria*, "contemplation, speculation; a looking at, viewing; a sight, show, spectacle"). It is this act of theoretical contemplation that enables him to see what the prisoners themselves are incapable of seeing—namely, that there is a truth beyond the puppet or marionette show in which they are captured: the forms. For Plato, of course, Socrates's fear, or suspicion, of theater as a form of representational dissimulation here is a symptom of his well-known animus against Homer, poetry, and mimetic art more generally in book 10 of the *Republic* because it allegedly "knows nothing of the reality but only the appearance."[4] If Plato's ideal polis famously finds no place for the Homeric poets, we might thus be tempted to read his allegorical cave as a dystopian parody or inversion of his republic that dramatizes the political threat posed by such unregulated mimesis. In the Platonic cave, we perhaps discover an embryonic version of the "theatrocracy" (*theatrokratia*, "sovereignty of the audience") he attacks in the *Laws* where the spectators, not the philosophers, rule.⁵

If Plato's philosophy thus appears to be essentially antitheatrical—which is to say that it seeks to establish an opposition and hierarchy between *theōria* and *theatron*, between theory and theater, between what (at least according to its metaphysical reception history) will become the pure, enlightened contemplation of the forms and the partial, contingent, and dimly lit viewing of a secondhand mimetic representation—it will be my hypothesis in what follows that this philosophical antitheater remains, nonetheless, a minimal or minimalist *theater* of sovereignty. It is always worth recalling that Plato himself famously recognizes that philosophy begins with an experience of *thauma* ("wonder," marvel," "astonishment," as well as "puppetry" and more generally "a thing to look at," from the root of "theater").⁶ As Socrates reminds Theaetetus in their dialogue, Iris (the messenger of the gods) is actually the daughter of Thaumas: "This sense of wonder [thauma] is the mark of the philosopher. Philosophy indeed has no other origin, and he was a good genealogist who made Iris the daughter of Thaumas."⁷ To return to Plato's labyrinthine allegory of the cave in this rather more ambiguous light, I cannot help but be struck by the fact that there is another, indeed metatheatrical, layer to his apparently antitheatrical allegory: Socrates places Glaucon in an exactly symmetrical theatrical position to his abject prisoners. For Socrates, recall, Glaucon (and, by extension, any reader of this philosophical dialogue as well) is effectively invited to undertake a thought experiment in which he must himself assume the position of a kind of privileged spectator upon the spectators of this miniature conceptual *marionettentheater*: "Picture men [*ide gar anthrōpous*] dwelling in a sort of subterranean cavern." In Plato's cave, what we really enter is thus a kind of abyssal theater *within* a theater where a group of allegedly free spectators or *theorioi* (us) are put in the specular position of looking at another group of allegedly captive spectators (the prisoners) and, like them, we end up convincing ourselves that what we are seeing in this *theatron* is pure and unmediated *theōria*.[8]

In this book, I explore what I want to call the "theater of sovereignty," which can be very provisionally and heuristically defined here as the obscure, disavowed, but real mise en abyme between theory and theater, political representation and theatrical representation, the political power to represent and the theatrical representation of power, across a set of diverse theatrical scenes from modern political theory, philosophy, and literature. It is now well documented, of course, that the two (apparently rival or antagonistic) forms of phenomenology that the Ancient Greeks call *theōria* and *theatron*—which is very crudely to say the allegedly pure or disinterested contemplation of truth itself and the allegedly suspect, situated, or mediated spectatorship of a mimetic representation of truth—are both derived from the same etymological root in *thea* ("to see, a view or seeing a place from which to see").[9] As Simon Critchley is only the most recent to testify, "theory" and "theater" thus exist from their very origin in a philosophical, historical and political proximity that seems entirely alien to us today: "Theater is always theoretical, and theory is a theater, where we are spectators on a drama that unfolds: *our* drama."[10] However, my focus here will be on a more specific scene in this drama—namely, the relation between theater and political theory. To begin with one very simple, almost tautological, hypothesis that we will progressively unpack in different ways over the chapters that follow, I want to propose that *sovereign is (s)he who is seen as sovereign*: (s)he who appears, is beheld, or is made manifest *as* sovereign to themselves and others, whether in the purely philosophical sense of "sight," "vision," or "appearance" as the center of a particular distribution or arrangement of sensible experience; the more political sense of an object of legitimacy, believability, or recognition; or the theatrical sense of a site of artistic, symbolic, or ritualistic representability.[11] If a sovereign must indeed "appear" in order to be sovereign, then I further want to suggest that we can begin to construct a political phenomenology—indeed, perhaps even something close to a political thaumaturgy—of sovereignty's particular modes, forms, and places of appearance: the throne or seat of power; the court, chamber, and antechambers of power; the insignia, regalia, and vestments of power; the images, icons, artefacts, and relics of power; the acts, gestures, rituals, and ceremonies of power; the grammar, rhetoric, and tropologies of power; the shows, spectacles, cosplays, and dramaturgies of power; the allegories, phantasmagoria, heuristic fictions, and thought experiments of power; and so on.[12] Finally, I want to contend that this theater of sovereignty also reveals a certain "sovereignty" of theater itself: what we call "theatricality" is not merely the decorative façade or surface of a preexisting realpolitik but something that penetrates all the way down into the allegedly raw or naked "real" of power itself. In order to introduce this book, however, I do not want to offer a general history of the relationship between theory and theater—which has already been the subject of many studies—so much as a miniature genealogy of the emergence of the precise form of theater I am calling "political theory" via readings of three very singular, different, even mutually antagonistic scenes from (early) modern political thought: Thomas Hobbes's antidemocratic philosophy of political representation in *Leviathan* (1651); Jean-Jacques Rousseau's direct democratic manifesto for republican theater or spectacle in his *Letter to Monsieur d'Alembert on the Theater* (1758); and the modern French political theorist Claude Lefort's famous theory of representative democracy as an empty space in his essay "The Permanence of the Theologico-Political?" (1981). What would it mean if the (apparently empty) antitheater we call modern political theory were itself an obscure theater of sovereignty?

AS IF IT WERE DISSOLVED

In Jonas Barish's classic verdict, Plato's *Republic* is only the beginning of a long-standing "antitheatrical prejudice" within political modernity that stretches from the Puritan-led Parliament's closure of all London theaters on the outbreak of the English Civil War in 1642 to the present.[13] To take here Paul Kottman's *Politics of the Scene* (2008), which is arguably the most sophisticated contemporary prosecution of this "antitheatrical" thesis, Plato institutes a fatal split or fissure at the heart of *thea* or sight between theōria and theatron that will establish "theory"—now conceived as the disinterested contemplation of the fixed, eternal, and present order of the Ideas—as our privileged mode of knowledge.[14] It is with the proper name "Thomas Hobbes," allegedly, that we can also glimpse the inauguration of something called "political theory," indeed political science, in the modern sense of a discipline that takes as its referent object a positive, material and wholly immanent artefact, the state, whose movements can be objectively mapped, modeled, and predicted across space and time. As the Long Parliament closed London's theaters on the grounds that such "Spectacles of Pleasure" were incompatible with a time of "sad and pious Solemnity," early modern political theory also purges any suspicion of theatricality, as a rival mode of singular, limited, or mediated knowledge, in order to make good its own pretension to become the "view from nowhere."[15] For political philosophers from Hannah Arendt to Jacques Rancière, who seek to challenge this antitheatrical prejudice, political modernity's self-appointed task has consequently been to heal the ancient Platonic fissure or wound between theōria and theatron, theory and theater: Arendt herself famously claims in *The Human Condition* (1958) that theater is "the political art *par excellence*" because it is the only art form that, in her view, successfully imitates the singularity, contingency, and relationality that constitutes political life.[16] However, what apparently complicates this quasi-Heideggerian story of theory's fatal "forgetting" of theater is the inconvenient fact that early modern political theory's own "antitheatrical prejudice" manifestly does not consist of a simple prohibition against theater—rather, something like the opposite. If modern political theory really is predicated upon a Platonic exclusion of the theatrical, this exclusion appears to take the perverse form of a hyperbolic retheatricalization of the political whose visible symptoms exceed any simple explanation in terms of, say, a psychoanalytic return of the repressed. In such classic works of early modern political theory as Niccolò Machiavelli's *The Prince* (1532), Francis Bacon's "Of Simulation and Dissimulation" (1625), and, as we will now see, Thomas Hobbes's own *Leviathan* (1651), a certain theatricality—which is here defined in very different terms as the capacity for actorly self-fashioning, simulation, or representation, and even for dissimulation and misrepresentation—is paradoxically nominated as something close to the very essence of the political itself.

To square this apparent circle between theory and theater, I want to argue that Hobbes's philosophy does not so much preside over a violent new Platonic disavowal of "theater" so much as the inauguration of a radical new form of theatricality under the guise of something called "political theory." It is already very well documented, of course, that Hobbes persistently draws on theatrical metaphors and analogies to unpack his celebrated theory of the political person, and political representation more broadly. As he famously argues in chapter 16 of *Leviathan*, "Of Persons, Authors, and Things Personated," the word *persona* in Latin "signifies the *disguise*, or *outward appearance* of a man, counterfeited on the Stage," and, further, that "from the Stage, hath been translated to any Representer of speech and action, as well in Tribunalls, as Theaters. So that a *Person*, is the same that an *Actor* is, both on the Stage and in common Conversation."[17] If Hobbes derives his theory of the political actor from the theatrical actor—and of political representation from dramatic representation—Kottman insists that the philosopher's political theory still remains essentially antitheatrical, because it effaces the dimension of singular and contingent human relations that the latter (following Arendt) regards as the essence of the theatrical. For Kottman, what Hobbes famously calls the "state of nature" is the "radically nondramatic, inactive (and apolitical) ontological ground" for his theory of the state because it consists, in essence, of nothing more than a collection of material bodies in motion.[18] In Kottman's larger critique, Hobbes's antitheatrical theory of the state of nature is what really underpins and legitimizes the English philosopher's (only superficially theatrical) theory of representation in the civil state, in which the civil sovereign seizes the political power to speak or act solely for themselves.

If Kottman concludes that Hobbes's political theory is a "politics without a scene"— a purely artificial theory of the political predicated upon the negation or expropriation of the contingent, here-and-now relationality of Arendtian dramatic interaction—it remains possible to argue that this apparent Hobbesian evacuation of theater into a materialist void remains, albeit in a very different sense, the *scene* of no scene.[19] It is worth recalling here the mise en abyme we encountered in Plato's allegory of the cave, where Glaucon must himself enter a kind of theater in order to experience what is allegedly pure, unmediated theory, because something like the same abyssal logic recurs in Hobbes's own allegory of the state of nature. As Kottman himself recognizes, Hobbes's state of nature is not quite a simple ontological ground in which there is nothing but matter in motion, but a "radical mythologeme" that describes a point of origin that is, strictly speaking, "mythical, atemporal, and immemorial."[20] Yet, in fact, this heuristic fiction of origins has a very modern origin, because it is nothing more than the negation of the social order that we currently inhabit, and so remains internal to society. To take his famous account in *De Cive* (1642)—a work that was first published in the same year as the Puritan closure of the theaters—Hobbes makes clear that what he calls the "state of nature" is the product of an eliminative or subtractive thought experiment that seeks to reverse engineer the representational machine that is the Commonwealth: "It is necessary, I say, not to take them insunder, but yet that they be so considered, *as if they were dissolved [ut tanquam dissoluta consideretur]*"; that is, that we rightly understand what the quality of human nature is, in what matters it is, in what not, fit to make up a civil government, and how men must be agreed among themselves that intend to grow up into a well-grounded state."[21] For Hobbes, what we encounter in the state of nature is less a real and prepolitical ontological ground, that precedes and underpins the order of political representation, than the (retroactively naturalized negative of political representation itself. By considering the Commonwealth as if it were dissolved, in other words, we do not immediately begin to contemplate a natural state before or without representation, but rather something closer to a pure or empty representation without world—or what we might call "the representation of no representation." In the Hobbesian state of nature, we enter what we will see to be modern political theory's own distinctive theater of sovereignty: an empty stage whose sole dramatis persona is representability itself.

In Hobbes's political antitheater, whose outline I can obviously do nothing more than sketch here, I thus want to propose that we do not observe a simple political ontological passage from theater to theory—which is to say from a contingent, partial and mediated mode of political vision to a new, neutral objective and regime of visibility—so much as from a premodern theater of sovereignty to a modern one: what we call modern political theory is *itself* a form of theater, albeit one that crucially obscures or eclipses its own contingent place, vantage point, or theatron, under the guise of absolute neutrality or objectivity. To supersede the old political theological theater of premodernity, whose system of representation famously makes visible an invisible entity in the form of the real presence of a sovereign person,[22] modern political theory constructs what we might call a new *metatheater* of power in which it is not the sovereign representative but the bare or empty fact of representationalism itself that increasingly becomes the principal political actor.[23] It was arguably Carl Schmitt who was the first to observe that, despite the philosopher's own explicit intentions, the omnipotent sovereign at the center of Hobbes's Commonwealth is no longer a metaphysical sovereign person like the Baroque absolutist prince, who finds his paradigm in James I's famous claim that the king is always on the "public stage," because Hobbesian sovereignty ultimately becomes nothing more than the empty space of a purely formal or juridical theater of representation.[24] As Schmitt claims in his *Leviathan in the State Theory of Thomas Hobbes* (1938), Hobbes's "sovereign-representative person is only the soul of the 'huge man' state" but very quickly this person becomes depersonalized; "the process of mechanization is not, however, arrested but completed by this personification," he continues, because this "personalistic element too is drawn into the mechanization process and becomes absorbed by it. As a totality, the state is body and soul, a *homo artificialis,* and, as such, a machine."[25] If Hobbes's theory of representation has a fatal flaw, according to Schmitt's diagnosis, it is that it is perversely *too* theatrical: every representer and representee alike are absorbed into a system of universally equivalent representation. For Hobbes, whose foundational mythologeme of a pure or empty representability without content begins to reveal its revolutionary implications here, what this theory of political representation ultimately sets in motion is a representing machine in which a "person," up to and including the sovereign person, is reduced to nothing more than a fungible token or currency in a general economy of representability where anything (human being, corporation or thing) can represent or be represented, or misrepresented, by anything else: "A Person, *is he whose words and actions are considered either as his own*, or as representing *the words and actions of another man, or of any other thing to whom they are attributed, whether Truly or by Fiction.*"[26] In Hobbes's theater of sovereignty, the sovereign is transformed from the first or principal representer in the Commonwealth, who animates the system of representation in its entirety, to just one more representee in a machine that increasingly runs by itself: representability itself—and not any real sovereign person—becomes "sovereign."

NOTHING, IF YOU PLEASE

In Jean-Jacques Rousseau's *Letter to Monsieur d'Alembert on the Theater* (*Lettre à M. D'Alembert sur les spectacles*, 1758), which famously takes the unfortunate Jean d'Alembert's modest proposal for the erection of a new theater in Geneva as an opportunity to give a sweeping indictment of the social, political, and philosophical pretensions of dramatic representation in general, we perhaps find the most celebrated post-Hobbesian effort to construct what I am calling a "political antitheater."[27] It is not merely that Rousseau disavows the theater on social, political, and economic grounds—in other words, that he sees it as a closed, dark, exclusive, unequal, passive, and even monarchical form of spectacle—because his principal objection is, once again, a philosophical one: a republic must be ontologically, not simply empirically, antitheatrical. As is well known, the Genevan philosopher has many critical things to say about the social and moral effects of contemporary French theater: we can find no positive moral "read-across" or correlation between, say, a theatrical performance of Molière's *Le Misanthrope*, where immoral behavior is satirized, and the moral impact the play has upon its audience, not to mention the social mœurs or behavior of that audience outside the theater. To be clear, however, Rousseau's real problem with the theater is less to do with what is represented *on* stage—the content of the play—but rather the bare fact *of* representation or theatricality itself. "Let us not be mistaken," Jacques Derrida observes in his famous discussion of the *Letter to d'Alembert* in *Of Grammatology* (1967), "what Rousseau criticizes in the last analysis is not the content of the spectacle, the sense represented by it, although that *too* he criticizes: it is re-presentation itself. Exactly as within the political order, the menace has the shape of the representative."[28] For Rousseau, this critique of theatrical representation in the *Letter to d'Alembert* thus explicitly mirrors his critique of political representation (and, in particular, of representative democracy) in the *Social Contract* (1762): both theater and politics create a fatal alienation between what is represented (the audience/

the people) and their external, transcendentalized representer (the actor/the monarch). If Molière's *Le Misanthrope* may well seek to expose the vice of social hypocrisy, for example, Rousseau's claim is that any apparent virtue in the content of the play is belied by its representational form: theater is *itself* a form of organized lying or hypocrisy whose principal goal consists, as Jacques Rancière observes, in the perfect reproduction of "the signs of feelings and thoughts on human bodies that *they do not have*."[29] In a final confirmation that theatrical representation is itself the problem with theater, Rousseau explicitly aligns his own critique of Moliere's plays with Plato's original decision to expel the Homeric poets: "What! Plato banished Homer from his republic and we will suffer Molière in ours!"[30]

To be precise, Rousseau does not call for the puritanical abolition of all forms of popular entertainment but, rather, demands the resurrection of a specifically *republican* genre of spectacle: "Ought there to be no Spectacles in a republic?" he asks in chapter 11 of the *Letter*. "On the contrary, there ought to be many. It is in republics that they were born, it is in their bosom that they are seen to flourish with a truly festive air."[31] It is with this kind of public spectacle (festivals, promenades, sporting competitions and prize-giving ceremonies as opposed to staged dramas) that we find the real theatrical equivalent to the pure, nonrepresentational expression of the general will (*volonté générale*) of the people. As the philosopher explains, this republican antitheater opens the closed, dark, and exclusive Platonic cave of monarchist theater to the (literal and figurative) light of day: "No, happy peoples, these are not your festivals," he claims, "It is in the open air, under the sky, that you ought to gather and give yourselves to the sweet sentiment of your happiness."[32] For Rousseau, whose call for a new and emancipated public theater that abolishes the space between actor and spectator will be repeated across the next two hundred years by drama theorists and practitioners as different as Antonin Artaud, Bertolt Brecht, Peter Brook, and Ngũgĩ wa Thiong'o, what really distinguishes spectacle from theater is the exorcism of any specter of representationalism that would divide the people from themselves.[33] If "theater" is where the people are represented by something they are not, a "spectacle" is where the people are naturally present as themselves and to themselves. In this account, a spectacle represents nothing, because it spontaneously *is* something—namely, the *presentation* of the people itself as and by itself: "But what then will be the objects of these entertainments? What will be shown in them? Nothing, if you please [*Rien, si l'on veut*]. With liberty, wherever abundance [*l'affluence*] reigns, well-being also reigns."[34]

If Rousseau's republican spectacle thus quite literally represents "nothing," whether theatrically or politically, it is because, once again, it is an antitheater of pure presence in which the people simply embody or perform their own general will by and as themselves without any alienated representational excess or residue whatsoever. To put it in the words of the philosopher's own deceptively simple invitation from chapter 11: "Plant a stake crowned with flowers in the middle of a square," he writes, "gather the people together there, and you will have a festival."[35] Yet it is only necessary to recall Derrida's reading of Rousseau in the *Grammatology* once again here to appreciate that this theory of theater as an artificial *supplément* to the civic life of the city—that is, as both an unnecessary addition to, and a dangerous falsification of, the latter's mœurs—equally exposes a lack or deficit within the alleged plenitude of the city itself, that paradoxically calls for theatrical supplementation in the first place. For Rousseau, recall, a new theater will allegedly corrupt the morals of the fine and upstanding Genevan people, but his attempt to prohibit its construction quickly begins to look very much like an attempt to shut the theater door after the moral horse has bolted: "One must not dissemble," he admits, "the intentions are still upright, but the morals [*mœurs*] already noticeably incline toward decadence, and we follow, at a distance, in the tracks of those same peoples whose fate does not fail to cause us anxiety."[36] In his own reading of chapter 11 of the *Letter to d'Alembert* in *Of Grammatology*, Derrida further observes how Rousseau insists that a genuine republican spectacle must necessarily take place *en plein air* but, just like in Plato's original allegory of the cave, it is harder to go outside into the daylight of the general will than it looks: this open-air festival must be substituted by an indoor ball for young marriageable couples in the cold weather of wintertime, the philosopher concedes, and the indoor ball is itself a substitute for potentially even more private liaisons between single men and women.[37]

In a very similar way to Hobbes's antitheatrical state of nature, Rousseau's natural republican antitheater—where nothing, if you please, is represented by nothing—constitutes a modern minimalist theater of sovereignty because, crudely speaking, even this "nothing" becomes, representationally, something. It is not necessary to dwell upon the various performative contradictions that attend his *Letter to d'Alembert* (whereby a former playwright and self-professed theater-lover, who liberally deploys theatrical metaphors throughout his political work, professes to attack theatrical spectacle) in order to prove this point because, even if we accept it on its own terms, Rousseau's philosophical distinction between spectacle and theater, presence and representation, is far more precarious than he alleges. After all, a bunch of flowers that has been placed in the middle of a square so that people can gather around it is obviously no longer just a "bunch of flowers." However, a republican spectacle that really did present nothing but the people themselves, without flowers, festivals, or competitions, would not escape the suspicion of representation, either. To recall Rousseau's precise formulation here, the people must *represent themselves to themselves* in the spectacle to genuinely become a unified people. By gathering the people in the public square, he argues, we "put the spectators on show [*donnez les spectateurs en spectacle*]; make them actors themselves; do it so that each sees and loves themselves in the others, so that all will be better united [*tous en soient mieux un*]."[38] If this call to make the spectators themselves the spectacle would seem to describe a perfect republican synthesis of representer and represented, actor and spectator, citizen and sovereign, which contains no trace or residue of alienation, it is nonetheless very clear from this account that there is still a certain excess or supplement of the representation *over* the represented. For Rousseau, as Jean Starobinski observes, each spectator is explicitly transformed from an atomized individual, who possesses only what the *Social Contract* famously calls "the will of all" (*volonté de tous*) into part of a "better united" people, endowed with the general will, via the theatrical medium of *recognizing themselves being represented* by the other.[39] In Rousseau's political antitheater, what he calls the "nothing" of representation ("Nothing, if you please") remains what we might call representation's *own* nothing: modern political theory is not the absence of representation but the representation of absence, a metatheatrical representation without content, an empty space.[40]

AN EMPTY SPACE

In Claude Lefort's essay "The Permanence of the Theologico-Political?" ("Permanence du théologico-politique?," 1981), we perhaps find the modern paradigm of the political antitheater.[41] To recall the thesis of this now classic essay, Lefort claims that what defines modern liberal democracy as an original form of sovereign power is neither the transcendental appeal to an absolutist "outside" (the gods, the city, or some sacred ground) nor the immanent appeal to a republican "inside" (the people, the community) but, paradoxically, the appeal to an *empty space*. "I have for a long time concentrated upon this peculiarity of modern democracy," he writes, "of all the regimes of which we know, it is the only one to have represented power in such a way as to show that power is an *empty place* [*lieu vide*] and to have thereby maintained a gap between the symbolic and the real [*l'écart du symbolique et du reel*]."[42] If earlier forms of sovereignty always seek to ground power in some foundation external to themselves that legitimizes their rule, and that they, in turn, can claim to speak on behalf of, liberal democracy's perverse genius is to nonviolently internalize or institutionalize the very *groundlessness* of the political—which is to say the absence of any agreed or common foundation for political order after the crises of modernity—as its own exclusive "source" of legitimacy. For Lefort, democracy thus preserves the *form* of the transcendental ground for politics but evacuates it of any political content so that, properly speaking, it cannot be occupied even by "the people" in whose name it is created without immediately dividing those people into competing parties: "It does so by virtue of a discourse which reveals that power belongs to no one [*qu'il n'apartient à personne*]; that those who exercise power do not possess it [*que ceux qui l'exercent ne le détiennent pas*]; that they do not, indeed, embody it [*ne l'incarnent pas*]; that the exercise of power requires a periodic and repeated contest; that the authority of those vested with power is created and re-created [*se fait et se refait*] as a result of the manifestation of the will of the people."[43] In Lefort's liberal democratic version of the political antitheater, what is "represented" in the empty space is neither god, king, people, nor community, but nothing more than the bare ongoing possibility of representability itself.

To a remarkable degree, Lefort's empty space thus lays bare what Hobbes's state of nature and Rousseau's natural republican spectacle both seek to cover over: what presents itself as a modern political antitheater is a new and singular theater of sovereignty. It is even possible to interpret his essay as a thoroughgoing critique of political theory's ongoing pretension (in the form of the political and social sciences) to detheatricalize politics by reducing it to a mere positum that can be localized within a given society. As Lefort goes on to show via a reading heavily indebted to his mentor Maurice Merleau-Ponty, any attempt to offer a purely immanent or autotelic account of society must fail, because the social realm, like Merleau-Ponty's own phenomenological realm, always contains an invisible excess or "opening" (*ouverture*) over its visible appearance as such. For Lefort, who here puts to work the influential modern conceptual distinction between "politics" (*la politique*) and the "political" (*le politique*), what we call "the political" names this presocial phenomenological *Umwelt* or "background" out of which any positive social or political order is instituted. If the political gives form to (*mise en forme*) society, it also supplies it with content by, secondly, giving meaning to (*mise en sens*) its social relations via grids of intelligibility and normativity and, finally, by *staging* (*mise en scène*) those relations via images that serve to make them signify for society's members: "We can say that the advent of a society capable of organizing social relations can come about only if it can institute the conditions of their intelligibility, and only if it can use a multiplicity of signs to arrive at a quasi-representation of itself."[44] In Lefort's verdict, "political theology" remains a quasi-permanent condition within secular political modernity, not because of any residual religious content within this society, but because "the religious" is the prototypical name for any work of thought that punctures the fiction of social self-immanence to reveal the constitutive opening onto the other that makes every society possible: "Every religion *states* in its own way that human society can only open onto itself by being held in an opening it did not create" (*une ouverture sur elle-même que prise dans une ouverture qu'elle ne fait pas*), Lefort famously writes. "Philosophy says the same thing, but religion said it first, albeit in a language philosophy cannot make its own."[45]

If every historical form of politics has staged this constitutive "opening" of the political differently—by peopling it with various transcendentalized bodies such as gods, kings, or the people—what distinguishes the mise-en-scène of liberal democracy is that, for the first time, a political order seeks to stage the opening *as such* in the form of an empty space that no one can permanently occupy. It may still be tempting here to read Lefort's theory of the empty space as the final stage in the long detheatricalization of political theory set in motion by Hobbes and continued by Rousseau, which definitively strips politics of any residual pretension to transcendental authority by revealing the realpolitik that lies beneath, but, on the former's account, this interpretation would be simply another doomed attempt to ground politics in an (equally fictive) self-immanence. As we have begun to see, what defines the democratic empty space in Lefort's account is precisely that it preserves the symbolic dimension of the other even or especially as it abolishes the real figure of the other itself. To the question of what, if anything, can be said to be "represented" upon this empty stage of power, Lefort's answer is, consequently, that democracy aspires to represent nothing more than the irreducibility of the gap between the symbolic and real dimensions of politics—the impossibility of any one particular form of politics embodying or monopolizing the political opening itself—or, if we want to put it less melancholically, a kind of pure or absolute representability that has the capacity to exist independently from any particular representation. By participating in representative democracy (whether as representer or represented) we do not thereby commit ourselves to the propriety of any one singular representation over all the others, but simply to the infinite work of representability itself: what matters is the repeated staging of political conflict in the nonviolent form of the electoral contestation of power rather than any final, teleological resolution of that contest. Finally, what we might term this metarepresentational dimension also explains why Lefort's democracy, more than any allegedly "realist" political form, must necessarily involve a theatrical mise-en-scène to give it meaning. In Lefort's political antitheater, we might even go so far as to say that democracy is nothing *but* its own mise-en scène: the metatheatrical staging of political staging itself.

In Hobbes, Rousseau, and Lefort's political theory, we thus bear witness to three—obviously very different, mutually agonistic, but nonetheless curiously sequential—scenes in the making, not so much of a political antitheater, but of a new and entirely modern metatheater of sovereignty that eclipses or occludes its own contingent theatrical position beneath a new and supreme fiction: the empty space. It may well appear, of course, that "democracy," whether liberal or republican, is predicated upon the exorcism of precisely the kind of theatrical ritual and ceremony associated with premodern forms of government. As Zvi Ben-Dor Benite, Stefanos Geroulanos, and Nicole Jerr have recently testified, however, the modern democratic "pretense to an absence of theater and the rejection of ornate regalia enforce new kinds of revolutionary theatricality, oftentimes at the most basic levels—theatricality in new claims of sovereignty, in competitions over it, in appeals to it, in dreams played out through it."[46] To reread Hobbes and his modern political theoretical heirs in this context, what becomes apparent is that each progressively substitutes (whether by accident or design makes little difference here) the real or fictive presence of a premodern sovereign body, who is deemed to animate or infuse the body politic with life, for the sovereignty of an empty or contentless representationalism itself: Hobbes's absolutist sovereign person is, as we have seen, inexorably depersonalized by the (entirely vacant) representational machine that is the modern state; Rousseau seeks to supplant the monarchical representationalism of traditional theater with a republican spectacle predicated upon the presentation of precisely nothing; and, finally, Lefort insists that the democratic stage must remain constitutively empty of any substantive political person or entity, even the people in whose name it is created. If modern political theory from Hobbes onward frequently prides itself upon its antitheatrical "realism"—which allegedly subtracts or eliminates what it sees as the old political theological fictions of Greek or Christian natural law theory, divine right sovereignty, and so on to reveal the materialist core of politics that lies beneath—it thus ironically presides over something closer to a total and absolute theatricalization of political life that (at least apparently) dispenses with any relation to the real whatsoever. For Hobbes, Rousseau, and Lefort, what premodernity originally conceived of as a real or personal system of representation, whereby the representee is really made present in the form of the representer, is thus (tragically, traumatically, or gloriously, depending upon one's political perspective) superseded by a very modern economy of pure, empty, and universal representability which promises and threatens that anything, natural or artificial, can be represented by anything else—or perhaps even by nothing. In Hobbes, Rousseau, and Lefort, this modern theater of sovereignty finds its privileged theatrical figure or place of the political, not in the dark, subterranean Platonic cave, but, revealingly, in the transparent, iridescent, and yet wholly empty, space.

THEORY, THEATER, THAUMATURGY

In bearing witness to the rise of our own modern theater of sovereignty, this book seeks to be neither a work of political theory nor a study of political theater, which might reestablish the boundary between theory and theater once and for all, so much as an exercise in what I want to call "political thaumaturgy": a political science of sights, wonders, marvels, miracles, artifices, optical illusions, special effects, and confidence tricks that may or may not be "real." It is predicated upon the suspicion that every political theorist of the theater of sovereignty must (like Plato's Glaucon) obscure the fact that they are—contingent, situated, and interested—players in that theater. Accordingly, what follows does not seek to prosecute its argument from some privileged abstract vantage point, but rather to *perform* that argument from within a series of (partial, contingent, and historically and geopolitically unrepresentative) textual scenes, events, and signatures. To be very clear about the particular place I am speaking from, I should thus forewarn the reader that this book *is* (formally and generically) what it is *about* (thematically): what follows consists of a set of unapologetically performative, improvisatory, indeed "theatrical" essays that seek to not only passively document but actively stage or perform sovereignty's own mise-en-scène.[47] If political theory aspires to a view from nowhere, this book instead offers a series of inescapably partial or restricted perspectives which always place us *somewhere*—in, under, between, or behind, a sovereignty that can never be seen face-to-face. In a coup de théâtre we will witness throughout this work, every attempt to critically unmask or demystify the theater of sovereignty—to exit the cave, pull back the curtain, or otherwise uncover the antitheatrical "reality" of power—will reveal only a sovereignty of theater itself.

To navigate our way through this thaumaturgical universe, I seek in each of the following chapters to rehearse a few scenes, fragments, and vignettes in the representational life of one privileged prop or property within the theater of sovereignty from the early modern period to the present. First, chapter 1 explores the representation of the royal throne, chair, office, or seat of power via readings of Shakespeare, Kant, Ionesco, and Bacon. Chapter 2 turns to depictions of the political theological ritual of royal anointment with oil in Shakespeare, Milton, and Melville. Chapter 3 analyses the figure of the veiled or secret sanctum sanctorum of power in Hobbes, Benjamin, Deleuze, and Derrida. Chapter 4 examines representations of the larger political court, chamber, or antechamber that surrounds the inner sanctum of power in Schiller, Kafka, Benjamin, and Schmitt. Chapter 5 considers dramatizations of the rite of political investiture with regalia or clothing in Montaigne, Kafka, Genet, and Agamben. Chapter 6 surveys the staging of the trope of the political puppet show or marionette theater in Aristotle, Cervantes, Benjamin, and Derrida. Chapter 7 reads the representation of the theatrical crowd or audience via Le Bon, Jarry, Kelsen, and Foucault. Finally, a brief conclusion rehearses the theater director Peter Brook's famous theory of modern theater as an empty space. In Brook's figure of the (allegedly) empty theatrical stage, I conclude, we also encounter the defining mise-en-scène of modern political power.

If we survey the diverse bodies, gestures and things that populate the (early) modern political stage, I hope we will begin to construct, not a thing theory, political ecology, or *dingpolitik*, but a political thaumaturgy of some of the *properties* (from the English fifteenth-century *propyrtes*, "object used in a play" but also the Latin *proprietatem*, "special character") that underpin our modern *theatrum politicum*.[48] It requires very little knowledge of the theater to appreciate that props are much more than simple accessories or appurtenances to be wielded by actors. As Andrew Sofer recalls, a prop is really a kind of "time machine" that accumulates meaning not only across linear stage temporality from the beginning of a play to the end, but also across theatrical history from performance to performance, from play to play, and, one might add, from stage to world.[49] To track the representational fate of thrones, regalia, oil, and so on across modern history, we do not merely observe a set of passive silos or vessels for pure power that are exploited at will by princes, priests, and the like, but rather the repositories of what we might call (in a manner redolent of contemporary artificial intelligence theories of so-called distributed cognition, memory, or intelligence) a "distributed sovereignty." By exteriorizing itself onto its material environment, sovereign power invests this environment with an uncanny agency of its own that enables it to operate quasi-autonomously: crowns, thrones, and regalia become political actors in their own right that animate us as much as we do them. In this sense, the real dramatis personae of this book are not the crowd of princes, philosophers, theologians, and artists who wield theatrical properties but the props themselves: Jarry's toilet brush, Benjamin's puppet, Ionesco's chair, Genet's robes.

In drawing this brief introduction to a close and opening the book proper, however, I want to end by reiterating that what follows consists of a set of singular, improvisatory, and largely free-standing political theatrical experiments that can, in fact, be read in any order the reader wishes, but, nonetheless, if taken together, attempt to stage an old, and perhaps even stagey or overfamiliar, drama in a new way. To rehearse this script here once more before we start: what this book seeks to perform or dramatize is a series of privileged theatrical scenes in literature, political theory, and philosophy that collectively describe the passage from early modernity to late capitalist or neoliberal democratic modernity; from a form of government characterized by political theological absolutism to one of liberal popular and democratic constitutionalism; from a political philosophy founded upon an allegedly real sovereign personalism to one predicated upon formal or juridical representationalism; from a political phenomenology grounded in a particular place or vantage point of appearance to a new theoretical, disinterested, and allegedly objective "view from nowhere"; from a political topology or geography in which the theatrical properties of power remain recognizably rooted in, and emerge out of, real, specific, and localizable traditions to one where they become (at least apparently) infinitely mobile, utile, and fungible; and, finally, from a political theological system of representation that is ultimately grounded in a real and personal sovereign representative (whether it be god, king, or people) to a form of political thaumaturgy in which a metatheatrical machine of representability effectively become its own political actor. In the modern theater of sovereignty, we always end up in the same—empty—space.

1

IN THE CHAIR

Shakespeare, Kant, Ionesco, Bacon

In the opening scene of Eugène Ionesco's *The Chairs* (*Les Chaises*, 1952), the curtain rises on a group of empty chairs standing in the middle of a sparsely furnished room.¹ To replay this self-styled *farce tragique* from the beginning, Ionesco's play depicts an Old Man and an Old Woman, who live together in a tower on a desolate, even postapocalyptic island, busying themselves arranging seats for their expected guests. It gradually emerges that the couple have invited a vast number of people—perhaps even the entire human race—to hear an important message that the Old Man wishes to communicate because he believes it will save the world.² As the play progresses, a long line of guests, including a Lady, a Colonel, and even the island's Emperor, thus arrive and the Old Man and Woman variously welcome, flirt with, and grovel in front of them before ushering each one to their assigned place. However, any reader familiar with Ionesco's play will already know that it contains a famous conceit, which it pursues to the point of apparent absurdity. If the old couple always treat their guests as real, flesh-and-blood people, this growing crowd remains totally *invisible* to the play's audience throughout, which inevitably raises the suspicion that they are simply a product of the Old Man and Woman's delusions. Finally, an Orator (who, alone among the invitees, can be seen by the audience) arrives to read out the important message and, satisfied that their life's work is now complete, the Old Man and Old Woman commit suicide by jumping out of the tower's window. In the play's final scene, the Orator attempts to deliver the message, but it turns out that he is deaf and mute and so cannot, despite increasingly desperate efforts, make himself understood to the "crowd."

To take up Ionesco's invitation and revisit *The Chairs* today, we appear to find ourselves ensconced in a simultaneously literal, figurative, and ontological empty chair.[3] Its creator was widely attacked in the 1950s and 60s for his alleged affirmation of an absurd or nihilist *"anti-theater"* over and against the fashionable conventions of Brechtian *episches Theater*, Sartrean *littérature engagée*, or English "kitchen sink" social realism.[4] According to Kenneth Tynan's famous 1958 attack in the London *Observer* on a revival of the play, the empty chair is a metaphor not only for the death of God, Marx, or the Romanian Iron Guard but also for the emptiness of Ionesco's own theatrical universe: *The Chairs* ushers in "a bleak new world from which the humanist heresies of faith in logic and belief in man will be banished forever."[5] However, in "Le Coeur n'est pas sur la main" (1959), a reply to Tynan's charge that his plays propagate an empty, anti-realist formalism, Ionesco claims that an empty form, in fact, possesses a powerful realism of its own. If we continue to visit "deconsecrated [*désaffectés*] temples, cathedrals, deserted palaces, uninhabitable old houses," he argues, it is not due to any substantive content or use-value they possess but because of the *"objective* reality of architectural principles" expressed within them: "They serve above all to reveal, to be the expression of, these architectonic laws."[6] For Ionesco, as he goes on to explain in the later essay "Propos sur mon théâtre et les propos des autres"

(1960), a work of art—like a vacant building—has no need to mimetically imitate or represent reality, because it is *itself* a real object: "a construction, an autonomous universe, a monument" that "becomes an objective reality."[7] In Ionesco's theatrical universe, an empty chair on a stage is still a chair, a real object in space and time that concretizes a particular Newtonian field of force, mass, and motion, and so never quite empty at all.

If Ionesco's theory of art aspires to a sort of sui generis objectivity, it is telling that his historical paradigm for the artwork remains a very particular kind of empty chair: a deconsecrated *cathedral* (from the Greek *kathedra* and Latin *cathedra*, a throne, seat, or chair). It is tempting to suspect that the Old Man and the Old Woman's chairs, which they prepare for their invisible guests, belong to a long line of theological and political chairs beginning with the Christian "empty throne" (*hetoimasia tou thronou*, throne of preparation) that was prepared for God alone in Revelation 4:1–11, Isaiah 6:1–4, and Ezekiel 1:1–2. As Charles Picard argues, the figure of the empty chair first began to be used for political ends in the Roman Empire to glorify an (absent or dead) emperor like Alexander the Great in the fourth century BCE.[8] Yet, from the Christian era onward, the absent emperor was replaced with the dead Jesus Christ and the imperial throne with a *hetoimasia* prepared for the second coming: a ninth-century Byzantine illuminated manuscript of the First Council of Constantinople (381), for example, depicts an empty throne with a Gospel at the center. To jump forward a millennia to the epoch of medieval and early modern European monarchy, Jacques Le Goff complicates the political theological picture further by arguing that the *sedes* or special seat reserved for the monarch in the 1250 Ordo or program for the coronation ceremonies of French kings can once again be compared to the "*hetoimasia* (empty seat of God or of the cross) in early Christian and Byzantine art."⁹ For Giorgio Agamben, whose recent *Kingdom and the Glory* (2013) has reignited critical interest in the significance of the hetoimasia, we can likewise observe a certain structural correspondence between the empty throne and Ernst Kantorowicz's famous fiction of medieval and early modern royal perpetuity—namely, the king's two bodies: "the throne, like the other insignia of regality," Agamben contends, "refers more to the office and the *dignitas* of the sovereign than to his person."¹⁰ In the material form of the (empty) royal throne, Julia Reinhard Lupton argues, we confront the king's "second, immortal body within an elaborate exo-skeleton of carved wood and cloth of gold, since the ghostly *dignitas* of father, king, or bishop requires bio-technical support to maintain its fragile charisma."¹¹

In this chapter, I seek to gather an apparently random set of empty chairs—royal thrones, papal seats, university chairs, and even common stools—for a new crowd of theatrical guests: Shakespeare, Kant, Bacon, and Ionesco. It is my aim to explore (recalling Ionesco's revealing metaphor of the deconsecrated cathedral) what we might call the profane, democratic "afterlife" of the empty throne in an epoch when it has apparently been evacuated of its original sacred use and returned to immanence. As Claude Lefort argues in his classic essay "The Permanence of the Theologico-Political? ("Permanence du théologico-politique?," 1981), a new and peculiarly secularized *amor vacui* emerges in the nineteenth century via such figures as Chateaubriand, Tocqueville, and Michelet that not merely seeks to reveal that "the throne is empty, and Humpty Dumpty, having fallen, cannot be put back together again," but to, paradoxically, install or ensconce *emptiness* itself as the symbolic, immanent, and autonomous seat of democratic power.¹² To introduce my argument in this chapter, I want to propose that Shakespeare, Kant, Bacon, and Ionesco dramatize the political movement of the empty chair from the early Christian *hetoimasia tou thronou* up to what Lefort famously calls the "empty space" of democracy: "I have for a long time concentrated upon this peculiarity of modern democracy," Lefort contends, "of all the regimes of which we know, it is the only one to have represented power in such a way as to show that power is an *empty place* [*lieu vide*] and to have thereby maintained a gap between the symbolic and the real [*l'écart du symbolique et du reel*]."[13] If the ancient royal throne was a permanent, inert fixture that signified the king's undying dignitas—which is to say the sovereign power to reign in perpetuity irrespective of the natural life of any one monarch—I will contend that this new, modern, and so-to-speak mass-produced democratic chair is, by contrast, symptomized by what we might call a certain virtual and real political *moveability* (from the Latin *mōbile* and the French *meuble*, literally a "moveable" and also, of course, "a piece of furniture"). For Lefort, what defines "democracy" is the fact that the seat or place of power is never fixed but remains permanently in circulation: democratic power belongs to no one, and those who temporarily exercise it neither possess nor embody it, but merely circle it infinitely.[14] In the short article "Sur la crise du théâtre," Ionesco likewise declares that "there is a crisis of theater when there is *immobility* [*immobilité*]" and I want to argue that his work stages the historical passage from the old political theological throne to a new political theater of the meuble, mobile, or moveable.[15] Who or what, then, sits in the empty chair today?

IN THE KING'S PLACE

In act 3, scene 4 of *Macbeth* (ca. 1606)—a tragedy that Ionesco will himself later rewrite as the black comedy *Macbett* (1972)—William Shakespeare depicts what is perhaps the most famous or notorious empty chair in theatrical history. It can be found in the so-called banquet scene, where Macbeth and his wife prepare a celebration for the Thanes of Scotland to observe his (suspiciously sudden) accession to power. As J. P. Dyson observed more than sixty years ago, Macbeth himself welcomes his guests by formally inviting them to "sit down," because, of course, this entire scene is about nothing other than the political gesture of sitting down.[16] The new king's banquet is no mere celebration but a "formal or gestural attempt to enthrone himself, to become the *true* king" in front of his people after the murder of Duncan.[17] Yet, of course, what the banquet scene really concerns is the new king's *inability* to legitimately occupy the throne he has acquired through regicide, and, revealingly, the injunction to "sit" has to be repeated no less than six times in this short scene. To Macbeth's horror, his attempt to preside over his own symbolic coronation will be frustrated by the appearance of an uninvited guest who invisibly takes the king's seat at the political table: "*Enter the* Ghost *of* BANQUO," Shakespeare's famous stage direction reads, "*and sits in Macbeth's place.*" If Macbeth is unable to take his eyes off this spectral *arrivant*, Banquo's ghost remains (like the crowd of guests in Ionesco's *The Chairs*) totally invisible to his wife, Lady Macbeth, and the rest of the assembled party: Ross and Lennox repeatedly invite the new king to sit in the empty chair that has been reserved for him, but the dumbfounded Macbeth, seeing the ghost of Banquo already sitting in his seat, can only reply "The table's full" (3:4, 44). In this moment of tragic farce, we can already begin to detect the absurdist ghost of Ionesco—Macbeth, like a prototypical Bérenger from *Rhinocéros* (1959), even pathetically dares Banquo's specter to turn into a "rhinoceros," so he can fight him (3:4, 99)— but what is rarely observed by scholars is that the seating arrangements in the banquet scene also leave one, apparently minor, detail unresolved. Which chair, exactly, to repose a question recently raised by Lupton, does Banquo's ghost sit on?

To answer this (seemingly pedantic) question, which actually speaks to a larger power shift that is taking place not only theatrically but also historically in the early modern period, we need to slowly rerun the tragic or farcical drama of standing versus sitting, mobility versus immobility, equality versus hierarchy, performed at Macbeth's royal banquet. First, the new king himself disarmingly declares his intention at the beginning of the feast to *not* sit on his formal throne of state (which would, in the early modern period, have been situated on a podium or platform at one end of the banqueting hall), but instead to "play the humble host," "mingle with society," and "sit i' th' midst" of his guests (3:4, 3–4, 9) by taking a place at what would in this period have been a long table in front of the raised dais furnished with stools or benches. It is not possible for him to take his chosen seat, however, because three uninvited guests—the murderers he had earlier hired to kill Banquo—next arrive to discreetly inform him (most likely somewhere away from the main table) that the latter now "bides" dead in a ditch (3:4, 24). After this brief interruption, which already reminds us that the new king does not really belong at his own royal banquet, Banquo's ghost appears and sits in the former's place at the feast—presumably leaving Macbeth still standing. For Macbeth, Banquo's rising up from his own final resting place in order to unseat him is a horrifying portent of the political theological counterrevolution his own unnatural seizure of the throne has set in motion: "the times have been, / That when the brains were out, the man would die, / And there an end," he famously muses. "But now they rise again, / With twenty mortal murders on their crowns, / And push us from our stools" (3:4, 76–80). If Macbeth himself undoubtedly "sees" Banquo sitting in his place at the table, Lady

Macbeth exasperatedly replies that the ghost is merely a hallucination, and he is staring at an empty chair: "Shame itself. / Why do you make such faces? When all's done, / You look but on a stool" (3:4, 63–65). In the mounting chaos, Macbeth apparently never gets to sit down at all, and the banquet is prematurely broken up by his wife, who orders the assembled party to all stand up and leave immediately: "At once, good night: / Stand not upon the order of your going, / But go at once" (3:4, 116–18).

If Banquo's reclamation of Macbeth's empty chair is obviously full of political significance in Shakespeare's play—because the old order is quite literally restored to its proper or rightful place—it is rarely observed that the king has not one but *two* possible places to sit at the banquet: his royal chair of state on the raised dais (where Lady Macbeth chooses to sit), and his stool in the middle of the long table among the other guests (where Macbeth himself has indicated he wishes to sit). To judge by most historical and modern staging practices, Banquo's ghost sits on the king's chair of state on the dais: Simon Forman's record of a 1610 performance of the play at the Globe Theatre, for instance, describes the ghost appearing directly *behind* Macbeth's royal throne.[18] It is not difficult to see why generations of directors should choose to position Banquo, who the Weird Sisters predict will be father to a line of kings that will culminate in the reigning English King James I, in the king's seat rather than on a common stool. After all, Banquo's spectral "coronation" in the sovereign's place, together with Macbeth's relegation back to the rank and file, plausibly symbolizes that the divinely ordained and patrilineal order of royal succession will reestablish itself following the regicide. However, as Dyson and, more recently, Lupton observe, what stands in the way of this reading of the play as an exercise in pure Jacobean propaganda is the inconvenient fact that Macbeth himself specifically identifies Banquo's ghost as sitting at the *lower*, rather than the higher, table. For the new king, recall, Banquo's ghost apparently takes his place, not on the chair of state, but upon the common stool he planned to occupy among his fellow guests: "They rise again, / With twenty mortal murders on their crowns, / And push us from our *stools*" (emphasis mine). In order to stand up the long-standing critical and directorial consensus that Banquo's ghost sits on the royal throne, Dyson and Lupton are obliged to read Macbeth's exclamation about the ghost pushing us "from our stools" nonliterally, as a symbolic expression of the usurper's traumatized sense of alienation or exclusion from the common "table" of humanity, but this ontological reading does not quite explain why the (conspicuously untraumatized) Lady Macbeth should also identify Banquo's situation as a stool rather than a chair: "You look but on a stool."[19]

Instead of arguing that Macbeth, Banquo, or even Shakespeare must somehow be "wrong" to sit the ghost in a commoner's place, I want to propose that what Lupton calls a "political theology of the stool" might, perversely, be the *right* target for Banquo's counterrevolution, because this common stool is the virtual placeholder of a democracy that can have no place within the ancient political theological order that the ghost seeks to restore.[20] It is necessary to offer an Ionescan anarchist rereading of Shakespeare's play—a reading that is always virtually present in the original, I think, regardless of its official support for James I—to turn the tables on the classic political theological interpretation of Banquo's ghost as the righteous avenging angel of Jacobean sovereignty: Ionesco's own version of Banquo ("Banco") is, revealingly, no innocent victim but every bit as steeped in blood as Macbeth.[21] According to Dyson's conventional reading of the banquet scene, it stages a political theology of natural hierarchy in which everyone knows their proper place from top to bottom: "You know your own degrees, sit down," Macbeth instructs his guests upon arrival, "At first and last, / The hearty welcome" (3:4, 1–2). Yet, unlike Duncan (an armchair general who inhospitably invites himself to spend the night at Castle Macbeth), Macbeth's own royal hospitality is a show, at least, of modesty, equality, and commonality: he wants to "sit i' the midst" of his guests, as we have seen, on a table where "both sides are even," so they can all "drink a measure / The table round" (3:4, 9–11). To be sure, Macbeth's desire to sit on a common stool among his people may well be an empty and cynical performance of the role of "good king," of early modern "commoning" (even an early exercise in Tony Blair-style "sofa government"), but it is worth remembering here that, in another Ionescan twist, the usurper's own bloody seizure of power from Duncan is itself a weirdly democratic coup against a dictator, and the new king a perversely constitutional monarch.[22] By overthrowing Duncan, recall, Macbeth is arguably just responding to an audacious power grab by the old king himself: he only decides to act after Duncan breaks with the historical tradition of electing Scottish kings by capriciously installing his son Malcolm as his heir, consequently depriving Macbeth himself of his own, arguably greater, claim to the succession (1.4.37–8).[23] If Macbeth self-consciously declares his preference for sitting on a common stool rather than the chair of state at the banquet held in his honor, we thus might plausibly see this as the (unfulfilled, betrayed, indeed very probably hypocritical from the very beginning) promise of a virtual and protodemocratic political theology "from below" that stands over and against the political theology from above, here represented by Banquo: what Banquo's ghost seeks to reclaim or reoccupy as the sole property of the ancien régime when he takes Macbeth's place on the empty stool—a common stool that actually belongs to no one—is thus curiously redolent of that other empty space that, as we have seen, Lefort calls "democracy."[24] For Shakespeare, whose play obviously remains deeply immersed in the old Jacobean political theological imaginary, a royal banquet that concludes with the guests being asked to democratically "stand not upon the order of your going, / But go at once" can only signify a descent into anarchy, civil war, or mob rule, but, with an Ionescan turning of the tables, this scene may equally be reimagined as something like the violent birth pangs of a popular sovereignty in which there are no longer any hierarchies or "degrees" but only a "most admired disorder" (3:4, 108). In *Macbeth*, which is just the first of a series of very different theatrical scenes that stage the meuble or movement from absolute monarchy to liberal democracy we will encounter in this chapter, a democratic theater of the empty stool thus begins to pull the chair out from under the supposedly permanent fixture that is the political theology of the throne—but whether the new occupant of this chair will be a legitimate elected leader or an illegitimate usurper or tyrant remains to be seen.

VACANT CHAIRS

In Immanuel Kant's *The Conflict of the Faculties* (*Der Streit der Fakultäten*, 1798), we encounter a new kind of empty chair: the vacant university chair of the professional philosopher. It is worth recalling here that the immediate political context of Kant's classic work on the idea of the university was another royal throne left suddenly empty, albeit in less suspicious circumstances than the regicide in *Macbeth*. After the death of the liberal Frederick the Great, Johann Christoph von Wöllner, minister of justice to the new Prussian king, Friedrich Wilhelm II, launched a policy of state-sponsored religious censorship against the Aufklärung that culminated in the prohibition of the second book of Kant's *Religion Within the Limits of Reason Alone* (1792). To explain his own idea of the place of the university within the state, Kant responded with an essay, "The Conflict of the Philosophy Faculty with the Theology Faculty" (1794), that famously proposes an internal division of the university between what he calls the "higher" faculties of theology, law, and medicine—which represent and are subject to the interests of the state—and the "lower" faculty of philosophy, which, crucially, is not: "It is absolutely essential that the learned community at the university also contain a faculty that is independent of the government's command with regard to its teachings," he argues, "one that, having no commands to give, is free to evaluate everything, and concerns itself with the interest of the sciences, that is, with truth: one in which reason is authorized to speak out publicly [*wo die Vernunft öffentlich zu sprechen berechtigt sein muss*]."[25] For Kant, as he goes on to expound in an intriguing long footnote, we can even draw an analogy between philosophy's place as the lower faculty within the ideal Prussian university and the House of Commons's position as the lower house within the real British parliamentary system:

> It is a principle (*Grundsatz*) in the British Parliament that the monarch's speech from the throne is to be considered the work of his ministers (since the House must be entitled to judge, examine, and attack the content of the speech and it would be beneath the monarch's dignity to let himself be charged with error, ignorance, or untruth [*Irrthum, Unwissenheit oder Unwahrhei*]). And this principle is quite acute and correct. It is in the same way that the choice of certain teachings which the government expressly sanctions for public exposition must remain subject to scholarly

criticism (*Prüfung der Gelehrten*); for this choice must not be ascribed to the monarch but to a state official whom he appoints to do it—an official who, it is supposed, could have misunderstood or misrepresented his ruler's will (*er könne auch wohl den Willen seines Herrn nicht Recht verstanden*).[26]

If Kant wants to argue here that the philosophy faculty should enjoy the same privileged position within the university as the House of Commons does in Parliament, in that both have the same freedom of expression upon, and right of inspection over, government policy, this parliamentary analogy was even more radical than he perhaps realizes: the British Parliament actually adopts the polite constitutional fiction or convention that "His Majesty's Most Gracious Speech"—which is the official title of the speech from the throne given on the opening of parliament—is the work of the king *himself*, when it is entirely written by his ministers. In a topological irony that will reverberate through the offices of Kant's ideal university, the king's throne, which allegedly precedes and authorizes the philosopher's own state-appointed chair, is itself a largely ceremonial seat that is empty of "real" power.[27]

To revisit *The Conflict of the Faculties* as a whole in the light of Kant's misplaced parliamentary metaphor for philosophy, I am tempted to suspect that his historical error is actually something of a Freudian slip, because, as a handwritten note on one of the manuscripts of the introduction reveals, his real ambition in this text is to make possible a kind of democratic or republican "glorious revolution" of the philosophy faculty against its alleged superiors: "The lower faculty must one day become the highest" (*Die Unterste Facultät muss einmal die Oberste werden*), he declares, "i.e., subject everything to the legislation of reason" (*der Gesetzgebung der Vernunft unterwerfen*).[28] It is true that the final published version of the text advocates this becoming-higher of the lower faculty in far more diplomatic terms, because, as Kant is at pains to stress, the lower faculty should not seek to exercise power directly but only by giving wise counsel to those in power.[29] Yet, all the same, a polite Kantian version of the Platonic philosopher-king, who would quietly dispense wisdom in the sovereign's ear without seeking to rule themselves, still cannot but upset the delicate balance of powers between the university and the government he has established. For Hent de Vries, Kant's parliamentary metaphor seems to open up an even more radical democratic and participatory place for philosophy in the political system than the latter's—principally negative and regulatory—role in the university because it becomes an early version of Lefort's "empty space": "the king's authority (more precisely, his 'speech from the throne,' ex cathedra)," de Vries argues, "resembles the empty signifier that some political philosophers—notably Claude Lefort and Ernesto Laclau—reserve for the place left open after the demise of theocracy and absolute monarchy." If de Vries reads the king's speech from the throne as establishing a kind of empty democratic space for debate ("That the monarch must be obeyed is beyond question," the former glosses, "but what he dictates through his ministers and his guardians is or, rather, seems to be up for discussion"), we must again add the historical footnote that we appended to Kant's original parliamentary metaphor: the English king's throne was, following the post-1688 constitutional settlement, *itself* empty.[30] In the Declaration of Right (1689), which decisively resolved the long struggle for sovereignty between the Crown and Parliament in the latter's favor, James II's absolute monarchy gave way to William III's constitutional monarchy: Parliament only "obeyed" the king's speech from the throne because the king had already constitutionally agreed to obey parliament.

If Kant's king speaks from an empty throne—which is to say that he neither historically nor textually possesses the sovereign authority necessary to act by himself in the first place—it is possible to argue that his cherished state-appointed philosopher, too, occupies an uncannily symmetrical "vacant chair" within the university that deprives them of their own defining vocation—namely, to speak truth to power without fear or favor.[31] To enter the Kafkaesque walls of the Kantian ideal university, with its seemingly infinite series of divisions and subdivisions between king and scholar, speech and action, conflict and war, inside and outside, lower and higher, layman, businessman, lawyer, doctor, biblical theologian, philosophical theologian and so on, we find at its center a singular philosophical void because Kant apparently leaves no place whatsoever for what is, in his view, the university's single most important occupant: the philosopher. For Jacques Derrida, as he observes in his essay "Vacant Chair: Censorship, Mastery, Magisteriality" (1984), the Kantian professional philosopher's allegedly unique position within the university, as the only scholar who has been given the freedom to teach nothing but pure reason with impunity, can be purchased or secured only at the perverse aporetic price of rendering them gloriously unemployed or redundant. By taking on this new official position, the philosopher may earn the right to speak, but they cannot do anything or even say what should be done without infringing upon the jurisdiction of the other faculties or the state censor;[32] they cannot occupy one localized faculty amongst others because they are mandated to maintain a purview over the truth-claims of the university as a whole,[33] and they cannot even fulfill their basic job description of teaching pure reason because, beyond a simple history of ideas, Kant himself confesses that "philosophy," as the rational knowledge of pure reason, remains essentially unteachable and unlearnable.³⁴ In Derrida's philosophical verdict, the Kantian philosopher thus finds themselves caught in a topological aporia or double bind that locates them both everywhere and nowhere in a university that can seemingly exist neither with nor without them: "This teacher of truth does not, in truth, exist," he argues. "He is nowhere to be found; he does not take place; he is not present," and, consequently, "the university itself does not take place: presently" either.³⁵

In *The Conflict of the Faculties*, then, Kant's speculative king and philosopher appear to exist less in a state of productive nonviolent conflict than a kind of political equivalent to a negative or entropic feedback loop where, so to speak, no one gives nothing to, and receives nothing from, no one. It is possible to detect a parallel here between the recursive logic that seems to operate within Kant's architectonic of the university system and that of the larger organic system of the natural world to which, as Derrida observes, the former still belongs.³⁶ As Kant explores in the second half of the *Critique of Judgment* (1790), which is the still little-read "Critique of Teleological Reason" on freedom and nature, we human beings claim to *receive* from nature our predisposition to free rational activity but, in actuality, we *give*, retroactively and anthropomorphically, this very power of causality to nature in the first place: "We say that we put [*legen*] final causes into things," he argues, "rather than, as it were, lifting them out of our perception of things."³⁷ To return to *The Conflict of the Faculties* in this context, we arguably find ourselves in a political version of this same circle: the king appears to give to the philosopher the power that he actually receives from him, whereas the philosopher appears to receive from the king the power that he actually gives to him, such that power *itself does not, presently, exist, reside or "take place" anywhere or with anyone* within the political system. If the king and the philosopher would seem at first blush to occupy what de Vries calls the two most extreme polarities within the spectrum of institutional possibilities that constitutes the modern state, which is to say that the king has the absolute freedom to act without having to speak and the philosopher the absolute freedom to speak without any possibility of acting, we might thus be tempted to conclude that, on the contrary, the extremities of empty throne and vacant chair in fact meet in a common or shared void: they are both defined by the impossibility of either speaking or acting from their own, allegedly "legitimate," place.[38] For Kant, whose strict logic here obviously departs from his own declared objectives, what this means is that every "conflict" that *The Conflict of the Faculties* was written to nonviolently negotiate or resolve—in other words, any constitutional, political or institutional crisis within the state, whether it assumes the form of political absolutism, popular revolution, unconstitutional overreach, or mission creep, trahison des clercs, unreason, error, or, finally, just "war"—is itself violently reproduced within the text in the form of its own supposed solution or resolution: every legitimate political speech act or philosophical truth claim is equally illegitimate, every form of political or rational representation a misrepresentation, every use of power an abuse, every conflict an act of war. In this Ionescan theater of the political, Kant's dream of a modern Platonic "philosopher-king," who would alone be capable of resolving the aporia of the king and the philosopher, power and truth, action and speech into a single office or seat, becomes a kind of tragic or farcical equivalent to the Orator in *The Chairs*: a speaker who says nothing to no one on behalf of no one.

EX CATHEDRA

In his "Screaming Popes," a series of more than fifty paintings inspired by Velázquez's *Portrait of Pope Innocent X* (1650), which he coincidentally began the year after the first performance of Ionesco's *The Chairs*, Francis Bacon depicts one more empty political theological chair: the papal *cathedra*. It is by now well documented that Bacon (arguably more than any other modern artist) depicts the human body in a state of repose—if never, of course, at rest. According to the most recent *Catalogue Raisonné* (2016), he painted no less than sixteen works titled *Seated Figure* and positioned many more subjects on chairs, sofas, beds, or, in the case of the haunting 1970s triptychs of George Dyer, collapsed on or near a toilet.[39] To put it in Gilles Deleuze's words from *Francis Bacon: The Logic of Sensation* (1981), Bacon is thus the painter of what we might call the body *in* rather than *ex cathedra*. "Bacon's figures are ordinary bodies in ordinary situations of constraint and discomfort," Deleuze writes in the preface to the English translation of his book, "A man ordered to sit still for hours on a narrow stool is bound to assume contorted postures."[40] If Bacon (like Ionesco) aspires toward an absolute, nonrepresentational, and neuroaesthetic realism in his art, which refuses all attempts to read social, political, or religious "messages" into it, his Screaming Popes nevertheless seem (again, like Ionesco) to locate the seated body in a very particular political theological chair that, uniquely in his body of work, *preexists* his own act of artistic sitting, composition or arrangement. "The Pope is unique," Bacon concedes in his interviews with David Sylvester. "He's *put in a unique position* by being the Pope, and therefore, like in certain great tragedies, *he's as though raised onto a dais* on which the grandeur of this image can be displayed to the world."[41] In Bacon's imaginary, what sets the Pope apart from the various subjects who sit for his paintings is that he is already *in cathedra*, so to speak, before the artist arrives on the scene, already "in the chair"—indeed, nothing but his chair.

To stand up his now classic thesis about Bacon as the painter of pure "sensation," Deleuze famously claims that the Screaming

Popes break away from any representational, narrative, or figural function by impacting immediately, and preconceptually, upon the spectator's nervous system.[42] It is not that the *Study After Velázquez's Portrait of Pope Innocent X* (1953) is "about" something or other—a real renaissance pope, say, screaming at some real scene of horror—because what the painting really presents is *sensation itself* devoid of any unified and unifying subject or object. As the French philosopher recounts, what is at stake in the Screaming Popes is really a scream that has no "why": "The Pope himself sees nothing, and screams *before the invisible*."[43] For Deleuze, Bacon's Popes are not Kantian subjects with attached percepts or affects but purely polymorphous bodies without organs upon which the invisible forces of sensation exert themselves: "When sensation is linked to the body in this way, it ceases to be representative and becomes real," he argues, "and *cruelty* will be linked less and less to the representation of something horrible, and will become nothing other than the action of forces upon the body, or sensation."[44] If Bacon is interested in the ordinary sitting or reclining body "to whom nothing visible happens," rather than the extraordinary body wracked by torture or brutality, it is not because this body is at peace or in repose but, on the contrary, because it makes clear that even here there is no such thing *as* "rest": what Deleuze calls the "*form at rest*"[45] is the only apparently still surface upon which this endless theater of pure sensation, uncaused by any external force, plays itself out.[46] Perhaps it would thus be more accurate to say that Bacon's static or immobile bodies exist—like the famous Eadweard Muybridge stop-motion photographs that influenced the artist so much—in a state of suspended or interrupted animation: "What fascinates Bacon is not movement, but its effect on an immobile body," Deleuze writes, "heads whipped by the wind or deformed by an aspiration, but also all the interior forces that climb through the flesh."[47] In Deleuze's verdict, what really "sits" in Bacon's art is not the human figure but movement itself: Bacon's movement is always "movement 'in-place' " (*mouvement sur place*).⁴⁸

If Deleuze is obviously even less interested in political theology than Bacon himself, I want to propose—and here I am following Eric Santner's remarkable reading of the Screaming Popes in his *Royal Remains* (2011)—that we may still be able to place this political physics of bodies at rest and in motion into dialogue with our own political and religious genealogy of the meuble, the mobile or "moveable": what is at stake in both remains a body in and ex cathedra.⁴⁹ To begin with, I find it significant that Deleuze himself is ultimately forced to marginalize the Screaming Popes in order to make good his thesis that Bacon is the "painter of sensation"—almost as if the former recognizes that they are clearly of a very different order to, say, Edvard Munch's *The Scream* (1893). It appears that even Bacon's celebrated desire to "paint the scream more than the horror"⁵⁰ still remains too mortgaged to what Deleuze regards as the representational fetish that there *is* a real horror "out there" that will explain the scream away, and, consequently, its pure power is "botched."⁵¹ Applying a curious representational benchmark of his own devising, Deleuze thus prefers to argue that Bacon's theater of cruelty only manifests itself in depictions of "ordinary bodies in ordinary situations of constraint and discomfort" to whom no visible and explicable violence ever happens: a figure sitting on a common stool, for instance, rather than a papal throne. However, Deleuze would again appear to part company with Bacon here, at least where the Screaming Popes are concerned. For Bacon himself, the Popes are ordinary bodies that are obviously placed in an *extraordinary* situation of constraint and discomfort by the symbolic violence of investiture or enthronement. By contrast to Deleuze, what fascinates Bacon (as the painter's remarks on the pope's unique status to Sylvester

FIGURE 1.1 Francis Bacon, *Study After Velázquez's Portrait of Pope Innocent X* (1953). Purchased with funds from the Coffin Fine Arts Trust; Nathan Emory Coffin Collection of the Des Moines Art Center, 1980.1. Photo Credit: Rich Sanders, Des Moines © Estate of Francis Bacon. All rights reserved. DACS 2023.

again reveal) is not the "becoming-animal" of the pope but the "becoming-pope" of the animal.[52] In returning the 1953 *Study After Velázquez* to this singular political theological context, I obviously do not mean to reject out of hand Deleuze's vitalist or energetic reading of the painting as a nonrepresentationalist theater of cruelty, nor to rehabilitate banal pseudoexistentialist or psychoanalytic interpretations of it as a "critique" of the Catholic Church or Nazism (or even of Pius XII's collaboration with the Nazis) so much as to construct what we might call a Baconian "political-theological-libidinal economy" where nature and politics, life and history, the laws of force, mass and motion and the normative symbolic grammar of political theology, bleed into one another.

In his *Study After Velázquez*, Bacon seems to turn Velázquez's original study in ex cathedra papal power inside out as if it were a dying star collapsing in upon itself. It is true, of course, that both painters (Velázquez and Bacon) depict the Pope's body as the still center of an at once symbolic and real, political, and physical vortex of power: Innocent's political appurtenances (e.g., a gilded throne, ermine robe, brocaded curtain) are equally atmospheric forces, torsions, and pressures. As Deleuze himself observes, Velázquez's apparently serene theater of representation was already a secret field of dynamic forces long before Bacon ever arrived on the scene: "The armchair [in Velázquez's painting] already delineates the prison of the parallelepiped," he writes, "the heavy curtain in back is already tending to move up front," "the mantelet has aspects of a side of beef" and "the attentive, fixed eye of the Pope already sees something invisible looming up."[53] Yet (upon my interpretation, at least) Bacon's own painting does not merely actualize—Deleuze's word is "hystericize"—a set of intensities that are already virtually present in Velázquez's original, so much as to immanentize, even perversely *democratize*, the original painting's political absolutism.[54] To libidinally "democratize" Velázquez's attempt to raise Innocent's body up to a place of total ex cathedra authority, Bacon's Pope painting chooses to stress what we might call the "gravitational" forces of resistance which that animal body experiences when it is elevated into a position of "unnatural" political theological power: what is striking about the *Study After Velázquez* is that power does not radiate outward or centrifugally from the chair into Innocent X's flesh, as it did in the original painting, but instead appears to collapse inward, centripetally, riveting Innocent's skeletal and transparent body to the chair. If the Pope's body seems to disappear into his chair, almost as if swallowed up by a black hole, the empty chair, by contrast, appears to enlarge and multiply formally beyond its own physical perimeters: Deleuze's "prison of the parallelepiped," the strange abstract prism in which Innocent, like so many of Bacon's figures, is positioned, expands to divide space and time themselves into empty, geometrical forms. Finally, Bacon's political theological counterrevolution of the chair against the throne perhaps also affords us a new and radically nonrepresentationalist answer to a question that, in spite of Deleuze's best efforts, continues to haunt the Screaming Popes. In Deleuze's own oddly moralizing verdict, Bacon's Popes remain ambivalent about the new libidinal universe they have midwifed into being —"Should these presences have been let loose?" the philosopher ventriloquizes the painter, "Were not things better, infinitely better, in Velázquez?"—but the residuum of political theology in the paintings that disappoints Deleuze is arguably the source of an energizing horror for Bacon: his own Pope screams at the horrifying empty space that will become democracy.[55]

IN THE EMPTY CHAIR

In the closing scene of Ionesco's *The Chairs*, the curtain falls on the same group of empty chairs sitting in the middle of a sparsely furnished room. To bring his tragic farce to a close, Ionesco thus appears to return it to the void from which it came: the Orator, frustrated that his message does not seem to have been properly received or understood by his invisible audience, exits the stage and leaves behind what seems, at least from the spectator's perspective, to be a totally empty space. However, as anyone familiar with *The Chairs* will already know, there is one very significant difference between the beginning of the play and its end. For Ionesco, as his dramatic final stage direction makes clear, what appears to be a perfect philosophical vacuum slowly but unmistakably begins to fill with a curious theatrical "oxygen":

> We hear for the first time the human noises of the invisible crowd (*les bruits humains de la foule invisible*): there are bursts of laughter, murmurs, shh's (*des chut*); ironical coughs (*toussotements ironiques*); weak at the beginning, these noises grow louder (*grandissant*); then, again, they progressively become weaker. All this should last long enough for the audience—the real and visible audience—to leave with this ending firmly impressed on its mind. The curtain falls very slowly.[56]

If this coup de théâtre would seem to force us to reassess everything we had thought we were seeing (or rather not seeing) up to that point—what if the invisible crowd of people was not just the Old Man and Woman's fantasy, as we might have assumed, but was really there all along?—I find it revealing that Ionesco himself, in his own interpretation of the ending of the play in a private letter to the director of the original 1952 Paris production, rejects what he calls such a "false . . . routine, mediocre" choice between psychological or rational reality and illusion.⁵⁷ In another letter about this cryptic final scene, Ionesco simply refuses to speculate about the existence or nonexistence of the crowd of human beings (a question which he clearly deems irrelevant) and instead focuses on what he calls the "life" of the furniture (*meubles*) itself: "The chairs, the décor, the void [*le rien*]," he writes, "would inexplicably come to life [*se mettraient à vivre inexplicablement*]."⁵⁸ What might it mean, though, to say that the empty chair itself, rather than its human occupant, "lives?"

To the question of who or what occupies the "seat of power" in political modernity, this opening chapter has proposed that Shakespeare, Kant, Ionesco, and Bacon could each be said to stage a curious game of political theological musical chairs in which the various players—king, pope, professor—all circle indefinitely around an essentially empty or absent place called "democracy." It is striking that all of these very different depictions of real or symbolic coronation, investiture, and inauguration conclude with what we might (in every sense of the word) call a moment of *dis-appointment* where everything is set in motion (*meuble*) but no one or nothing ever "takes place." After the old political theological music stops, all the players in this game belatedly discover that there is no longer anywhere for them to sit down: Shakespeare's Macbeth is a usurper, Kant's philosopher-king is neither king nor philosopher, and Bacon's pope is a pure scream without a body. Yet, in case we are tempted to reply that this is precisely the perverse genius of democracy—which is to say that it is the only political system where no one ever gets to sit down at the table of power permanently—what this chapter has sought to demonstrate is less the genius than the perversity of the democratic empty chair. For Shakespeare et al., what "dis-appoints" the pretenders to the empty throne is not so much the historical retreat of sovereign absolutism that empties their claim to power or legitimacy so much as the new political vacuum *created* by democracy itself: Macbeth, Innocent, and company are not the (tragic or comic) remnants of an old political theological epoch who no longer have any place within the new democratic order, but the peculiar metastases of an emerging democratic system that creates a new form of Demogorgon or "people-monster" in whom legitimacy and illegitimacy coincide. They are each studies in what we might call "screaming sovereignty." If democracy is really an empty space that can be permanently occupied by no one, after all, then every legitimate, even elected, occupant of the democratic seat of power is, unless or until they vacate that space, always virtually illegitimate, a potential dictator, imposter, or usurper: what distinguishes the empty place of power that is Lefortian democracy from a predemocratic society with legitimate rulers and violent or illegitimate usurpers, Slavoj Žižek observes, is that, "within the democratic horizon, everyone who occupies the locus of power is by definition a usurper."[59] In Shakespeare, Kant, Ionesco, and Bacon, we discover that the promise and threat to democracy always comes from *within*, and may even just be, the empty space of power itself: *democracy is its own usurpation.*

If Ionesco's *The Chairs* really does depict a postapocalyptic world, as many critics of the play allege, it often seems to be one that has been created or destroyed by a kind of dramatic equivalent to the neutron bomb: a thermonuclear weapon also invented in the 1950s that could annihilate all life but, theoretically at least, leave the buildings standing for future use. It is not necessary to endorse the Catholic theologian Hans Urs von Balthasar's explicitly apologetic attempt to place Ionesco within the long history of "theo-drama" here to recognize that Ionesco's devastated landscape of empty towers, deconsecrated cathedrals, and abandoned palaces nonetheless remains here in certain important respects a recognizably political theological one that can be reoccupied differently by new inhabitants.[60] As Nicole Jerr has recently argued, Ionesco's kings never quite die or exit the historical stage so much as enter a sort of spectral biopolitical afterlife in modernity: *Rhinocéros* (1959), *Le Roi se meurt* (1962), and *Macbett* (1972) all call "attention to the responsibilities and burdens of sovereignty the common individual inherits."[61] Yet it is actually the common meubles or furniture, the rows of empty chairs which may or may not ever be occupied, that, I would argue, bear the burden of sovereignty in this play. To reread even the opening scene of *The Chairs* in this political theological context of the "remains" of sovereignty, I find it striking that Ionesco's own empty chairs already recognizably bear the historical impression of a very different set of empty chairs—namely, the thrones of the deposed, unseated, or overthrown kings of prerevolutionary France. For Ionseco, recall, the Old Woman warns her husband in their very first exchange to stop leaning out of the tower's window and sit down, lest he should befall the same fate as the sixteenth-century French king François I, whose own final resting place was desecrated during the French Revolution, with the monarch's corpse apparently even being thrown into the latrines. In this moment of real and symbolic (de)position, Ionesco's play thus already begins to position itself within the—first tragic and later farcical—historical passage from the empty throne of royal or absolute sovereignty to the empty space of modern democracy: the Old Man is, revealingly, quite blind to the lesson of his unfortunate predecessor ("Still more examples from history!" he chides his wife. "Sweetheart, I'm tired of French history"),[62] but both characters will, of course, end up committing suicide by jumping out of the window and vacating the space of power for their assumed representative, the Orator.

What kind of "democracy," though, is taking place in the empty space of Ionesco's postwar tragic farce? To return to the cryptic final scene of the play one last time, I want to conclude by hypothesizing that, contrary to the once-fashionable but now distinctly passé critical orthodoxy promulgated by Tynan, *The Chairs* does not describe an absurd existentialist universe in which human existence no longer has any meaning so much as an empty structuralist or functionalist one in which, so to speak, meaning continues to exist without humanity: what Ionesco's drama depicts is a total, autonomous, and self-regulating political order—encompassing everything from bare acts of politesse, function, employment, norm, ritual and office, up to authority or sovereignty—which is capable of enduring even or especially when all the empirical human beings who occupied it have ceased to exist. It would be quite premature to conclude that the deaf and mute Orator simply fails to deliver the Old Man's important message to the assembled crowd, or that the message could not be delivered, or that there was never any such message in the first place, because Ionesco's desire, as he revealingly puts it in his reply to Tynan, is "to make the *decor* speak [*faire parler les décors*]" rather than the people.⁶³ After all, Ionesco's theatrical decor or environment already contains all the constituent parts of what, less than five years earlier, the renowned information theorist Claude Shannon had called a "communication system," even if no act of communication ever takes place in the play: a source (the Old Man); a transmitter (the Orator); a channel (the Orator's speech or action) and a receiver (the guests).⁶⁴ For Ionesco, what is successfully communicated by the inexplicable figure of an empty chair coming to life in a world where all human beings have died may thus be nothing more than the bare, formal, and objective possibility of ongoing communication itself: the meuble, to misquote Marshall McLuhan, is the message. If Lefort's "The Permanence of the Theologico-Political" defines democracy as a kind of self-regulating symbolic economy that no longer needs to communicate with any substantive inside or outside (i.e., a god, king, community, or even the people) in order to function, then we might speculate that Ionesco's own political theater *empties even that empty space itself* of its last vestige of political theological depth or profundity: what is taking place in the uncanny posthuman tableau at the end of *The Chairs*, where a crowd of objects come to life all by themselves and are capable of speaking to one another freely, equally, and collectively in the absence of any human users or occupants, is perhaps the beginning of a new kind of taking place, a new arche or rule, without any demos. In Ionesco's democracy without people, the empty chair itself presides.

2

ANOINTED WITH OIL
Shakespeare, Milton, Melville

> *Be thy Head anointed with holy Oil: as kings, priests, and prophets were anointed: And as Solomon was anointed king by Zadok the priest and Nathan the prophet, so be thou anointed, blessed, and consecrated Queen over the Peoples, whom the Lord thy God hath given thee to rule and govern, In the Name of the Father, and of the Son, and of the Holy Ghost. Amen.*
> —Anglican Liturgical Library, *The Form and Order of the Service That Is to Be Performed and the ceremonies that are to be observed in the Coronation of Her Majesty Queen Elizabeth II*

In the 1953 coronation of Queen Elizabeth II of the United Kingdom, which was the first coronation ceremony in history to be broadcast live on television, one sacred ritual remained deliberately out of sight of the audience of twenty million viewers. It began with the new Queen being divested of her royal cloak and jewelry and then seated upon the ancient throne of King Edward. As Handel's coronation anthem "Zadok the Priest" was sung, four knights of the Garter erected a gold canopy above the throne to protect the monarch from public view. To perform the so-called Act of Consecration, the archbishop of Canterbury, Geoffrey Fisher, then applied what he called a "holy oil" (which was composed of orange, roses, cinnamon, musk, and ambergris from the intestines of whales, according to a centuries-old recipe) onto the Queen's hands, breast, and the crown of her head, while making the sign of the cross and speaking the words "so be thou anointed, blessed, and consecrated Queen over the Peoples, whom the Lord thy God hath given thee to rule and govern." In this thaumaturgical gesture of anointment with oil, Elizabeth Windsor was apparently transformed into the sacred monarch Elizabeth Regina.[1]

To pull back the golden canopy that conceals the monarch's sacred body and look behind it, however, we quickly find that this ancient tradition of anointment with holy oil, which allegedly stretched unbroken from Solomon to Elizabeth, is also the site of what we might call a long political theological "oil war." It is well documented, of course, that the ritual of anointment does extend all the way back to the anointing of the first kings of Israel in the Hebrew Bible: the Hebrew *mashiach* (messiah), as well as the Greek *christos* (Christ), literally translate into English as "the anointed."[2] As many scholars have recounted, the ritual of consecrating someone or something with oil, which is to say setting them apart from common use, was applied to an astonishingly wide range of people and objects in the Hebrew Bible, including priests, prophets, the altar in the Temple, kings of Israel (Saul, David, Solomon), and even the pagan Persian king Cyrus the Great. For the crowning of Solomon in the Book of Kings, we are told that "Zadok the priest took a horn of oil out of the tabernacle, and anointed Solomon. And they blew the trumpet; and all the people said, God save king Solomon" (1:39). If Jesus Christ was said to be anointed as king by the Holy Spirit rather than oil in the New Testament—"The Spirit of the Lord is upon me, because he hath anointed me to preach the gospel to the poor" (Luke 4:18)—the original Hebrew ritual of anointing with a physical oil or unction survived to become part of Roman and early medieval European coronation ceremonies. In 672 CE, for example, a Visigoth Catholic monarch, Wamba, was reported to have been anointed with holy oil by the archbishop of Toledo during his coronation ceremony.[3]

If Elizabeth's anointing was presented as belonging to an uninterrupted history going back to the Hebrew Bible, though, we need only recall Marc Bloch's classic study *The Royal Touch* (1923) to appreciate that the Act of Consecration was actually the site of a millennium of political theological dispute between church and state before her coronation. Its precise meaning or meanings—whether anointment with oil was a sacrament or a ritual, a real act, or merely a symbolic gesture, an indelible signifier of divine office, or an ephemeral and conditional trace that can be removed—changed radically over time.[4] According to the eleventh-century Benedictine theologian Peter Damian, for example, royal anointment was one of no less than twelve, rather than seven, sacraments of the Church and bestowed a quasi-priestly status upon the monarch. To take a figure like the Norman Anonymous, who was probably the most vocal medieval spokesperson for the divinity of anointment, holy oil also transformed the king into a *persona mixta* possessed of both temporal and spiritual properties.[5] However, on the other side of the argument, Pope Gregory VII's 1076 deposition of Henry IV (who was self-declaredly king "through the holy ordination of God") during the Investiture Controversy was predicated on the claim that royal anointment was categorically *not* a permanent sacrament of the Church, and so could be removed from its bearer.[6] For Thomas Cranmer, who presided over the coronation of Edward VI at the height of the English Reformation in 1547, royal anointment inevitably carried the taint of Catholic ritual and so was accorded no religious significance whatsoever. "The oil, if added, is but a ceremony," Cramner argued, "if it be wanting, that king is a perfect monarch notwithstanding, and God's anointed, as well as if he was inoiled."[7] In a 1924 letter to Gershom Scholem, written from Capri, Walter Benjamin perhaps symptomizes holy oil's modern fall from grace when he sees the "anointed" head of the fascist leader Benito Mussolini as a signifier, not of some residuum of divine appointment, but of an altogether more repulsive Weberian sovereign charisma: "Mussolini set foot on this island at noon today," he writes. "He does not look like the lady-killer the postcards make him out to be: corrupt, indolent and as arrogant as if he had been generously anointed with rancid oil."[8]

In the case of Elizabeth II's mass media anointment, I want to propose that what took place was thus not simply the latest application of an ancient political theological substance but a kind of political chemistry experiment with this highly volatile material and semiotic liquid called "holy oil." It is this chapter's aim to reimmerse us in the long and fluid history of oil or unction from the English Reformation, through the Civil War, up to the period that Zygmunt Bauman metaphorically names "liquid" modernity.[9] As we have already begun to see, what is at stake in the history of the mysterious ritual of royal anointment is ultimately nothing less than the origins of the political or religious legitimacy of the "anointed one" themselves, whether it be the divine Wamba, the dictator Mussolini, or the constitutional monarch Elizabeth. To divine what we might call the "political theological fluid mechanics" or "energetics" of anointment, this chapter seeks to explore holy oil's extraction and production; importation and exportation; liquefaction and coagulation; application and removal; ablution and emulsification by other liquids like tears, blood, and seawater from William Shakespeare, through John

Milton, to Herman Melville. If we trace the global flow or circulation of unction over (early) modern time and space—from the Welsh coast to Nantucket Bay, from the England of the Middle Ages to modern capitalist America, from the forehead of a deposed divine right king to the cranium of a hunted sperm whale—we may also begin to read the signs of an increasingly *unholy*, profane, or immanent rite of anointment that does not descend vertically from God, but rather spreads out horizontally, like an oil slick, across, through, and between different political land masses, apparently bestowing its supernatural legitimacy on everything from divine right monarchy to global capital. In the coronation of Elizabeth II's son and heir, King Charles III, we will finally bear witness to the metabolization of anointment with oil from a sacred imprimatur into the kind of political metabrand that William Mazzarella, Eric Santner and Aaron Schuster recently called "Sovereignty, Inc."[10] Who or what, then, is anointed with the "sovereignty ink" that is holy oil today?

NOT ALL THE WATER IN THE ROUGH RUDE SEA

In act 3, scene 2 of Shakespeare's *Richard II*, the increasingly embattled king arrives back on the shore of Wales from Ireland, kisses the soil of his kingdom, and delivers what is arguably the single most celebrated assertion of divine right monarchy in political history: "Not all the water in the rough rude sea / Can wash the balm off from an anointed king," he proclaims. "The breath of worldly men cannot depose / The deputy elected by the Lord."[11] To begin this genealogy of anointment with Shakespeare's history play, I want to propose that *Richard II* is not (as it is often read) simply a drama about the clash between two political theological solid bodies—Richard versus Bolingbroke, the theological body politic versus the realpolitik body natural, the divine right king versus the profane Machiavellian prince—but between two, famously immiscible, liquids: "holy" balm or oil and "rough rude" sea water. If Richard's great soliloquy on the Welsh coastline represents the apparent zenith of the sacramental theology of anointed kingship, the moment of "peak" holy oil in the West, Ernst Kantorowicz's famous reading of Shakespeare's tragedy in *The King's Two Bodies* (1957) reveals that divine unction was, in fact, already a finite and fast-diminishing resource by this stage in (real and imagined) history: the king's supposedly indelible balm will, as any contemporary spectator of the play familiar with medieval history would have known, indeed be washed away by the rising tide of Bolingbroke's rebellion.[12] In *Richard II*, though, Richard's oil and Bolingbroke's water also meet, recombine, and even *emulsify* into a new and uncanny political theological substance: tears.

To reenter Shakespeare's theater of sovereignty, we of course find anointed royal bodies everywhere: Blunt admonishes Hotspur that "You stand against anointed majesty" in *Henry IV, Part 1* (ca. 1597);[13] the ghost of Henry VI tells Richard III, "My anointed body / By thee was punched full of deadly holes" in *Richard III* (ca. 1597);[14] Gloucester speaks of Goneril sticking her "boarish fangs" into Lear's "anointed flesh" in *King Lear* (ca. 1605);[15] and Macduff announces the death of Duncan by declaring, "Most sacrilegious murder hath broke ope / The Lord's anointed temple" in *Macbeth* (ca. 1606).[16] It would be premature to conclude that the history plays simply endorse the medieval idea of anointment as an inalienable sign of divine office, though, because they also constantly bring the sacred immiscibility of oil into question. As Henry VI ruefully acknowledges following his deposition by Edward IV in *Henry VI, Part 3* (ca. 1591), holy oil can indeed be washed away by water: "Thy place is filled, thy sceptre wrung from thee, / Thy balm washed off wherewith thou wast anointed."[17] For Shakespeare's kings, anointment with oil serves to confirm their position in a lineage stretching back to saintly predecessors like Edward the Confessor, who apparently possessed the thaumaturgical power of "healing benediction" called the royal touch and bequeathed it to the "succeeding royalty" (*Macbeth*, 4.3.155–57).[18] Yet we can also find distinctly more pagan, even demonic, forms of anointment in his plays that complicate any simple opposition between the sacred and the profane, oil and water. If Samuel Johnson was right to observe that the editors of an early folio version of *Macbeth* had misread the Weird Sisters' order *"Aroint thee, Witch!"* (1.3.7) as *"Anoint thee, Witch!"* in his "Miscellaneous Observations on the Tragedy of *Macbeth*" (1745), for instance, it was an understandable editorial error, because witchcraft and anointment remain in uncanny proximity throughout the Scottish play.[19] Shakespeare suggests a number of curious parallels between the diabolical Weird Sisters, who hail Macbeth as King of Scotland in a kind of pagan coronation ceremony, and the Jewish or Christian priests who anoint kings. In *Macbeth*, the Weird Sisters apparently even possess the same sovereign "gift of prophecy" as the anointed Edward the Confessor (4.3.159): they, too, have the power to "look into the seeds of time / And say which grain will grow, and which will not" (1.3.58–59).[20]

If we return to *Richard II* in the context of this complex political ecology of anointment, we can witness something like the same process of emulsification (from the Latin *ex-mulgere*, literally "to milk out," in the sense that milk is itself an emulsion of fat and water) at work: Shakespeare's tragedy figuratively and literally mixes oil and water together to make a new political theological "milk." It may well appear from many influential readings of the play, of course, that this is nothing more complex than a story of the political ablution, or even dissolution, of Richard's embalmed body by the sheer physical force of Bolingbroke's rising seawater. As Kantorowicz himself puts it in an intriguing choice of fluid metaphor, Richard's body endures the *"cascading"*—literally a short or steep fall of water—"from divine kingship to kingship's 'Name,' and from the name to the naked misery of man" over the course of the tragedy.[21] However, according to Victoria Kahn's protoconstitutionalist rereading of Kantorowicz's celebrated account, Richard's divine right kingship may only ever have been a theatrical performance in the first place, and holy oil a form of cheap greasepaint. To recall her disenchanted interpretation of Richard's soliloquy on the Welsh coastline in *The Future of Illusion* (2014), Kahn finds a sovereign who, for all his grand actorly speeches, already suspects that the political tide is turning against him: the King who so confidently declares, "Not all the water in the rough rude sea / Can wash the balm off from an anointed king," can be found greeting one of his few remaining defenders immediately afterward with the revealingly profane question "How far off lies your power?" (*Richard II*, 3.2.63).[22] For Shakespeare, though, I want to argue that Richard's deposition from the throne may be neither Kantorowicz's political ablution or cleansing of holy oil by popular water nor Kahn's demystificatory revelation that holy oil was only ever a form of water in the first place, but rather a process of what we have called "political theological emulsification," in which oil and water combine into new and potent substances. In his famous reading of the deposition scene in act 4, scene 1 as an act of symbolic decoronation, for instance, Kantorowicz famously observes that Richard's "ecclesiastical ritual of undoing the effects of consecration is no less solemn or of less weight than the ritual which has built up the sacramental dignity": water, it seems, can paradoxically be every bit as holy as oil.[23]

In response to Bolingbroke's question "Are you contented to resign the crown?," the beleaguered Richard famously instigates a ceremony of self- or autodecoronation that specifically includes a rite of what we might call "deconsecration":

> Now mark me how I will undo myself;
> I give this heavy weight from off my head,
> And this unwieldy sceptre from my hand,
> The pride of kingly sway from out my heart;
> With mine own tears I wash away my balm. (*Richard II*, 4.1.203–7)

To dialectically transform the political theological conflict of oil and water we have been tracing in the play, Richard here injects a new substance into the mix that is neither quite sacred nor profane but something closer to what Philip Lorenz has ambivalently named the "tears" of sovereignty.[24] It is Richard's remarkable conceit in this scene to symbolically position himself as *both* priest and king, Zadok and Solomon, in a ritual of not simply decoronation but of *reverse anointment*. After his earlier disavowal of the "rough rude sea" in act 3, scene 2, Richard now appears to concede that it *is* possible to wash the balm off an anointed king—but, crucially, what he has in mind is a very different, but recognizably still holy, kind of "salt water" (4.1.245): "With mine own tears I wash away my balm." If the king's assertion of a lachrymose sovereignty at this moment has any direct theological precursor, it would presumably be the anonymous woman's anointing of Jesus with her tears in the house of Simon the Pharisee as described in Luke 7: 37–38: "And, behold, a woman in the city, which was a sinner, when she knew that Jesus sat at meat in the Pharisee's house, brought an alabaster box of ointment, And stood at his feet behind him weeping, and began to wash his feet with tears, and did wipe them with the hairs of her head, and kissed his feet, and anointed them with the ointment." By effectively weeping at his *own* feet, though, Richard's tears become a signifier, not simply of Kantorowicz's cascade from divine kingship into the naked misery of man, but of the setting-apart of a sacred king whose majesty endures despite, or rather because of, his abject position: *a king's own tears are the only way to remove a king's anointment*. For Richard's peculiar political theological imaginary, oil and water thus *do* ultimately mix in his own tears of sovereignty, which both anoint and disanoint his body at the same time: "O, that I were a mockery king of snow, / Standing before the sun of Bolingbroke, / To melt myself away in water-drops!" (*Richard II*, 4.1.260–62). Finally, and in anticipation of the debates surrounding the execution of Charles I to which we will now turn, I find it significant that Richard II's political theological emulsion of oil and water quickly spreads over the remainder of the play to "anoint" not simply the deposed monarch, but the new King Henry IV—namely, Bolingbroke himself. In another dialectical reversal of Richard's original boast that "not all the water in the rough rude sea / Can wash the balm off from an anointed king," Henry ends the play by himself seeking a form of spiritual ablution for his own profane "anointment" in his predecessor's blood: "I'll make a voyage to the Holy Land / To wash this blood off from my guilty hand" (5.6.49–50).

STAINED WITH THE BLOOD OF THOUSANDS

In his famous *Defensio pro Populo Anglicano* (*Defence of the People of England*, 1651), a work of republican counterpropaganda commissioned during Cromwell's Protectorship in response to Claudius Salmasius's *Defensio Regnia pro Carolo I* (Royal defense on behalf of Charles I, 1649), John Milton claims that Charles I's holy oil had been washed off, not by water, but *blood*: "shall a nation have scruples about condemning to death their own anointed," he asks in a rewriting of the biblical blood of the lamb, especially one who was smeared with the blood of citizens and who had blotted out that unction whether sacred or civil by such long enmity?"[25] It had, of course, been the conceit of the pseudonymous work of royal propaganda *Eikon Basilike* (Portrait of the king, 1648)—which claimed to be the spiritual autobiography of the king himself—to portray Charles as a Christian martyr in the image of Shakespeare's Richard II. As his sanguinary metaphor reveals, though, Milton instead prefers to cast Charles as a Henry IV (or even a Richard III), who uses holy oil to wash the blood off his hands. To rebut Salmasius's royalist claim that the Parliamentarians had effectively committed parricide when they executed a paternal Christian king who was accountable only to God, Milton expands upon his familiar argument—already rehearsed at length in earlier tracts like *Eikonoklastes* (Iconoclast) and *The Tenure of King's and Magistrates* (both 1649)—in support of killing the king as a legitimate act of popular tyrannicide. For Milton, whose republican argument directly reverses the theory of the divine right of kings, the people had made Charles king in the first place, and, by resorting to violence against them, the king had forfeited whatever popular "anointment" he had allegedly received—and so this could now be removed by any means necessary. If the debate between Salmasius and Milton, which is to say between royalism and republicanism, the king and the people, might once again be described as a clash between two immiscible liquids, Milton is thus clear that, politically speaking at least, blood is thicker than oil. In his *Defensio pro Populo Anglicano*, the people's blood also becomes something like a "new" holy oil: the sacred substance of a popular or republican anointment.

To grasp what is at stake in Milton's bloody polemic against the anointed Charles, we first need to put it in the context of a larger set of debates around the political theology of anointment that were taking place in the first half of the seventeenth century. It is hardly surprising that the smoldering controversy over the rite of anointing kings we have been describing reignited during the English Reformation because it spoke so directly to the political and religious legitimacy (or lack thereof) of Henry VIII's successors. As both Roman Catholic and radical Protestant dissenters alike questioned the authority of James I, Anglican theologians who supported the king sought to resolve once and for all the question of whether holy oil was a spiritual or literal unction, a divine gift or an ecclesiastical ceremony, an inalienable right or a contract with strict conditions attached. For Lancelot Andrewes, who delivered an entire sermon on the politically charged biblical verse "Touch not mine anointed [*Nolite tangere Christos meos*]" (1 Chron. 16:22) in front of James in 1610, the title of "Anointed" is a gift from God alone; a title reserved exclusively for kings; an office free of any trace of Catholic ceremony or Puritan covenant; and, crucially, a wholly untouchable (inalienable, inviolable) right no matter what the beliefs or conduct of the holder. If religious dissenters really do believe that "*His Anointed* may forfeit their tenure, and so cease to be *His*, and their *anointing* drie up, or be wiped off, and so kings be *unchristed*," writes Andrewes less than five years after the Gunpowder Plot, then they have not read 1 Chronicles 16:22 properly: "Gods claime never forfeits: His character never to bee wiped out, or scraped out, nor Kings loose their right."[26] In stark contrast to Andrewes, however, John Donne's Sermon 13 on the Hebrew prophets, "Lord, Who Hath Beleeved Our Report?"

(*Domine, quis credidit auditui nostro?*, 1628) less than twenty years later, sees the title of "my Anointed" as something of an empty or floating signifier, whose meaning circulated freely in the Hebrew Bible among kings, priests, prophets and objects, and this very ambiguity was the reason why the divine office of the Hebrew prophets was often not recognized by the Jewish people themselves. "This word *Meshiach*, which signifies *Anointing*," he argues, "is not restrained to that very action, a real unction, but frequently transferred, and communicated in a Scripture use, to every kind of Declaration of any Election, any Institution, any Inauguration, any Investiture of any person to any place. And, lesse than that, *of any appropriation, any application of any thing to any particular use.*"[27]

If Milton's own republican counterpolemics of the late 1640s and early 1650s deploy the full range of their author's considerable rhetorical arsenal, from low ad hominem slurs to painstaking biblical exegeses, they consistently deploy one cunning line of attack—namely, to turn the royalist enemy's own weapon against itself. To defend the trial and execution of the king, Milton can thus be found symbolically (re)claiming the political theological "fuel" of sovereignty—blood, tears, and oil—for his own republican cause: the people, not the king, now bleed, weep, and, crucially, *anoint*. It is already well documented, of course, that the *Eikon Basilike* depicts Charles as a Christlike martyr king, whose prayers, tears, and blood will serve to expiate the sins of his enemies: "But O let the blood of Me, though their King, yet a sinner, be washed with the Blood of My Innocent and peace-making Redeemer," Charles allegedly prays, "for in that thy Justice will find not only a temporary expiation, but an eternal plenary satisfaction; both for my sins, and the sins of my People."[28] After the king's trial and execution in 1649, Pierre du Moulin's royalist apology *Regii sanguinis clamor ad coelum* (The cry of the royal blood to heaven, 1652)—whose title compares Charles to the unjustly murdered Abel in Genesis 4:10—further reinforces this theological reading of Charles's "royal blood," while simultaneously condemning "bloodless" defenders of regicide like Milton.[29] Yet, instead of simply refusing the sacrificial trope of "royal blood" altogether as a kind of crypto-Catholic recidivism, Milton's political writings perform what we might call a political theological "blood transfusion" that rhetorically extracts the allegedly sacred blood from the body of the martyred Charles and injects it into the corpses of the martyred people in order to symbolically reanimate them. For Milton, Charles is less a Christlike martyr, whose only weapons are the "Prayers and Teares" that the ancient Christians were wont to use against "thir Persecuters," than the Christian Church's pagan persecutor-in-chief.[30] "There hath bin more Christian blood shed by the Commission, approbation, and connivance of King Charles," he writes, "then in the Ten Roman Persecutions."[31] In another political theological reversal of Charles's alleged claim in the *Eikon Basilike* that his death will be a "temporary expiation" for the "sins of my People," Milton's *Defensio* makes the counterclaim that the people killed the king in order to expiate his own sins against *them*: we have "atoned for the countless deaths of good countrymen," he claims, "by the punishment of the man responsible.[32]

What, then, might a republican ceremony of anointment look like? To squeeze a few more drops out of Gil Anidjar's remarkable Christian genealogy of "blood," I want to propose that what is taking place in Milton's own political theological machine may be the rhetorical production and refinement of a new holy oil or unction out of the *people*'s blood.[33] It is possible to trace the origins of this act of popular anointment back to the English poet's contrapuntal reading of 1 Chronicles 16:22—"Touch not mine anointed"—where he observes (contra Andrewes and pro Donne) that what is frequently taken to be an endorsement of divine right monarchy is actually a divine *delimitation* upon kingly power. As Milton correctly observes, God's commandment is in fact an instruction to *kings* not to touch prophets rather than the other way around ("Touch not mine anointed, and do my prophets no harm") but, polemically, the *Defensio* goes on to render "prophets" as "people": "But God himself forbade kings to touch his anointed . . . that is, his people," he writes. "He put the anointing of his people before the anointing, if there was any such thing, of kings."[34] For Milton, this "people's anointment" is older than, and takes precedence over, any royal anointment and thus Charles remains permanently accountable to the people for his crimes against them under divine and natural law: "You will never induce me to grant you that all kings are the anointed of the Lord, and say that for this reason they are above the laws and should not be punished for any crimes whatsoever."[35] Perhaps most revealingly, however, this popular consecration—and later deconsecration—of the king is performed via the medium of the new "holy oil" that is the people's blood. If we reread Milton's sanguinary description of Charles's descent from king to tyrant in *Eikonoklastes*, for example, we can see that this fall, like the earlier "decoronation" of Richard II in Shakespeare's play, is solemnized by a grotesque or obscene rite of popular anointment with the blood of his own people. By killing so many people, the king is said to be "dipt from head to foot and staind over with the blood of thousands that were his faithfull subjects" and then "clad in an ignominious and horrid purple-robe of innocent blood."[36] Finally, the people's blood also (as we have seen) has the power to remove or wash off—to divest or disanoint—Charles's original anointment in holy oil: "Be he King, or Tyrant, or Emperour, the Sword of Justice is above him," he writes in

The Tenure of Kings and Magistrates, "in whose hand soever is found sufficient power to avenge the effusion, and so great a deluge of innocent blood."[37] In a republican equivalent to Bolingbroke's "rough rude" sea in *Richard II*, Milton thus reanoints "the people's blood" as a retributive deluge of divine violence unleashed on behalf of the multitude.

THE SWEETEST OF ALL OILS

In chapter 25 of Herman Melville's *Moby-Dick* (1851), Ishmael ruminates upon the strange fact that "a king's head is solemnly oiled at his coronation": "What kind of oil is used at coronations?" he asks, "Certainly it cannot be olive oil, nor macassar oil, nor castor oil, nor bear's oil, nor train oil, nor cod-liver oil, What then can it possibly be, but sperm oil in its unmanufactured, unpolluted state, the sweetest of all oils? Think of that, ye loyal Britons! we whalemen supply your kings and queens with coronation stuff!"[38] It is tempting to read Ishmael's famous defense of the whaling industry—which was removed from the first English edition of the novel by Melville's publisher, Richard Bentley, lest it offend presumably delicate royalist sympathies—as a profane riposte to Richard II's original boast that "not all the water in the rough rude sea / Can wash the balm off from an anointed king." After all, Ishmael's counterclaim reminds us that the main ingredient of the holy oil historically used in English coronation ceremonies, ambergris, is extracted from the bowels of the sperm whale, and so emerges out of that "rough rude" sea in the first place. To read Melville's magnum opus in the context of the political theological genealogy of anointment we have been tracking so far, I want to propose that this is neither simply a novel about land and sea (Carl Schmitt);[39] blood (Gil Anidjar);[40]

nor even flesh (Jason Frank and Bonnie Honig) but *oil*:⁴¹ what figuratively and literally keeps *Moby-Dick* afloat is a superabundance of unction that variously anoints, lubricates, saturates, immerses, and even liquidizes the solid bodies of Ishmael, Ahab, and the crew of the *Pequod*. If Melville's novel is frequently narrated by modern political theorists such as Frank, Honig, and Santner as a struggle between two rival figures of sovereignty—which is to say Ahab versus Starbuck; political theology versus political economy; a biblical-style "king" obsessed with blood sacrifice or vengeance versus a modern mercantile entrepreneur pursuing a profit on the open market of the high seas—I instead want to pursue Honig's remarkable insight that whale oil (which she prefers to call "flesh") may represent another "third term" or substance in the dialectic of blood and water that she does not hesitate to anoint as "democratic," but that I want to associate with a more open or ambiguous political possibility.⁴² In *Moby-Dick*, whale oil is not the harbinger of a democratic future so much as of a liquid modernity, where all that is solid melts into oil.

To track the fluid motion of whale oil across *Moby-Dick*, I first want to insist upon that novel's status as not only perhaps the supreme political allegory of nineteenth century literature — whose story of the quest for the white whale has becomes a signifier of everything from royal or imperial power, (post)colonialism, slavery, extractive capitalism and terrorism up to environmental catastrophe—but, more radically, as a meta-allegorical exploration of the politics of allegoresis itself: the whale becomes, as many scholars have observed, a kind of Rorschach Blot onto which the desires and fears of Ahab and the crew of the *Pequod* are variously projected or extracted from. It is holy oil, the political theological floating signifier that, as John Donne already observes, describes "any appropriation, any application of any thing to any particular use," that literally and figuratively greases the wheels of this metarepresentational machine. After all, anointment with oil, whether for baptism, consecration, extreme unction, embalmment or other more utilitarian purposes, is a master trope or trope of tropes in a novel that is famously stuffed to the gills with metaphors of kings, queens, emperors, and presidents: Father Mapple's chapel sermon calls Jonah an "anointed pilot-prophet,"[43] Tashtego ends up totally immersed in sperm oil when he accidentally falls head-first into a decapitated whale's cranium;[44] Queequeg is said to have "anointed" the bottom of his boat with grease to make it run smoothly through the water;[45] Ishmael gets up to his elbows in oil squeezing the globules of coagulated sperm back into liquid;[46] and, finally, Ahab anoints the harpoon with which he plans to kill Moby-Dick with the "baptismal blood" of the crew.[47] If Melville's legendary white whale is both literally and metaphorically fugitive—which is to say that it forever escapes any game of "hunt-the-symbol" by we aspiring readerly Ahabs—then its sperm is arguably even more difficult to pin down: whale oil is variously identified as sacred and profane in this novel, transcendental and immanent, sublime and utilitarian, a pure gift, token of exchange and a commodity fetish, the locus of freedom, sexuality, and death. In the same way as the whale itself, whale oil thus ceases to be simply one more "figure" amongst others in this book, whose meaning can be caught, killed, and extracted by a hermeneutic equivalent to a harpooner, and instead becomes something like the metafigure of a pure, unfigurable liquidity or performativity that both makes possible and overflows every attempt to contain it.

If Jason Frank undoubtedly gets his hooks into something crucial when he reads the famous sperm-squeezing scene in chapter 94 as a moment of "democratic absorption" that "resists incorporation into the terrible logic of Ahab's quest," for instance, it is possible to argue that even a weak democratic reading of whale oil as a metaphor for constituent power inevitably becomes somewhat extractive in its desire to make political capital out of the novel's essential liquidity.[48] It may be significant here that an earlier admirer of Melville's novel, who was rather less sympathetic to the promise of American democracy, extracts something very different from this exact same bucket of whale oil. According to Ernst Jünger in a 1941 letter to his friend Carl Schmitt, the *Pequod* crew's processing of the spermaceti is less the inaugural site of an American equivalent to Rousseau's general will than a diabolical mise-en-scène (redolent of the Weird Sisters' cauldron in *Macbeth*) in which the cosmic power of the biblical Leviathan is boiled down into something close to a pure or total utility: "The interest of the economic world in these magnificent [*herrlichen*, masterly, sovereign] animals is that of a cover-up [*eine abdeckerei*]," he writes. "The lowly-demonic plays a role and becomes visible in the dim fires of the sperm oil boilers."[49] To immerse ourselves fully into Ishmael's own, deeply ambiguous, account of this moment of sensuous labor, we arguably find not only the promise but the threat—the *jouissance* in the full Lacanian sense of the term—of total liquefaction into a collective that annihilates even the minimal "consent" that Ahab obtained for his own (suicidal) version of the social contract: "I squeezed that sperm till I myself almost melted into it," he recalls. "I squeezed that sperm till a strange sort of insanity came over me."[50] For Bonnie Honig, whose own reading of *Moby-Dick* also discovers an immanent democratic politics within the hunt for the white whale, Tashtego's plunge into the "sanctum sanctorum" of the severed whale's head in chapter 78 constitutes a symbolic dethronement of the Hobbesian Leviathan,[51] "whose head is flesh and is therefore in no position merely to govern flesh or make it governable through incorporation under the head of reason," but, once again, this powerful interpretation arguably extracts one particular meaning (which in this case is something like Jane Bennett's democracy of things) from the vast hermeneutic reservoir that is whale oil: a model of sovereignty in which a man very nearly drowns in a Leviathan's spermaceti is not obviously to be preferred to a Hobbesian social contract that, for all its faults, at least secures the bare lives of its members.[52] In playing Schmitt and Jünger off against Frank and Honig—in other words, sovereignty against democracy, the demonic against the redemptive and so on—I obviously do not mean to say that the one reading of holy oil is right and the other wrong, but rather to ask why exactly the same substance can legitimize such diametrically opposite response, and my answer is this: what Melville's novel presides over is the final metabolization of oil or unction from the bitterly contested referent of different political theological regimes of legitimation into a pure and contentless signifying machine whose imprimatur can legitimate everything.

What species of sovereignty, then, is anointed by that uncanny "coronation stuff" called sperm whale oil in *Moby-Dick*? To return to Ishmael's provocative reclamation of the English coronation ceremony for North American whalers in chapter 25, I prefer to argue that Melville's novel instead announces the quite literally liquid or floating *performativity* of anointment that overflows and liquefies the political theological boundary between the sacred and the profane and converts everything into utility: what was once applied exclusively to the head of a king to separate his body from common use is now applied equally and just as usefully to the head of a salad, the inside of an engine or the bottom of a boat.[53] It may be worth recalling here Heidi Scott's observation that whale oil was the "petroleum" of the late eighteenth and early nineteenth century in its seemingly universal utility.[54] As she shows, sperm was deployed extensively both domestically and industrially as, for example, the leading source of lamp oil, the main ingredient for candles and as part of the manufacturing process for soap. Yet, again, I hesitate to anoint this political theological oil spill too quickly as "democratic"—regardless of whether the latter is defined as the constituent power of the people (Frank); the democracy of things (Bennett), or the sabbatical power of jubilee or debt forgiveness (Honig)—because it does not simply liquify the king but *everything* into the stuff of a pure performativity or potentiality. For Melville's narrator, what happens when oil comes into contact with solid bodies throughout this narrative is less a pure, egalitarian liquefaction than something closer to total *liquidation*: Ishmael muses that a man who rubs oil into his hair "has got a 'quoggy [mushy, boggy]' spot in him somewhere," for instance, and "can't amount to much in his totality;"[55] he squeezes the whale oil sperm until "I myself almost melted into it,"[56] and speculates that, if Tashtego had indeed drowned in the severed whale's head, it would have been "a very precious perishing; smothered in the very whitest and daintiest of fragrant spermaceti; coffined, hearsed, and tombed in the secret inner chamber and sanctum sanctorum of the whale."[57] If this modern political theological melting pot is obviously open to many possible interpretations, where it may become the harbinger of everything from pleasure to horror, emancipation to interpellation, a new materialist immersion of human exceptionalism into the political ecology of things to a capitalist embalmment of the solid object or thing in the molten flux of commodity fetishism, what I want to propose here is that its real signifying power may consist in being, precisely, the possibility of "political possibility" itself: whale oil stands for a kind of pure, surplus potentiality or performativity out of which every possible political "solid body"—individual, community, state—is formed and to which it can equally be returned. In its raw "unmanufactured, unpolluted state," Melville's coronation stuff thus becomes the political ontological lubricant of that permanent state of molten political flux that Bauman calls "liquid modernity."[58]

AS THEY ANOINT MACHINERY

In the 2023 coronation ceremony of King Charles III of the United Kingdom—which was once again broadcast live on television to an audience of more than eighteen million—the Act of Consecration remained shielded from the cameras behind a screen, but, in one small respect, the anointment of the new king did break with centuries-old tradition. To reflect Charles's longstanding passion for the environment, Buckingham Palace announced before the ceremony that a new "animal cruelty-free" recipe for holy oil had been created for the coronation that, for the first time, dispensed with the use of ambergris or whale sperm oil.[59] If Ishmael's proud boast that "we whalemen supply your kings and queens with coronation stuff" metonymized the rise of extractive capitalism to global political and economic power in the nineteenth century, Charles's well-publicized decision to render the whale hunters literally and symbolically redundant by changing the recipe for the "coronation stuff" in the name of protecting the environment might, a little cynically, be read as signifying the ascendancy of that baroque new form of twenty-first-century political economy called "woke capitalism" whereby major brand names, franchises, and corporate structures seek (whether sincerely or performatively) to align themselves with social justice agendas. In its metabolization from ancient signifier of the sacred into a very modern kind of virtue signal, holy oil thus now takes its place on the market as a kind of political theological equivalent to "ethically responsible" products like the plant-based hamburger.

To expose the sacred body of the anointed monarch to the profane gaze of critique, however, this chapter has argued, we discover that this body is the site of a political theological oil war: holy oil is a symbolic fuel of political legitimacy that has been historically fought over, captured, and economized in the same way as any natural resource. It does not simply dry up or wash away as it flows down from the English Reformation into industrial America, as if in a kind of fluid equivalent to secularization or disenchantment, but is exported into new and emerging markets to legitimize new lines of products or commodities. If holy oil was always a politically mercurial substance from the beginning, which slipped far too easily between people, places, and things to be captured once and for all by any regime of power, this very liquidity itself now becomes its unique selling point: a new set of political actors from English republicans to American mercantile capitalists begin to extract, channel, and refine its symbolic reservoir of all-purpose transcendental power in order to legitimize new sovereign bodies (the people, the individual, capital) and new species of political performativity (democracy, industrial or extractive capitalism, and neoliberal global finance capitalism). In the language of William Mazzarella, Eric Santner, and Aaron Schuster's *Sovereignty, Inc.* (2020), "holy oil" finally ceases to be a solid body or object (we have already seen how its physical or chemical composition changes radically over time) and begins to assume the simultaneously empty and excessive—which is to say liquid— power of the contemporary advertising brand: what we call the "brand name" (e.g., Apple, Nike, Gucci) represents a kind of post-Marxian pure surplus value that is no longer extracted from the real production process but rather precedes the existence of the object and constitutes it as worth consuming in the first place.[60]

If Elizabeth II's original anointing with oil in 1953 was narrated to the millions of viewers watching on television as a moment of sacred prehistory—which was precisely why it had to be protected from the profane eye of the camera—the Act of Consecration's solemn observance of a reified sacred "tradition" that, as we have seen, never really existed in the first place ironically rendered it unctuous in every sense of the word. To present what we might, channeling Walter Benjamin, call "monarchy in the age of mechanical reproducibility," the Coronation Committee of 1953 still felt it necessary to preserve (or retroactively project?) a unique political theological "aura" that lay behind the all-seeing democratic gaze of the camera, but the golden canopy that protected Elizabeth from public view risked turning the sacred into nothing but democracy's own photographic negative—a kind of trompe l'oeil or special effect created at the very beginning of the age of mass media where, apparently, there could be nothing more sublime or transcendent than being deemed unscreenable. For Charles III's anointment in 2023, the king's retreat from the television cameras to commune with God was renarrated in distinctly profane terms as something close to an A-list celebrity demanding privacy ("No photos, please!") from paparazzi: Buckingham Palace's official Order of Ceremony explains that a "Screen shields The King from view as he sits in the Coronation Chair for this most solemn and personal of moments."[61] In the same way as Richard Bentley's removal of the profane coronation scene in Melville's *Moby-Dick* ("Think of that, ye loyal Britons! we whalemen supply your kings and queens with coronation stuff!"), the Coronation Committee's decision to censor the television cameras did not serve to conceal the real presence of "the sacred" from the democratic gaze, so much as the still more real anxiety over its possible absence, the fear that there may be nothing sacred left to see.

In the original and unexpurgated chapter 25 of Melville's magnum opus, though, Ishmael offers one final intriguing answer to the old question of why the English like to pour oil on to the heads of their kings and queens. "Can it be," the whaleman speculates, "that they anoint it [the monarch's head] with a view of making its interior run well, as they anoint machinery?"[62] It was not quite as profane or impertinent a speculation as it may now appear, because sperm whale oil was, of course, extensively employed throughout the nineteenth and well into the twentieth century as a lubricant for industrial machinery. Astonishingly, American cars ran on whale oil until as late as 1973: sperm remained the main additive in automatic transmission fluid for the U.S. car industry all the way up to its prohibition by the Endangered Species Act. If Elizabeth II's seventy-year reign as Queen of the United Kingdom from 1952 until 2022 is also frequently taken by royal historians to coincide with the transformation of the British monarchy itself from a venerable political theological institution into a modern political economic "firm," franchise or corporation—whose sole remaining grounds for legitimacy reside (just like that of, say, the American auto industry) in the value it delivers to its consumers, the profit it serves up to its shareholders, and increasingly, today, the preservation and burnishing of its own brand name and image via a public commitment to "social justice" issues like environmental protection and sustainability—then Ishmael's revealingly profane question in *Moby-Dick* about what, if anything, might enable this mass-produced automaton to carry on running, more or less smoothly, becomes timely once again: "Can it be that they anoint it with a view of making its interior run well, as they anoint machinery?" In Elizabeth II's anointment, holy oil is chemically transformed into a species of high-performance engine oil that greases the wheels of that modern machine called "constitutional monarchy."

3

BEHIND THE CURTAIN
Hobbes, Benjamin, Derrida, Deleuze

In Abraham Bosse's frontispiece to the original edition of Thomas Hobbes's *Leviathan* (1651), which was apparently designed according to the author's own specifications, we find one seemingly gratuitous theatrical embellishment.[1] To zone in on this curious detail, Hobbes's famous image of a vast artificial sovereign standing over the city he rules depicts the author's proper name, Thomas Hobbes of Malmesbury, and the book's full title, *Leviathan: Or The Matter, Forme, and Power of a Commonwealth Ecclesiasticall and Civil*, as embroideries upon a large, tasseled curtain that is positioned between a famous series of representations of civil and ecclesiastical power. It is not, as strange as it may seem, the first such curtain to appear in Hobbes's work. Almost ten years earlier, Jean Maltheus's frontispiece for *De Cive* (1642) placed between its representations of the state of nature (*"Libertas"*) and civil society (*"Imperium"*) a similarly imposing drape upon which is inscribed the title of the work and, rather than the author's name, a quotation from the Book of Proverbs 8:15: "Per me Reges regnant et legum conditores iusta decernunt" (By me kings reign, and rulers decree what is just). If Hobbes scholars have devoted abundant critical labor to decoding the complex iconography of Bosse's frontispiece over the centuries,

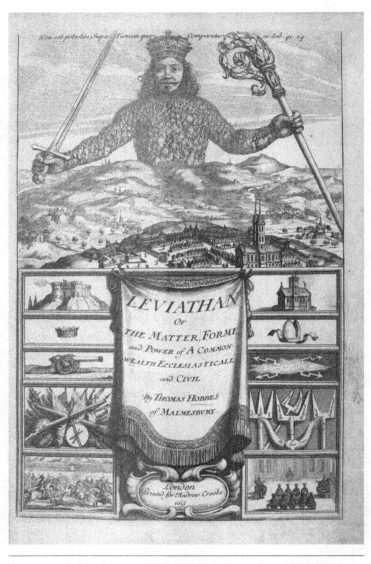

FIGURE 3.1 Abraham Bosse, Title Page of *Leviathan, or The Matter, Forme, & Power of a Common-Wealth Ecclesiasticall and Civill* by Thomas Hobbes, 1651 (engraving) © British Library Board. All Rights Reserved / Bridgeman Images.

it is thus all the more remarkable that, with one or two significant exceptions, this particular detail has largely been passed over in silence as presumably nothing more than a conventional Baroque decoration. In both a literal and a philosophical sense, Hobbes's curtain—which marks the precise spot between the state of nature and society, heaven and earth, God and man— occupies the absolute center of his work.

To tear down the iconographical curtain on Hobbes's frontispiece, whose presence inevitably appears to both conceal and reveal some kind of inner political sanctum sanctorum, we immediately enter a long political theological history of veils, curtains, and facades that stretches all the way back to the Book of Exodus. It is worth recording here that the art historian Horst Bredekamp (who is one of the few commentators to speak of it at all) insists that the curtain in *Leviathan* "signifies more than a baroque playfulness in the treatment of a façade. Following the model of the veils of the tabernacle described in the Old Testament, it alludes, through its alternating hints at revelation and concealment, to the notion that the text of Hobbes's own 'LEVIATHAN' is itself a fount of arcane knowledge."[2] As Exodus 26 famously recounts, Yahweh instructs Moses to cover the "Holy of Holies" (*Qodesh Ha-qadashim*), the inner sanctuary of the Temple that was only accessible to the High Priest at Yom Kippur to offer the blood of sacrifice, with a "vail [*parochet*] of blue, and purple, and scarlet, and fine twined linen of cunning work" that "shall divide unto you between the holy place and the most holy" (31–33). For the Apostle Paul, Jesus's incarnation and death, which famously coincides with the rending of the veil of the Temple, reveals him to be at once the high priest, the blood sacrifice, the veil (*katapetasma*), and the embodiment of the new covenant between God and Man: "Having therefore, brethren, boldness to enter into the holiest by the blood of Jesus, By a new and living way, which he hath consecrated for us, through the veil, that is to say, his flesh" (Heb. 10:19–20). In this context of old and new—Jewish and Christian, complete and torn—veils, Hobbes's frontispiece perhaps raises a larger question about the possible Jewish filiation or provenance of his own, allegedly Christian, Commonwealth: *Leviathan*'s veil, of course, remains firmly in place and intact, as if Christianity simply never happened.[3]

If Bosse's frontispiece has a more contemporary source than the veil of the tabernacle, then (as Bredekamp also suggests) it might be the Baroque idea of the façade, which reconfigures this ancient dialectic between interior and exterior, concealment and revelation in a modern way. To turn to a cryptic November 12, 1947, entry in Carl Schmitt's *Glossarium* (1991), for instance, we find Schmitt declaring that Hobbes is the "true philosopher of the Baroque" (*eigentliche Philosoph des Barock*) because, rather than the hidden interior or arcanum, he always prefers to highlight the "façade" (emphasis in the original): "The Leviathan itself is a façade," he continues, "the façade of dominion [*Herrschaftsfassade*] in front of power [*Macht*]," before specifically noting what he calls "those mysterious curtains on the cover of the Leviathan." It would be wrong, though, to speak of the Leviathan as a "'mere' façade"—"merely illusion or appearance"—because this façade is the signifier of "prestige, glory, honor, representation, omnipotence [*Allmacht*]" albeit "only an external omnipotence." As Schmitt makes clear here, the Baroque façade was not (yet) a "façade" in the modern pejorative sense of a mere artificial surface or veneer upon the naked truth. However, this early modern idea of the façade, which is still recognizably the public face (*facia*) of interiority, nonetheless stands on a historical threshold, because it will soon give way to the modern liberal theory of the public image as nothing more than a superficial external appearance that conceals a private, unadorned interiority. For Schmitt, political liberalism will eventually strip away the historic grandeur of the Baroque façade to reveal, not so much a new Holy of Holies, but the allegedly profane and authentic "truth" of power that lies behind it. "The whole sociology and psychology of unmasking imply a dismantling [*Abbau*] of the Baroque façade," he concludes, "and the unveiling of the pure core of power [*reinen Machtskernes*]."[4] In his own recessionary dismantling of the supersessionary history of the veil of the Temple, Schmitt's own *Leviathan in the State Theory of Thomas Hobbes* (1938) will notoriously blame iconoclastic "liberal Jews" like Spinoza for tearing down Hobbes's very own Christian veil and exposing the arcanum of power it conceals to the liberal light of day.[5]

In the Hobbesian curtain, I want to propose that we thus find one particular fold in what, after Walter Benjamin, we might call a larger political "curtainology" (*rideaulogie*).[6] It is already well documented by scholars as diverse as Hans Blumenberg, Jacques Derrida, and Pierre Hadot, of course, that the history of truth from ancient Greece to modernity is *itself* a history of the veil—whether it takes the form of pre-Socratic *aletheia* or unconcealment (Plato, Nietzsche, Heidegger); Aufklärung, Enlightenment, and visibility (Descartes, Hobbes, Kant, Hegel); or, conversely, the modern theory of truth as a process of historical materialist or genealogical masking and unmasking (Marx, Nietzsche).[7] As we are beginning to see, however, the particular history of political truth-telling, from Greek *parhhesia* (Euripides), through early modern (dis)simulation (Machiavelli, Bacon) and ideological (de)mystification (Marx), up to liberal disenchantment or transparency (Weber), is equally, if not more so, a dialectic of (un)veiling. To unveil my own argument in what follows, this chapter seeks to read three proper names embroidered upon the curtain of sovereignty—Walter

Benjamin, Gilles Deleuze, and Jacques Derrida—as signifiers of an originary *inexplicability* (from the Latin *inexplicabilis*, literally "what cannot be unfolded or disentangled") of the political inside and outside, appearance and essence, surface and depth. If Benjamin's curtainology, Deleuze's fold, and Derrida's prayer shawl or tallith each draw, fold, or pleat the curtain of sovereignty differently, I want to propose that they all seek to fashion, not so much a political theology, as what we might half-seriously call a political *rideaulogy*: all significant political concepts of the modern theory of the state are (if I may rewrite the signature thesis of Carl Schmitt's *Political Theology*) secularized *rideaulogical* concepts.[8] For Derrida, the veil or curtain that divides the inner sanctum of the Judaic Temple from the outside, together with the Christian division of that division, remains something like the primal scene of every philosophical, political, or theological division or separation, as well as every identification or reunification, of the same and the other. "The veil tearing down the middle, is that the end of such a separation, of that isolation, that unbelievable solitude of belief?" he asks in his late essay "A Silkworm of One's Own (Points of View Stitched on the Other Veil)" (1996). "I know of no other separation in the world, or that would be commensurable with that one, analogous, comparable to that one which allows us to think nonetheless every other separation, and first of all the separation that separates from the wholly other."[9] In the mysterious curtain on the cover of Hobbes's *Leviathan*, I will conclude that we do not encounter a divide or threshold between a political "inside" and some a-, pre-, or extrapolitical outside—which is to say between society and the state of nature, the inner sanctum of sovereignty and the lawless, anarchic *Bellum omnium contra omnes*—so much as the turning-inside, redoublement, or folding back upon itself of this outside. What if the sovereign does not lie behind the curtain but, inexplicably, just *is* the curtain itself?

CURTAINOLOGY

In and among his many uncompleted projects, Walter Benjamin apparently once planned something called a "curtainology" (*rideaulogie*): "Today I've obtained significant results in my study of curtains," he once wrote to Greta Karplus (later Greta Adorno) from Ibiza in May 1933, "for a curtain separated us from the balcony that looked out on the city and the sea."[10] To judge by his *Berlin Childhood Around 1900* (2006), Benjamin seems to have been fascinated, even haunted, by *Vorhänge* from a very early age: a child who "stands behind the doorway curtain" during a game of hide-and-seek, as he recalls in the fragment called "Hiding Places," "himself becomes something white that flutters, a ghost."[11] It often seems that the curtain occupies a privileged position in the secret life of objects, ornaments and accoutrements experienced by the young Benjaminian flaneur in his parents' Berlin apartment. As he recalls in another vignette, "A Ghost," Benjamin had a childhood dream about a specter who resided behind the "faded purple velvet curtain" in his parents' bedroom and who stole silks. For the young Benjamin, what lay behind this particular curtain was a psychosexual version of the Judaic sanctum sanctorum: "the darkness on the other side of the curtain was impenetrable," he writes, and "this corner formed the infernal pendant to the paradise that opened with my mother's linen closet."[12] If the early Benjaminian curtain constitutes an Oedipal threshold between childhood and adulthood, it will later come to represent the political threshold between the private individual and collective history. In "Paris, the Capital of the Nineteenth Century" (1938), for example, Benjamin accuses the nineteenth-century bourgeois Parisian, living in one of the new apartment buildings erected under Louis-Philippe, of effectively having drawn their curtains upon the outside world and retreated into a predatory individuality: "To have lived in these interiors was to have woven a dense fabric about oneself, to have secluded oneself within a spider's web, in whose toils world events hang loosely suspended like many insect bodies sucked dry."[13]

To obtain the "significant results" in his study of curtains mentioned in the 1933 letter to Karplus, Benjamin apparently undertook a very special kind of fieldwork: he spent the day smoking opium with the writer and translator Jean Selz at the latter's home in the old town of Ibiza. It is in his set of notes toward his legendary, albeit once again unfinished, project on drugs that the German thinker reenvelops himself in the *Vorhängwelt* (the curtained world) of his *Berlin Childhood Around 1900*.[14] As Benjamin's description of the hash-smoker's den in his "Main Features of my Second Impression of Hashish" (1928) reveals, the Ibizan opium addict may not be the decadent enemy of the Parisian property-owner so much as their secret sharer. "It is like being wrapped up," he writes in a metaphor that immediately recalls his description of the Hausmann-era apartment in the *Arcades Project*, "enclosed in a dense spider's web in which the events of the world are scattered around, suspended there like the bodies of dead insects sucked dry."[15] However, the bohemian figure of the drug-taker—who also dwells permanently behind drawn curtains and detests sunlight, fresh air and the great outdoors—pursues the bourgeois dream of a curtained-off existence to the point of destruction. For Benjamin, the hashish-smoker transforms the entirely passive nihilism of the self-enclosed bourgeois subject into an active, indeed diabolical, nihilism: "Such nihilism is the innermost core of bourgeois cosiness," he writes in the *Arcades Project*, "a mood that in hashish intoxication concentrates to satanic contentment."[16] If the bourgeois resident seeks to absolutely exclude the "outside" world from its self-enclosed space—or to domesticate that outside into merely another domestic interiority very much like its own, such as the apartment of a next-door neighbor—the hashish-smoker, by contrast, seems to turn that interiority inside out like the fingers of a glove: they inhabit an internal subjective space so intense and claustrophobic that it paradoxically becomes external or radically alien to them. In Benjamin's drug experiments, the medium of this turning-outside of the inside is, once again, the curtain.

If a bourgeois private individual living in their nineteenth-century domestic interior weaves a "dense fabric" around themselves to keep the city out, Jean Selz (Benjamin's companion in the opium experiment) recalls that the opium-smoker instead experiences a curious *fabrication*—a quite literal "becoming-fabric"—of the city itself. To return to the scene of his own rideaulogie in Selz's apartment (a curtain, a balcony, a city, and the sea), Benjamin begins to unfold a set of stoned phenomenological reductions in which subject and object are inexplicably woven into one another. First, the opium-smoker gazing upon the billowing curtain begins to see that curtain as a kind of spatial or visual equivalent to an Aeolian Harp which the invisible, sensual world endows with visible form: "Curtains are interpreters of the language of the wind," he writes, "They give to its every breath the form and sensuality of feminine forms."[17] Yet this Romantic apprehension of the Absolute is almost immediately folded back upon itself as the smoker becomes a decadent avatar of the Kantian transcendental subject, whose a priori conditions of cognition ("the curtain") inevitably govern or pattern the appearance of their sensible perceptions ("the city"). For

Benjamin, a patterned or filigreed curtain "will in some measure supply the smoker with patterns, which he lays on the landscape in order to transform it in the oddest ways."[18] Finally, and most strangely, however, Benjamin's phenomenological meditation also anticipates Howard Caygill's hypothesis that this Kantian transcendental synthesis within Benjaminian experience may *itself* be nothing more than the "fold" of a larger natural or cosmic synthesis of city, sky and sea that imposes its own speculative conditions (or "fabric") upon the conditioning subject.[19] In his fascinating memoir of Benjamin's opium experiments, to which we will return throughout this chapter, Jean Selz captures this uncanny process whereby the smoker begins to encounter an exteriority that is woven "inside" their very subjectivity:

> The view from the open window, through the white muslin curtain, was the repeated focus of [Benjamin's] musings. The terraced roofs, the curve of the bay, and the line of distant mountains, captured by the curtain or swathed in its folds, undulated along with it when it stirred—ever so slightly—in the hot evening air. The city and the curtain soon ceased to be separate things. And if the city had become fabric, that fabric had become the stuff of a garment. It was *our* garment, but was moving ever farther away from us. We then observed that *the opium was divesting us of the country in which we were living.* Benjamin added the humorous remark that we were engaging in "curtainology" (*rideaulogie*).[20]

In response to the inevitable question of what lies "behind the curtain" of Benjamin's curtainology—which is to say what, if anything, is at stake in this intoxicated phenomenology—I find it helpful to recall a famous passage from his essay "Surrealism: The Last Snapshot of the European Intelligentsia" (1929) in which, all too soberly, he speaks of a *"profane illumination*, a materialist, anthropological inspiration, to which hashish, opium, or whatever else, can give an introductory lesson." To reread his rideaulogy in this context, what shines through or illuminates Benjamin's curtain as he stares down upon the city in a stoned haze is not the Protestant ethic of property-owning capitalism but the profanity of historical materialism: hallucinogenic drugs are merely a propaedeutic to the *real* consciousness-raising experience that is politics.[21] It is worth remembering here that Benjamin's own drug trips were rarely solitary experiences, but, rather, communal and collaborative projects carried out together with like-minded comrades like Jean Selz and Ernst Bloch. As he recounts to Greta Karplus, his pharmacological experiments took place in a political—indeed communist—laboratory where master and servant, abstract and material labor, and even nature and history were woven together upon a single immanent and horizontal plane or curtain. "The role of assistant, which requires great care, was divided between us [Benjamin and Selz], in such a way that each of us was at the same time servant and beneficiary of the service," he writes, "and the conversation was interwoven with the acts of assistance in the same way that the threads which color the sky in a Gobelin tapestry are interwoven with the battle represented in the foreground."[22] However, it is not just the "human solidarity" enjoyed by the participants that provides Benjamin with his political buzz here, because what brings this special form of really-existing communism to life is the relational phenomenology furnished by the experience of intoxication, of being stoned, itself. For Benjamin, what is at stake in the persona of the Ibizan opium-smoker, gazing down on the city through the curtained window, is really a kind of immanent political critique of the bourgeois Parisian property-owner who seeks to, quite literally, curtain themselves off from the city in their extravagantly decorated domestic interior. By weaving the fabric of the city around themselves in exactly the same way as the bourgeois property owner, even to the point of turning that fabric into a "garment" that they can wear almost like a believer's prayer shawl or tallith, the opium smoker, however, comes to the entirely contrary conclusion that this garment can never become their own "property": "It was *our* garment, but was moving ever farther away from us," Selz cryptically observes. "*The opium was divesting us of the country in which we were living.*" If the bourgeois subject's curtain serves to create a dividing line between interiority and exteriority, which serves to constitute both subject and object, self and world, as separate entities, the smoker's garment is, on the contrary, symptomatic of the unfolding or doubling back of interiority into an absolute exteriority extending beyond city, state or world ad infinitum: what is or should be most proper, intimate and internal to subjectivity—my "own" investment or garment—becomes inexplicably improper, extimate, divested (from the Latin *vestire*, which is itself from *vestis*, "garment," and so literally "removing the garment"). In a kind of dialectic negative of the nineteenth-century bourgeoisie's cozy domestic interior, in which there is no longer any outside, Benjamin's opium smoker's den reveals to us that, mutatis mutandis, there is no *inside*: the outside is already inside "us," it is us.

INEXPLICABLE

In *The Fold: Leibniz and the Baroque* (*Le Pli*, 1991), Gilles Deleuze draws a famous diagram of a Baroque house that contains a room "decorated with a drape diversified by folds" (*tapisée d'une toile diversifiée par des plis*).[23] To quickly recall its place within his larger philosophical schema, Deleuze's celebrated theory of the fold (*le pli*) becomes the basis of what Alain Badiou correctly calls a remarkable "anti-Cartesian" philosophy of modern subjectivity that extends from Gottfried Leibniz to Michel Foucault.[24] It seeks, in particular, to challenge the notorious series of philosophical dualisms (e.g., mind and body) upon which the Cartesian theory of the subject is erected. As Deleuze famously argues, everything that is apparently most "inside" the Cartesian subject (the *ego cogito*, thought, or consciousness) is nothing more than its *outside*, surplus or excess material redoubled or "folded back" upon itself. For Deleuze, what the later Foucault calls the process of "subjectivation" (*assujettissement*) of the subject by regimes of power/knowledge is arguably the defining modern instance of this contingent "turning-inside" of the outside. "Foucault seems haunted by this theme of an inside which is merely the fold of the outside," he famously writes in *Foucault* (1986), "as if the ship were a folding of the sea."[25] If Deleuze's theory of the fold appears to have almost infinite applicability (from the Latin *applicare*, "to fold" or "fasten")—which stretches from philosophy (Aristotle, Leibniz, Heidegger, Foucault); through art (Donatello, Tintoretto, Caravaggio, Klee, Hantaï, Pollock); architecture (Wölfflin, Rousset, Le Corbusier); to science (Huyghens, Leibniz, and even the supposed "superfold" of evolutionary biology and new technologies)—it is because the very activity of thought itself, up and including even the gesture of unfolding, consists of the production of new folds, pleats, or redoublings.[26] "The Baroque invents the infinite work or process," he writes. "The problem is not how to finish a fold, but how to continue it, to have it go through the ceiling, how to bring it to infinity."[27] In Deleuze's Baroque house, just as in Benjamin's apartment, this work of infinite inexplicability is signified by the curtain.

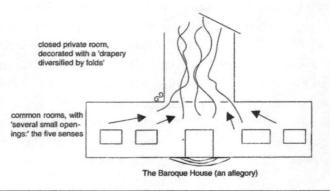

FIGURE 3.2 Gilles Deleuze, diagram of "The Baroque House (An Allegory)." © Gilles Deleuze, *The Fold: Leibniz and the Baroque*, trans. Tom Conley (Minneapolis: University of Minnesota Press, 1993). Copyright 1993 by the Regents of the University of Minnesota. Originally published in *Le Pli: Leibniz et le baroque* © 1988 by Les Editions de Minuit, Paris. Used by permission of Minnesota University Press and Bloomsbury Publishing Plc.

To return to Deleuze's diagram, we quickly grasp that his Baroque house is itself, of course, an architectural allegory for a particular assemblage of post-Cartesian subjectivity: Leibniz's monad. It depicts a two-storey building that comprises a lower common room with five small apertures—which represent matter and the five senses, respectively—and a self-enclosed upper room, which represents the famously "windowless" space of the monad itself. As depicted by Deleuze, the Leibnizian soul is "decorated with a drape diversified by folds" that entirely (or almost entirely) conceals its interiority from the outside world: "Leibniz's most famous proposition is that every soul or subject (monad) is completely closed, windowless and doorless," he says in a contemporary interview, "and contains the whole world in its darkest depths, while also illuminating some little portion of that world, each monad, a different portion."[28] Yet, as we will see, what really concerns Deleuze in this Baroque allegory is what he calls the "almost schizophrenic tension" between the "open façade" and the "hermetic inner volume" of Leibniz's philosophical house, "each being independent of the other and both regulated by a strange preestablished connection."[29] For Leibniz, in his essay "A New System of the Nature and Communication of Substances, and also of the Union that Exists Between the Soul and the Body," (1695), the soul and body do not exist in any direct causal relation, but there is nonetheless a divinely preestablished harmony between them: "God first created each soul and other real unity in such a way that everything in it arises from its own depths, with a perfect *spontaneity* as regards itself—i.e. with no causal input from anything else—and yet with a perfect *conformity* to things outside it."[30] If we inspect Deleuze's diagram of the Leibnizian monad more closely, we see that this conformity between the (apparently separate) lower and upper stories of the house is represented by a dotted line that marks both their division and connection: "The Baroque contribution *par excellence* is a world with only two floors separated by a fold that echoes itself, arching from the two sides according to a different order."[31] In addition to what Deleuze calls the "pleats of matter" and "the folds of the soul," we thus find what he calls a "fold between the folds," which is here allegorized by the mysterious curtain that unfurls to cover both the upper and the lower level of the house alike: the Baroque fold "separates or moves between matter and soul, the façade and the closed room, the outside and the inside."[32]

If Deleuze obviously occupies a radically different monad from Benjamin (their shared investment in Baroque allegory notwithstanding), I think it is possible to read his "drape diversified by folds" as another metaphysical refolding of the latter's original curtainology.³³ It restages an uncannily similar philosophical tableau—a curtain, a domestic interiority, a set of hallucinations,³⁴ and even a sovereign vantage point over a city—to Benjamin's thought experiment.³⁵ As with Benjamin, Deleuze's *Fold* is a study of the *Herrschaftsarchitektur* of political modernity: what he identifies at work in that seventeenth-century phenomenon called "the Baroque" is, among other things, the political ontological origins of the "world interior" of capitalist modernity that will culminate in Benjamin's nineteenth century Paris.³⁶ To take just one revealing detail here, Deleuze's diagram is itself something of a Baroque construction, because this drawing only chooses to depict the façade or front elevation of the house and obscures the interiority: "Baroque architecture," he writes in what could almost be a ventriloquism of Carl Schmitt in the *Glossarium*, "can be defined by this severing of the façade from the inside, of the interior from the exterior, and the autonomy of the interior from the independence of the exterior."³⁷ However, as his description continues, Deleuze's Baroque house increasingly begins to resemble an even more modern political attempt to effect a total separation of the exterior and interior so that they no longer have anything to do with each other—namely, Benjamin's Parisian apartment building. For Deleuze, Leibniz's divide between the soul (which is entirely self-enclosed) and the body (which exists in the common world of matter) does not simply describe an architectural division between the upper and lower levels of a house but the political division between the upper level private apartments and the lower "common" lobby or entrance of the identikit bourgeois Hausmann-era building: "In the upper area, we have reasonable monads," he writes, "like private apartments that are not connected to one another, that do not act upon each other, and that are variants of the same interior decoration."³⁸ In the chapter entitled "To Have a Body,"

Deleuze also goes on to position Leibniz's famous theory of the "dominant monad," where the rational soul subjugates and appropriates for itself the lower or dominated order of monads that make up the body, as a protocapitalist acquisition of "private property" in a metaphysics of power:

> Finally, a monad has as its property not an abstract attribute—movement, elasticity. plasticity—but other monads. such as a cell, other cells, or an atom, and other atoms. These are phenomena of subjugation, of domination, of appropriation that are filling up the domain of having, and this latter area is always located under a certain power (this being why Nietzsche felt himself so close to Leibniz). To have or to possess is to fold, in other words. to convey what one contains "with a certain power." If the Baroque has often been associated with capitalism, it is because the Baroque is linked to a crisis of property, a crisis that appears at once with the growth of new machines in the social field and the discovery of new living beings in the organism.[39]

In the same way as Benjamin's original curtainology, however, Deleuze's theory of the fold will show that Leibniz's' "drape diversified by folds" *expropriates* the "private property" that is his philosophical Baroque house: what allegedly lies behind the curtain in some impenetrable interiority turns out, once again, to be nothing but a fold in an infinite metaphysical curtain. It is Leibniz's crucial claim, recall, that there is a preestablished "fit" or harmony between the two absolute singularities of the soul and the body: the soul still exists in "perfect *conformity* to things outside it." As Deleuze elaborates, what this means is that the two apparently distinct floors of the Leibnizian monad must remain "inseparable by dint of a presence of the upper in the lower"—and, as we have seen, the medium or interface of this (in-)separability is the fold that lies between them.[40] To put it in Deleuze's words, what Leibniz calls the soul is thus a "folding inside" of the outside that is the body, and the body, vice versa, a "folding outside" of the soul, such that it becomes possible to speak of an "intermediate, or rather, original zone"—which is to say a constitutive ontological *inexplicability*—that precedes and organizes what will subsequently become the two separate spheres of soul and body:

> Each soul is inseparable from a body that belongs to it, and is present to it through projection. Every body is inseparable from the souls that belong to it, and that are present to it by requisition. . . . But the belonging makes us enter into a strangely intermediate, or rather, original, zone, in which every body acquires individuality of a possessive insofar as it belongs to a private soul, and souls accede to a public status; that is, they are taken in a crowd or in a heap, inasmuch as they belong to a collective body. Is it not in this zone, in this depth or this material fabric between the two levels, that the upper is folded over the lower, such that we can no longer tell where one ends and the other begins, or where the sensible ends and the intelligible begins?[41]

If Deleuze is not quite proposing a metaphysical version of Pierre-Joseph Proudhon's famous claim that all property is theft here, I think he is asserting that all "property"—in other words, all the soul's attempts to have a body and the body's attempt to belong to a soul—is the effect of an originary fold that, strictly speaking, can belong to no one and nothing: what can be folded inside by one monad can, as he makes very clear in his discussion of Leibniz's dominant monad, be just as easily be refolded back outside by another. For Deleuze, a soul's "possession" of a body is thus categorically not "a relation of the proprietor and property that could be easily established once and for all" but one that, on the contrary, "introduces into possessions factors of inversion, turnaround, precariousness, and temporalization": what I call "my body" itself consists of monads inside monads, all the way down to cells and atoms, that are themselves in a constant state of flux and renewal.[42] Finally, we can perhaps begin to see here why Deleuze's Baroque theory of the fold also doubles up (or down) politically upon Benjamin's original curtainology in which, as we have seen, the proper is always being expropriated—divested or removed of the garment—of its own property: "It was *our* garment, but was moving ever farther away from us." In Deleuze's inexplicable universe, what we persist in calling the absolute "inside" of political ontological sovereignty (e.g., the Cartesian subject, the Hobbesian sovereign, the Leibnizian monad, the Benjaminian property-owner, or the Schmittian "pure nucleus of power") is, once again, turned inside out.

DERRIÈRE LE RIDEAU

In *Glas* (1974), his monumental (in every sense of the word) text on G. W. F. Hegel and Jean Genet, Jacques Derrida confesses that he always finds his dead father's proper name—and, therefore, his own name as well—hiding behind one particular French word: "*Derrière*: every time the word comes first, if written therefore after a period and with a capital letter, something inside me used to start to recognize there my father's name, in golden letters on his tomb, even before he was there. *A fortiori* when I read *Derrière le rideau* [Behind the curtain]."[43] To return to the vast tapestry of work signed in the proper name "Derrida," whose corpus describes nothing other, of course, than a state of originary impurity or contamination between inside and outside, we find a sustained and remarkable reflection upon the question of what, if anything, lies behind our collected philosophical, political, and theological curtains: *Glas* itself, as we will see momentarily, rereads Hegel's Christian supersessionary account of the lifting of the veil of the Temple in Exodus; "The Double Session" (1970) traces the figure of the hymen, threshold and curtain in the poetics of Mallarmé; "To Speculate—on Freud" (1980) reanalyzes Freud's famous interpretation of his grandson's *fort/da* game via the figure of the child's curtained bed or crib; and, most explicitly, "A Silkworm of One's Own (Points of View Stitched on the Other Veil)" (1996) explores the possibility of what it calls a different history of truth—which exists quite apart from the exhausted Greek and Christian concept of truth as *aletheia* that extends from Plato to Heidegger—in the Jewish prayer shawl or *tallith*. If I hesitate to draw any shared theme from these diverse series of texts, events and signatures, it is nonetheless possible to read them all as meditations upon a certain shared "Jewish" inheritance, filiation or law, descending, somewhat profanely, from father to son, and which, contrary to the logic of Christian iconoclasm, insists once again upon the *inexplicability* of the curtain or veil. "You poor thing," one (Judaic?) point of view in "A Silkworm" chides the other (Christian?) one, "finishing with the veil will always have been the very movement of the veil; un-veiling, unveiling oneself, reaffirming the veil in unveiling."[44] In seeking to remove the veil once and for all, we paradoxically remain *derrière le rideau*.

To pull back the speculative curtain upon Judaism, which it notoriously sees as only an unhappy, alienated religion of the law, Hegel's early essay "The Spirit of Christianity and Its Fate" ("Der Geist des Christentums und sein Shicksal," 1798) recalls the Roman General Pompey the Great's shocking discovery of what actually lay inside the Holy of Holies at the temple:

nothing. It seems certain, Hegel writes, that the pagan general would have approached the "center [*Mittlepunkt*] of adoration" with the hope or expectation of discovering in it "the root of the national spirit, to find indeed in one central point the life-giving soul of this remarkable people, to gaze on a Being as an object for his devotion, on something significant for his veneration." As Hegel narrates it, Pompey would thus have been "astonished on entering the arcanum to find himself deceived so far as some of his expectations were concerned, and, for the rest, to find himself in an empty room [*in einem leeren Raum*]."[45] For Hegel, who is here ventriloquized by Derrida in *Glas*, what we might call the "empty space" (*lieu vide*) in the temple comes to symbolize the absolute and unbridgeable divide or curtain between God and Man—which is to say between the infinite and the finite, the transcendental and the sensible—that plagues Judaism itself:

> The Jewish hearth forms an empty house. Certainly, sensible to the absence of all sensible form, the Jews have tried to produce an object that gave in some way rise, place, and figure to the infinite. But this place and this figure have a singular structure: the structure encloses its void within itself, shelters only its own proper interiorized desert, opens onto nothing, confines nothing, contains as its treasure only nothingness: a hole, an empty spacing, a death. A death or a dead person, because according to Hegel space is death and because this space is also an absolute emptiness. Nothing behind (*derrière*) the curtains.[46]

If Hegel notoriously claims that it will only be with the birth of the incarnate God of Christianity (whose tearing of the veil of the temple is clearly anticipated or prophesized by Pompey's own pagan act of desecration) that a new religion will be able to fill this empty space between God and Man, *Glas* dedicates itself to demonstrating the *impossibility* of this triumphal Christian supersessionary philosophy of religion: "Judaism" will become one of Derrida's strategic answers (alongside woman, the bastard child and, of course, the homosexual Jean Genet himself) to the question of what structurally "remains" outside of, and unsublatable by, Hegelian *Savoir absolu*.[47] In seeking to reveal the truth that Judaism has no "inner truth" to reveal, though, Hegel (like the naive Christian voice in "A Silkworm of One's Own") remains committed to the theory of truth *as* revelation—and so the Judaic curtain remains intact even or especially as it is torn in half.

If the absence of anything whatsoever behind the veil of the temple is apparently final proof of Judaism's fatal commitment to a purely abstract or formal law handed down by an unknowable lawgiver—which is why it will require sublation by Christianity—I find it very revealing that Hegel repeats the same metaphor of the "empty room behind the curtain" a few years later in the very different context of the *Phenomenology of Spirit* (1806) to demonstrate the equally necessary supersession of post-Kantian transcendental philosophy by his own speculative philosophy. It is the Protestant Kant who perversely plays the role of the "Jew" to Hegel's own "Christian" in the *Phenomenology* because, upon the latter's reading, Kantian transcendental philosophy ends up repeating Judaism's enslavement to the absolute law of an unknowable "nonworld." As Derrida himself observes (though, oddly, he only cites in passing the passage from the *Phenomenology* I am referring to in a footnote to "The Double Session"), "Kantianism is, structurally, a Judaism" in Hegel's system because it still promulgates a "formal and abstract morality (*Moralität*)."[48] Yet, if Kant is a philosophical "Jew," then what Derrida calls the unsublatable Jewish "remnant" [*reste*] in Hegel's own allegedly Christian philosophy—that is, its inability to escape a logic of veiling—might equally express itself in the form of a certain residual, indeed Kantian, dualism. To Kant's defining claim that the noumenon remains absolutely unknowable to consciousness, recall, Hegel famously replies in the "Force and The Understanding" chapter from the *Phenomenology* that, behind the curtain of phenomena, consciousness still only ever experiences itself:

> This curtain (*Vorhänge*) [of appearance] hanging before the inner world is therefore drawn away, and we have the inner being [the "I"] gazing into the inner world—the vision of the undifferentiated selfsame being, which repels itself from itself, posits itself as an inner being containing different moments, but for which equally these moments are immediately *not* different—*self-consciousness*. It is manifest that behind the so-called curtain which is supposed to conceal the inner world, there is nothing to be seen unless *we* go behind it ourselves, as much in order that we may see, as that there may be something behind there which can be seen.[49]

By arguing that the allegedly transcendental divide between the phenomenal and the noumenal is in fact already immanent to the speculative movement of consciousness itself, Hegel effectively presents himself as a nineteenth century version of that proto-Christian iconoclast Pompey the Great, who tears down the "Jewish" veil of the Kantian temple to reveal that there is nothing to reveal. For Hegel, what lies behind the curtain of transcendental philosophy is not the invisible object of the thing-in-itself, but rather an empty room waiting to be filled by whatever speculative consciousness itself will put there, but, revealingly, we must still go "behind the curtain" in order to know the truth that there is no curtain: "It is manifest that behind the so-called curtain which is supposed to conceal the inner world, there is nothing to be seen unless *we* go behind it ourselves, as much in order that we may see, as there may be something behind there that can be seen." In revealing that nothing lies behind the curtain of the Kantian temple but the space of consciousness itself, Hegel's Christian iconoclasm thus arguably still participates in the revelatory structure of a certain Judaism whose veil or curtain thereby remains intact: what is "revealed" in this Christian coup de théâtre is not the unrepresentable otherworld of an irretrievably transcendental God, but the nonworld behind that illusory other world, the true inner sanctum of a pure nothingness.

In his late essay "A Silkworm of One's Own (Points of View Stitched on the Other Veil)," a dialogue or polylogue between at least two (Jewish and Christian, female and male?) anonymous voices, we find one more attempt to locate within Judaism what Derrida calls a *"verdict* [a *veredictum* or speaking of the truth, but also a *ver-dit* or speaking of the silkworm]" that breaks with the long history of truth as (un-)veiling from Plato to Heidegger: "Where we're going, before the verdict falls," he writes, "another figure perhaps upsets the whole of history from top to bottom and upsets even the meaning of the word 'history': neither a history of a veil, a veil to be lifted or torn, nor the Thing, nor the Phallus nor Death, of course, that would suddenly show itself at the last *coup de théâtre*, at the instant of a revelation or an unveiling."[50] It returns to the project, begun almost twenty years earlier in *Glas*, of recuperating Judaism as the religion of a heteronomous law—which is exemplified by the empty room of the temple—from the Christian supersessionary caricature to which it is subjected by Hegel in his "Spirit of Christianity." As Derrida observes of Hegel, "Absolute knowledge [*savoir absolu*] will never accept this unique separation, that in the veiled place of the Wholly Other, nothing should present itself, that there be Nothing there that is, nothing that is present."[51] However, revealingly, "A Silkworm of One's Own" also discovers a particular text or textile that does not so much break with this long and exhausted political and theological dialectic of veiling and unveiling—because the very idea of a break or tearing of the veil is, of course, entirely of a piece with that dialectic—so much as to live or experience the truth of its inexplicability without seeking to "know" or unveil it once and for all. To recall Derrida's own surprisingly intimate verdict in this essay, his own Jewish prayer shawl or tallith (a textile or fabric that "veils or hides nothing" and "shows or announces no Thing") is one figure that breaks without breaking history's veil:[52]

> My reference cloth was neither a veil nor a canvas (*une toile*), but a shawl. A prayer shawl I like to touch more than to see, to caress every day, to kiss without even opening my eyes or even when it remains wrapped in a paper bag into which I stick my hand at night, eyes closed. And it is not an article of clothing, the tallith, although one wears it, sometimes right against one's skin. *Voilà* another skin, but one incomparable to any other skin, to any possible article of clothing. It veils or hides nothing, it shows or announces no Thing, it promises the intuition of nothing. Before seeing or knowing (*le voir ou le savoir*), before fore-seeing or foreknowing, it is worn in memory of the Law.[53]

For Derrida, whose phenomenology of the shawl again redoubles Benjamin's original curtainology, the prayer tallith is neither a veil nor a curtain, neither seen nor known, neither skin nor clothing—indeed, what he persistently calls "my shawl" (a believer's tallith is not supposed to be exchanged or given to another) is, once again, radically im- or ex-proper: "But this is the property (the for-self) which at bottom does not belong and is there only to recall the Commandments."[54] If Derrida is careful to never suggest that the tallith somehow stands totally "outside" the history of the veil—in fact he concedes that we still see "*through*" it, albeit quite "differently than (*through*) a veil or behind a veil to be lifted"—the question thus arises of who or what exactly we do see differently through the prayer shawl, and his curiously theological anthropological answer is not God, truth or revelation, but ourselves, whoever "we" may be: "One says '*my* shawl' only by obeying Iahve's order.[55] And by beginning to wonder: who am I, I who have already said 'here I am?' What is the self?"[56] Perhaps we may be tempted to find something residually Hegelian—indeed Christian—in Derrida's claim that it is the subject who was behind the curtain all along, but the "I" described here could not be more different from Hegel's self-consciousness: Derrida's subject (like the silkworm) lives and works in the dark; it neither sees, knows, nor owns itself and carries inside its body an unsublatable, heteronomous outside. In putting *ourselves* rather than God behind the curtain, Derrida's prayer shawl once again turns the logic of the veil inside out: what the tallith conceals and reveals is the outside *within* ipseity, propriety, the sovereign self.

POLITICAL RIDEAULOGY

In book 35 of his *Naturalis Historiae*, "An Account of Paintings and Colours," Pliny the Elder tells the famous story of a competition between the renowned Greek painters Zeuxis and Parrhasius to determine who was the greater artist. To quickly recall this tale from chapter 36, "Artists Who Painted with the Pencil,"

Pliny recounts how Zeuxis painted a picture of a bunch of grapes that was so lifelike it even deceived a flock of birds, who immediately flew down and started pecking at the painting. Yet, as he goes on to relate, Parrhasius's own picture appears to be concealed behind a curtain, which Zeuxis—delighted by the positive verdict passed on the verisimilitude of his work by the birds—demands be drawn back, so that his rival's effort can be judged alongside his own. In seeking vainly to get behind the curtain and view the real picture, though, Zeuxis suddenly realizes that he has lost the competition: Parrhasius has deceived not only a flock of birds but also a fellow master painter because, of course, the curtain *was* the painting.[57]

To the classic question of who or what may lie behind the curtain of sovereignty, this chapter has argued that Benjamin, Deleuze, and Derrida's answer turns out to be neither the Judeo-Christian god, the Roman general, the Baroque prince, the Leibnizian monad, the Parisian bourgeois subject, nor any other allegedly pure or naked nucleus of power, but a political trompe-l'oeil worthy of the master painter Parrhasius: the curtain *is* the sovereign. If the political veil, curtain, or threshold apparently separates interiority from exteriority, Benjamin's curtainology, Deleuze's theory of the fold, and Derrida's testimony about his prayer shawl are all, albeit in radically different ways, predicated upon a certain originary *inexplicability*—"what cannot be unfolded"—that precedes and constitutes the opposition between the individual and the world, the same and the other, the private and the public or common. In the unfinished (and perhaps unfinishable) project of political rideaulogy, we might say that the Hobbesian political theology of sovereignty is turned inside out: sovereignty is not a decision (from the Latin *de-cision*, literally "to cut off") that cuts the political field into two (inside and outside, order and disorder, friend and enemy) but a contingent *fold* that can always be unfolded or refolded differently.

If I can return to the artwork with which we began, Hobbes scholars have proposed many answers to the question of what lies behind the curtain on the frontispiece of *Leviathan*—whether it be a sacred Holy of Holies (Bredekamp) or a profane Wizard of Oz pulling the levers of power (Schmitt)—but I would like to suggest that the philosopher's magnum opus might itself be a Parrhasiusian trompe-l'oeil.[58] To read Hobbes's *Leviathan* as a political equivalent to Baroque art like Adriaen van der Spelt and Frans van Mieris's *Trompe-l'oeil Still Life with a Flower*

FIGURE 3.3 Frans van Mieris the Elder (1635–1681) and Adriaen van der Spelt (Dutch, 1630–1673): *Trompe-l'Oeil Still Life with a Flower Garland and a Curtain*, 1658. Oil on panel, 18 1/4 x 25 1/8 in. (46.5 x 63.9 cm). Wirt D. Walker Fund, 1949.585. Art Institute of Chicago, Chicago (IL), USA. Public Domain. Creative Commons CC0 1.0 Universal Public Domain Dedication.

Garland and a Curtain (1658), which was painted eight years after the publication of the former's own work, what begins to emerge is that the Hobbesian curtain cannot "conceal" the work of art because it is *itself* the work of art and, moreover, the particular work of art called the modern political state.[59] Perhaps we can find one example of what such an inexplicable state might look like—one that, like Parrhasius's painting, contains its own outside within itself—in Giorgio Agamben's proposition that, in Hobbes's political theory, the state of nature is not spatially or temporally "outside" the political state but is folded *inside* its warp and woof: what we call the Hobbesian "state of nature" is not "a prejuridical condition that is indifferent to the law of the city," Agamben argues in *Homo Sacer* (1995), but, rather, "the exception and the threshold that constitutes and dwells within it."[60] For Agamben, the Hobbesian commonwealth thus represents what he calls the state of nature's "incorporation [*inglobamento*, "absorption" or "inclusion"]" into the political state in the form of the state of exception.[61] In Agamben's logic of inclusive exclusion, Hobbes's curtain between the state of nature and society would thus signify less a threshold between the outside and the inside than yet another turning-inside or *inglobamento* of the outside itself: the curtain is the commonwealth.

In order to finally draw the curtain upon this chapter, though, I want to double back toward another curtain, another city, and, perhaps, another sovereignty. To return one more time to the scene of Walter Benjamin's original curtainology, as described in his 1933 letter to Greta Karplus, I cannot help but find within this tableau a curious refolding or redoubling of Abraham Bosse's original frontispiece for Hobbes's *Leviathan* in which, so to speak, a sovereign stares out through a curtain upon his own proper realm: "Today I've obtained significant results in my study of curtains," Benjamin writes to Karplus from the island of Ibiza, "for a curtain separated us from the balcony that looked out on the city and the sea." For Benjamin, however, what he calls "curtainology" appears to make possible a very different sovereign perspective or vantage point upon this classic Hobbesian panorama of curtain, city, sea, and sky. If Bosse's celebrated image is a dream of absolute sovereignty over the city, whose curtain signifies the unbridgeable divide between ruler and ruled, Jean Selz's memoir "An Experiment by Walter Benjamin" describes how Benjamin's own historical materialist reverie once again turns this Hobbesian fantasy of mastery inside out so that the curtain instead becomes a fold that symbolizes the absolute *impossibility* of separating sovereign from subject. In Benjamin's political rideaulogy, we do not see through the curtain so much as the curtain sees through *us*:

> The view from the open window, through the white muslin curtain, was the repeated focus of [Benjamin's] musings. The terraced roofs, the curve of the bay, and the line of distant mountains, captured by the curtain or swathed in its folds, undulated along with it when it stirred—ever so slightly—in the hot evening air. The city and the curtain soon ceased to be separate things. The city and the curtain soon ceased to be separate things. And if the city had become fabric, that fabric had become the stuff of a garment. It was *our* garment, but was moving ever farther away from us. We then observed that *the opium was divesting us of the country in which we were living*. Benjamin added the humorous remark that we were engaging in "curtainology."

4

IN THE ANTECHAMBER

Schiller, Kafka, Benjamin, Schmitt

And I—my head oppressed by horror, said:
"Master, what is that I hear? Who are
Those people so defeated by their pain?"

*And he to me: "This miserable way (*misero modo*)*
*Is taken by the sorry souls (*l'anima triste*) of those*
*Who lived without disgrace and without praise (*sanza 'nfamia
e sanza lodo*)*

They now commingle with the coward angels,
The company of those who were not rebels
*Nor faithful to their God, but stood apart (*per sé fuoro*).*

The heavens, that their beauty not be lessened,
*Have cast them out, nor will deep Hell (*profondo inferno*)*
receive them—

Even the wicked cannot glory in them."
—Dante Alighieri, *Inferno*, canto 3, lines 31–42

In canto 3 of the *Inferno* (ca. 1308–1320), Dante enters a liminal space between the shores of the River Acheron and the gates of Hell that scholars have often called the "vestibule of Hell." It is populated by the lost souls of those who, in life, chose not to choose between good and evil, but instead pursued only their own self-interest. As Virgil explains, they include such figures as Pope Celestine V, those who "lived without disgrace and without praise," and even those cowardly angels who took neither God nor Satan's side in the rebellion in Heaven. To give the occupants of Hell's vestibule a collective name, they are what we might call history's *bystanders*—who stood apart (*per sé fuoro*), as Virgil puts it, in the great existential struggle between good and evil—which is why the *Divina Commedia* reserves a special place in, or rather adjacent to, Hell for them. In the first great *contrapasso* of the *Inferno*, which famously condemns every sinner in Hell to a punishment that fits their particular sins, Celestine and the other venal bystanders of history are sentenced to sit eternally on the very fence between good and evil, salvation and damnation, that they sought to occupy in life: they dwell in neither beautiful Heaven, nor in deep Hell, but in Hell's own antechamber.

To open the door to Dante's premodern vestibule of Hell, we immediately begin to see that it is the archetype of every early modern and modern representation of the political vestibule or antechamber. It is only necessary to recall some of the more celebrated antespaces in the (early) modern political imaginary to appreciate that this threshold—neither inside the place of power nor entirely outside it—is home to the modern equivalent to Dante's "lost souls." After all, the occupants of the modern political antechamber are also condemned to remain infinitely without entering or exiting: the valet or attendant, the secretary, the supplicant, the petitioner, the lawyer, the scholar, the lobbyist,

FIGURE 4.1 Gustave Doré, Dante und Vergil am Eingang zur Hölle—Illustration von zu Dantes Göttlicher Komödie, Band I, Tafel 8 bpk / Kupferstichkabinett, SMB / Volker-H. Schneider.

the mistress, the hanger-on, the gossip, the eunuch, the clown. For Roland Barthes, writing in his book *On Racine* (1960), the antechamber (*l'Anti-Chambre*) thus becomes "the eternal space of all subjections, since it is here that one *waits*."[1] If we think of some of the abject dramatis personae of the (early) modern antechamber of power—William Shakespeare's Rosencrantz and Guildenstern in *Hamlet* (ca. 1599);[2] Franz Kafka's man from the country in "Before the Law" (1919);[3] Jorge Luis Borges's librarians in "The Library of Babel" (1941);[4] or even the itinerant populations of those transient, anonymous spaces like hotel rooms, waiting rooms, or airport departure lounges that Marc

Augé describes in his book *Non-Places* (1992)—it is no coincidence that they each experience this liminal space as a kind of Dantescan metaphysical netherworld.⁵ In a very modern contrapasso, though, Dante's vestibule to Hell is today transformed into something like its opposite: our own special version of Hell might just be a permanent, inescapable vestibule.

If the modern antechamber is the (non)place of political impotence, though, it also becomes the—paradoxically exclusive or privileged—location of new forms of power. It is too simple to dismiss the antespace as just the "outside" of power, because, as the sole point of access to, and egress from, the sovereign, it really constitutes something like power's *own* outside. As Helmut Puff observes in his social history of such antespaces, "It would be erroneous . . . to see the *anticamera*'s purpose squarely as prohibiting visitors or audience seekers from entry. Rather, this room type assisted the production of social status via spatial layouts and temporal protocols."⁶ To police the space between the chamber and the antechamber, patrolling the corridors of power and deciding who enters the inner sanctum and who must wait outside, we thus find the emergence of such shadowy real and fictional political actors as Baldassare Castiglione's courtier in the *Book of the Courtier* (1528),⁷ Niccolò Machiavelli's adviser or counsellor in *The Prince* (1532),⁸ Henry VIII's chief minister Thomas Cromwell in Holbein's portrait (ca. 1532), and even the ambitious young secretary Thomas Hobbes as depicted by Aubrey in his *Brief Lives* (1696).⁹ Perhaps we might also see the appearance of a new breed of self-consciously "modern" courtiers like the Marquis of Posa in Friedrich Schiller's play *Don Carlos* (1787), who succeeds the old "Machiavellian" Renaissance courtier to become the rational, cosmopolitan, and enlightened adviser to Philip II of Spain, as the harbinger of a liberal political architectonic in which the balance of power begins to shift inexorably from what Foucault calls sovereignty to governmentality, from the king to the counsellor, and from the chamber to the antechamber of power.[10] In the modern liberal state, of course, the antechamber will go on to become an autonomous and permanent sphere of power in its own right as the seat of that politically neutral professional bureaucrat who, unlike Dante, finds positive virtue in not choosing one side or the other.

In Dante's vestibule of Hell, we thus enter what is only the first and most celebrated of a series of antechambers, vestibules, corridors, foyers, and lobbies in the Herrschaftsarchitektur of political modernity from Friedrich Schiller to Carl Schmitt. It is perhaps symptomatic of its traditionally lowly or ancillary status—whether socially, politically, or architecturally—that a general history of the anteroom from the Roman *vestibulum* to the Italian Renaissance *antecamera* remains unwritten.[11] As far as we can tell, this obscure social space performed diverse historical functions from ancient Rome onward—affording privacy, shelter, aesthetic decoration, and, increasingly, a kind of social "triage" system for assorting the stream of visitors seeking access to the inner sanctum.[12] Yet, as Puff reminds us, the antechamber was always political insofar as it organized and distributed power relations via strict spatial and temporal divisions: "Anterooms . . . gave architectural expression to a hierarchical society," he writes, "they offered spaces where social differences became manifest."[13] To introduce this chapter, I seek in what follows to offer a political cartography or architectonic of what Carl Schmitt calls the "antechamber of power" (*Vorraum der macht*)—the *vestibulum*, *vorraum*, *anticamera* or *antichambre*—that will argue that this historically marginal nonplace is actually (and here I am obviously following such readers as Benjamin, Derrida, and Agamben) the privileged space of an originary *partage*, partition, or division of sovereignty: "power" cannot strictly be held by anyone anywhere. If Jean Bodin famously defines sovereign power as "indivisible" in his *Six livres de la République* (1576), because it can never be shared, divided, or pooled without being destroyed, Schmitt's little-known essay "Dialogue on Power and Access to the Holder of Power" ("Gespräch über die Macht und den Zugang zum Machthaber," 1954) traces what we might call a certain originary self-division of sovereignty into what Jacques Derrida famously calls "plus d'un" (more than one, no more one) sources or places of power.[14] In Schmitt's "Dialogue on Power," contra his classic apology for sovereign personalism in earlier texts like *Political Theology* (1922), sovereign power can never be wholly incarnated in the singular body of the sovereign, who is master of his own house or chamber of power, because from the very outset it divides itself into a potentially infinite series of new political bodies, who, as we will see, reside in new political antechambers: Schiller's counsellor, Kafka's bureaucrat, Benjamin's clerk. What remains of sovereignty, then, when it enters the antechamber of power?

IN THE ANTECHAMBER OF POWER

In a July 29, 1954, article in *Die Zeit*, "Im Vorraum der Macht" (In the antechamber of power), which was subsequently published in expanded form as "Dialogue on Power and Access to the Holder of Power" (1954), Carl Schmitt offers what is (to my knowledge) the only study of the antechamber in the history of political theory.[15] It goes without saying that (despite his protestations of "impotence" throughout the essay) this former state counsellor of Prussia under the Nazi regime was himself no stranger to the corridors of power.[16] As we may expect, though, his earlier references to the political "antechamber" are uniformly hostile: Schmitt dismisses the neo-Kantian legal normativism of Hans Kelsen as stuck "in the antechamber of jurisprudence" (*die Antichambre der Jurisprudenz*) in *Political Theology* (1922),[17] whereas his *Crisis of Parliamentary Democracy* (1923) endorses the Count of Cavour's epigram that "the worst chamber is still preferable to the best antechamber" and later describes parliament as little more than "a gigantic antechamber [*riesige Antichambre*] in front of the bureaus or committees of invisible rulers."[18] To reread Schmitt's political theory in the context of a proposed genealogy of the antechamber, we may thus be tempted to conclude that he is an unapologetic defender of what we might call *der politische Raum*: sovereignty is personal, decisionist, concrete, and situational, he famously argues, not distributed across the endless debating chambers, committee rooms, and bureaucratic offices of the liberal *Vorraum* in which nothing ever gets decided once and for all. If the early Schmitt of *Political Theology* seeks to emancipate sovereignty from the fetters of liberal normativism and proceduralism—which is to say to free the political *Raum* from the depoliticized *Vorraum*—what concerns the later Schmitt of the "Dialogue on Power" is, however, something he intriguingly calls the "inescapable internal dialectic of power and impotence [*die unentrinnbare innere Dialektik von Macht und Ohnmacht*], into which every human holder of power falls."[19] In Schmitt's account, this internal political dialectic between power and impotence expresses itself as an architectural dialectic between the chamber and the antechamber: "In front of every chamber of direct power [*Raum direkter Macht*] an antechamber of indirect influences and powers [*Vorraum indirekter Einflüsse und Gewalten*] constructs itself," he writes, "a path of access to the ear, a corridor to the soul of the holder of power. There is no human power [*menschliche Macht*] without this antechamber and without this corridor."[20]

To explore the *Machtarchitektur* of the "antechamber, back stairwell, foyer, lower hold [*Hintertreppe, Unraum, Unterraum*]," Schmitt begins by drawing a distinction between the absolute nature of sovereign power in itself and the inevitably weak, frail, and mortal body of the sovereign in whom that power resides.[21] "Power is an objective, autonomous quantity [*Größe*]," he asserts, "with respect to any human individual who at any given time holds power in his hand."[22] It is precisely because the human "holder" of power (*Machthaber*) cannot wield absolute power all by himself that he requires counsellors to assist him. As Schmitt writes, "The human individual, in whose hand the great political decisions lie for an instant [*Augenblick*], can only form his will under given presuppositions and with given means" such that "even the most absolute prince is reliant on reports and information and dependent on his counsellors."[23] Yet, as the sovereign comes to depend more and more upon his counsellors, the latter inevitably begin to acquire significant power of their own: "He who holds a lecture before the holder of power or informs him, already has a part in power [*Anteil an der Macht*], regardless of whether he is a responsible counter-signing Minister or whether he knows how to attain the ear of the holder of power in an indirect way."[24] If the sovereign is still the one who decides, as Schmitt's famous definition holds, the trusted counsellor thus also begins to participate in sovereignty by becoming the one who, so to speak, *decides upon what is or is not up to the sovereign to decide*: "It suffices for him to transmit impressions and motives to the human individual in whose hand the decision [*Entscheidung*] lies for an instant."[25] In the instant before this instant of sovereign decision, where the court assembles to advise the king what to do, we find what Schmitt calls the "Vorraum der Macht": the antechamber of power.[26]

If no sovereign can entirely secure or concentrate power within himself, given the limits that human finitude imposes upon absolute sovereignty, then the chamber of power must inevitably overflow into this antechamber. "No institution, however wise, no organization, however well thought out, can wholly extirpate [*ausrotten*] the antechamber itself," Schmitt writes in what could almost be a critique of his own earlier critique of liberal parliamentary democracy, "no burst of outrage against the camarilla or the antechamber can completely dispatch with it. One cannot circumvent [*umgehen*] the antechamber itself."[27] It is here that what he calls the "internal dialectic" between power and impotence—the chamber and the antechamber—is set in motion. As a chamber of power begins to establish itself, he writes, so "an antechamber to this power promptly organizes itself as well. Every heightening of direct power also thickens and condenses the vaporous circle of indirect influences [*Dunstkreis indirekter Einflüsse*]."[28] For the later Schmitt of the "Dialogue on Power," this obscure antechamber of power is thus no longer the abstract, liberal cul-de-sac occupied by legal normativists like Kelsen, nor even the infinite *salle d'attente* that is the parliamentary democratic system, but rather something close to the necessary outworking of a permanent and structural "impotence" that haunts power. Inasmuch as the Schmittian sovereign simply has no choice but to share power with those who surround his throne (e.g., the ministers, counsellors, bureaucrats, mistresses), the birth of the antechamber inevitably creates the possibility of the subdivision, diminution, or dissolution of that power by plot, intrigues, palace coups, or, later, a bicameral (literally "two chambers") liberal parliamentary system.[29]

In rereading Schmitt's essay today, we can begin to see that his theory of the antechamber—which sees it as an apparently extraneous, but somehow essential, supplement to power—not only revises his own earlier apology for sovereign personalism in a manner we might be tempted to call "Benjaminian" but also anticipates Jacques Derrida's later critique of his work from *The Politics of Friendship* (1997) to *Rogues* (2004).[30] To recall Derrida's hypothesis, sovereignty is, far from being indivisible, founded upon an originary partition, distribution, or *divisibility* of power: the sovereign *decider* (from Latin *decision*, literally "to cut off") is himself de-cided, in a death of a thousand cuts.[31] It would only be possible for the Schmittian sovereign to remain singular, absolute, and exceptional if he never exposed himself to the other, Derrida argues, because the moment he enters time, space, and language, his sovereignty begins to divide, alienate, or exteriorize itself. "As soon as I speak to the other," he goes on, "I submit to the law of giving reason(s), I share a virtually universalizable medium, I divide my authority."[32] Yet, as Schmitt's own architectonic of power already reveals, this theoretical space of absolute political singularity prior to all time, language, and difference never actually exists: the sovereign is already exposed to a "flowing, infinite sea" of counsel "day by day and hour by hour" from which he can at most "ladle out a few droplets."[33] For Schmitt, the sovereign's political chamber thus inevitably subdivides into not simply a dialectic but a vertiginous mise en abyme of antechambers inside antechambers:

> In any case, in the course of world history, a motley and mixed society has found itself assembled together in this antechamber of power. Here the indirect assemble themselves. Here we meet ministers and ambassadors (*Botschafter*) in grand uniform, but also father-confessors (*Beichtväter*) and personal physicians (*Leibärzte*), adjutants and secretaries, chamberlains (*Kammerdiener*) and mistresses. Here stands the old Fredersdoff, Frederick the Great's

chamberlain, next to the Empress Augusta, Rasputin next to the Cardinal Richelieu, an *eminence grise* next to a Messalina. Sometimes clever and wise men are in this antechamber, sometimes fabulous managers and dependable *major domos* (*Hausmeier*), sometimes dumb careerists (*Streber*) and swindlers.[34]

If Derrida's claim is that there is no, and can never be, a private sovereign who resides alone in his own chamber of power—which is to say no space of pure ipseity or autoaffection of a self who, so to speak, requires no counsel[35]—Schmitt anticipates this originary subdivision or bicameralism of sovereignty by insisting upon the irreducibility of power itself to the finite body of the sovereign who happens to wield it at any given moment: "Power is an objective, autonomous quantity with respect to any human individual who at any given time holds power in his hand."[36] In his human, all too human body, which can only ever be a temporary vessel for the infinite majesty of sovereignty, the Schmittian sovereign thus occupies the original antechamber of power.

THE MARQUIS IS TO ENTER UNANNOUNCED

In the final line of act 3, scene 10 of Friedrich Schiller's tragedy *Don Carlos* (*Don Karlos: Infant von Spanien*, 1787), Philip II of Spain grants his new counsellor, Roderigo, the Marquis of Posa, the extraordinary right to freely enter the King's private chamber whenever he so wishes: "Count," the King commands his courtier, "in future the Marquis is to enter, / unannounced [*ungemeldet*]" (3.10.841–43; translation modified). It is with the dramatic entrance of Schiller's great Enlightenment hero Posa into the Renaissance sanctum sanctorum of power, Schmitt argues in his "Dialogue on Power," that the internal dialectic between power and impotence—chamber and antechamber—also announces itself. As Schmitt puts it in an intriguing "Intermezzo" to this essay, Schiller's drama of familial and political intrigue turns on the essential political question of the antechamber: "Who has immediate access to the King?"[37] To quickly recall the play's labyrinthine plot, the liberal, cosmopolitan Marquis of Posa rises from nowhere to become the new confidante of the despotic Philip II, but Posa's real plan is to pursue political and religious emancipation—*Gedankenfreiheit*, or freedom of thought—for the Spanish Netherlands by installing Philip's son and heir, Don Carlos, as leader of the growing Dutch Rebellion against the Hapsburg Empire. However, Posa's own dramatic entry onto the scene of sovereignty turns out to be short lived and his palace coup a total failure: Posa scapegoats himself to save Carlos from Philip's wrath after his elaborate plot collapses, but Philip sends his son to his death for treason at the hands of the Inquisition anyway. If the aging and isolated Philip's increasing dependence on his new favorite "son," Posa, undoubtedly anticipates Schmitt's theory of the fatal self-division of sovereignty from chamber into antechamber and from king to counsellor, though, Schiller's drama also exposes an internal *subdivision* within the new seat of power occupied by Posa—namely, the antechamber itself. In Schiller's theater of the antechamber, the counsellor who appears to be the "real" power behind the throne turns out to be as devoid of power as the king himself.

To trace Posa's remarkable rise to power, we must first go back to act 3, scene 5, where Philip dismisses all his old, discredited counsellors from his private bedchamber and utters the following anguished prayer: "Now, Providence, good Providence, send me /

A man," he asks. "You have been generous to me, / Now bless me with a man" (*Don Carlos*, 3.5.316–18). It is apparently a moment of total personal and political isolation—the "KING *alone*" reads the stage direction—but we need only recall Schmitt's critique of the human, all-too-human *Machthaber* to ask whether a sovereign like Philip can ever really be "alone" in his own chamber of power. As his soliloquy reveals, Philip's private chamber immediately becomes a new antechamber because the King reduces himself to a mere petitioner or supplicant to the real absolute "sovereign" (Providence), who will decide for him: "You [Providence] are alone, / Because unaided, you see everything" (3.5.318–19). For Schmitt, the King's inability to be politically alone, to fully occupy or monopolize his own chamber of power, is why Schiller's play becomes, in his view, a political theater of the antechamber: *Don Carlos*'s real dramatis personae are not so much kings, queens, and princes but the counsellors, father-confessors, grandees, mistresses, and attendants who navigate the cabinets, corridors, and private chambers of the royal household practicing the time-honored courtly arts of conspiracy, intrigue, and machination. If the Grand Inquisitor rebukes Philip for his human weakness in needing a man like Posa at all—"Why do you need a man? Mankind is numbers, / Nothing but numbers" (5.10.644–45)—Schiller makes clear that even this supposed representative of pure sacral power is not immune to the political arithmetic of the antechamber either, because his real anxiety appears to be that Philip should have any other adviser than *himself*. "What could he be to you?" he asks. "What could he say / That our good words have not prepared you for?" (5.10.635–36). In order to escape the "many thousands / Who flutter to the flame of royalty" (3.5.330–31), the King thus appoints as his principal advisor the only man who tells him he does *not* want to enter his service: "I cannot pledge allegiance to a lord" (3.10.516) but, as we will see, not even Posa can escape the fatal subdivision of sovereignty.

If Posa's privileged status at court is the apparent embodiment of the new liberal republican order he wishes to bring into being—he is free, equal, rational, devoid of self-interest, and able to speak truth to power with impunity—the Marquis's pursuit of his ultimate political goal of freedom for the Spanish Netherlands falls victim to a classic Schillerian confusion of means for ends—or, more precisely, of antechambers for chambers. "Can your good cause [*gute Sache*]," Queen Elisabeth asks the newly elevated Posa, "Transform the evil of its means [*Mittel adeln*] to honour?" (4.3.50–51). It is Posa's tragic fate to become the secret police of his own enlightened despotism as his increasingly unaccountable power begins to terrorize the court in a manner that anticipates the French Terror of only a few years after Schiller's play: "Without one aide, no matter what his name, / To interrupt me in my undertakings, / No matter what I have to do" (4. 11.519–21). To defend his cherished Gedankenfreiheit, for instance, Posa must invade not only Carlos and Elisabeth's personal space, entering their private chambers and reading their correspondence, but also the supposedly free chambers of their hearts and minds: "Get close to my son," Philip commands him. "Inquire into the queen's heart [*Erforscht das Herz der Königin*] / You have the right to speak to her in private" (3.10.836–37; translation modified). By convincing himself that he can best serve the King by *not* executing the latter's orders, the counsellor stops serving him at all and goes freelance: "I mean to serve him . . . with more honour than he looks for" (*Gedenk' ich diesmal redlicher zu dienen, / Als er mir aufgetragen hat*; 4.3.57–58). Finally, this staunch defender of liberty comes to believe that he can only protect Carlos by persuading Philip to issue a precautionary arrest warrant for the king's son—"It would remain a secret of the state / Until its use, of course" (4.11.537–38)—and then immediately goes on to execute that warrant. In a drama of uncanny doppelgängers (Carlos and Posa, Elisabeth and Eboli), Schiller's play even raises the possibility that the enlightened Posa's dark twin may be none other than the sinister figure of the blind, fanatical Grand Inquisitor, who is equally happy to invent noble reasons for fathers killing sons:

KING:
Could you invent a fashion of belief
That would condone (*vertheidigt*) the murder of a child?
GRAND INQUISITOR:
To make amends (*sühnen*) for his eternal justice (*Gerechtigkeit*)
The son of God died on the cross (5.1.680–83).[38]

In *Don Karlos*, however, Posa's fate is not simply a tragic downfall nor a culpable descent into corruption, but another iteration of what we have called the self-division of sovereignty from chamber to antechamber. To explain the Marquis's political demise, Schiller's subsequent *Briefe über Don Karlos* (1788) makes clear that Posa is not merely the innocent victim of the powerful vested interests of church and state (represented by the Grand Inquisitor and the Duke of Alba, respectively), because he is himself guilty of the classic Enlightenment plague of *Schwärmerei*, excessive enthusiasm or sentiment, which leads him to privilege an abstract love of "the People" in general over his allegiance to actual individuals like Carlos, Elisabeth, and Philip. "I do not intend to have acquitted the Marquis of *Schwärmerei*," Schiller writes. "*Schwärmerei* and enthusiasm [*Enthusiasmus*] touch one another so closely, their line of distinction is so fine, that in a state of passionate excitement [*leidenschaftlicher Erhitzung*] it can all too easily be crossed."[39] It may be possible to find a different political explanation for Posa's downfall, though, in another recurring but far less historically overdetermined trope in the play: "confidence" (*Zuversicht, Glauben, Sicherheit*). As well as Schwärmerei (enthusiasm, feeling, or overconfidence), Schiller's tragedy also explores "confidence" in the sense of that far more precarious trust, the faith or intimacy that exists between lovers, friends, fathers, and sons, and, of course, kings and counsellors. Carlos declares: "You are today so amazingly confident [*sicher*]" (*Don Carlos*, 4.5, 223; translation modified) to the elevated Posa; Posa recognizes that Philip has placed his trust or confidence (*glauben*) in him and deserves to be repaid (4.6, 282–83), and the Marquis finally admits to Carlos that his "confidence was madness" (*Raserei War meine Zuversicht*; 5.3.143). Yet, in a paradoxical sense, Posa's tragic error is not the political confidence he places in others but that which he places in *himself*: he confesses to Elisabeth that he is the victim of his excessive desire or ambition to "play with heaven so confidently" (*so zuversichtlich mit dem Himmel spielen*; 4.20.825–26; translation modified). If Philip's trust or confidence in his counsellor Posa turns out to be misplaced because the latter has effectively been serving himself all along, Posa's overconfidence in his *own* powers of political machination finds itself equally betrayed by the counsellor himself: the Marquis is perversely his own worst or most disloyal servant. For Schiller, the Marquis of Posa, like the King before him, can never be alone even when he is by himself: the sovereign counsellor's ipseity or subjectivity phenomenologically splits into a "court" (the other counsellors, the counsellors in himself*)* with whom he must share power. In *Don Carlos*, Posa's new antechamber of power thus cannot help but produce its own antechambers—into which yet more Posas may enter unannounced.

UNKNOWN ANTECHAMBERS

In a famous 1903 letter to his friend Oskar Pollak, Franz Kafka observes that "some books seem like a key to unfamiliar chambers [*fremden Sälen*] in one's own castle."[40] To pursue this political architectonic into the twentieth century, I want to nominate Kafka—who began his working life as a legal clerk, who lived through the final collapse of the decaying Hapsburg Empire, and whose fiction is populated with tragicomic petitioners, messengers, and servants vainly seeking entry to mysterious rooms jealously guarded by gatekeepers—as Schiller's successor to the official position of cartographer of our modern political antechambers. It is surprising, given the vast critical labor devoted to allegoresis of Kafka's philosophical universe, that little or no attention has been paid to its peculiar architecture. As Walter Benjamin famously observes in his essay "Franz Kafka: On the Tenth Anniversary of his Death" (1934),[41] Kafka's world is a "world of offices and registries, of musty, shabby, dark rooms" but the antechamber remains largely a closed room in the secondary literature.[42] For Kafka, what seems to be at stake in his own political architectonic is less the claustrophobic Benjaminian "becoming-antechamber" of the world—which is to say its shrinking down to a solitary, windowless room—than the infinite, Escherian opening up or "becoming-world" of the antechamber. If Schiller's *Don Carlos* begins to reckon with the self-division or multiplication of sovereign power, Kafka's fiction calculates this political arithmetic, as Jorge Luis Borges famously recognizes in his "Kafka and His Precursors" (1951), almost to infinity: sovereignty becomes infinitely divisible into a series of near identical and anonymous microspaces like attics, doorways, entrance halls, lobbies, offices, stairwells, and vestibules populated by seedy bureaucrats, clerks, secretaries, mistresses, clowns, and, finally, that curious itinerant, Odradek.⁴³ In the labyrinthine castle of Kafka's own books, it seems there are only ever unknown antechambers.

To reread the celebrated short story "The Great Wall of China" ("Beim Bau der Chinesischen Mauer," 1917), for example, we find another fiction that seems to anticipate the fatal Schmittian self-division of sovereignty.⁴⁴ It is the story of another all-too-human sovereign ("a man like us") who, again, falls victim to his own antechamber. Around the emperor, Kafka's narrator recounts, we find a "brilliant and yet ambiguous throng of nobles and courtiers" who represent a "counterweight to the imperial power" and "perpetually labor to unseat the ruler from his place."⁴⁵ However, the people of the narrator's own remote village remain utterly oblivious to the Schillerian intrigue happening far away at the imperial court in Peking: they are like "strangers in a city" standing at the end of a busy "side street" while "the execution of their ruler" is taking place in the "Market Square at the heart of the city."⁴⁶ For Kafka's narrator, this unbridgeable cosmological gulf between the sovereign and the people is best captured in a famous parable (which was published separately as "An Imperial Message" ("Eine kaiserliche Botschaft") about a dying emperor who wants to send a message to "you, the humble subject": the imperial herald carrying the message from the Emperor's deathbed is, the parable recounts, "only making his way through the chambers [*Gemächer*] of the innermost palace," and, even if he managed to do so, "the courts [*Höfen*] would still have to be crossed, and after the courts the second outer palace [*der zweite umschließende Palast*], and once more stairs and courts; and once more another palace; and so on for thousands of years."⁴⁷ If "Before the Law" ("Vor dem Gesetz") is a fable about the impossibility of the "man from the country" gaining access to the law, what seems to be taking place in "An Imperial Message" is thus a kind of *Nach dem Gesetz*: this is a parable about the impossibility of the *law* gaining access to the common people, of the infinite subdivision of the chamber of power, of the literal impossibility (to recall Schmitt again) of circumventing power's antechambers. In the sense that he cannot but expose his sovereign power to the throng at court, the emperor is already politically "dead"—divided, shared, diminished—even when he physically lives on: "he's speaking of a dead man as if he were alive," the villagers mock the imperial official who pays a once-in-a-lifetime visit to hand down the real, live Emperor's instructions. "This Emperor of his died long ago."[48]

If "An Imperial Message" is a story about the political death of one sovereign at the hands of his antechamber, then "The Cares of a Family Man" ("Die Sorge des Hausvaters," 1919) can be read as a study of another finite "sovereign," the *Hausvater*, and his melancholy fear that his own antechamber will outlast him. To approach what is arguably the single most overinterpreted figure in the whole of Kafka's work, Odradek, I again find it more productive to put allegoresis to one side and focus on the story's distinctive architectonics, because this uncategorizable "creature" is obviously yet another occupant of the musty, shabby, and dark anterooms of power. It—whatever "it" is—is indistinguishable from the marginal, transitional spaces in which it can habitually be found loitering: Odradek claims to have "no fixed abode," the family man relates, and instead "lurks by turns in the garret [*Dachboden*], the stairway [*Treppenhaus*], the lobbies [*Gängen*], the entrance hall [*Flur*]."[49] As Benjamin observes in his own famous early reading of the story, Odradek's temporary places of residence (e.g., lobbies, entrance halls) carry a very specific political or juridical resonance that the creature itself signally lacks: they do not belong in the domestic home, he argues, so much as in the "court of law."⁵⁰ Yet this creature may not necessarily be a guilty defendant awaiting a death sentence at the prehistoric court of justice, as Benjamin memorably suggests, so much as a perversely modern iteration of the royal courtier, counsellor, or bureaucrat whose role is to administer or pronounce that sentence. For Kafka, Odradek resembles the final form sovereignty takes when it has, so to speak, divided or devolved itself (almost) to death: a functionless or dysfunctional fonctionnaire, a "perfectly finished" but "senseless" object or machine, a "faithful" but rogue attendant who permanently hovers on the threshold before entering unannounced (like a wooden, star-shaped Marquis of Posa) in order to deliver the news of the sovereign's demise with empty, hollow laughter.⁵¹ In the same way as the herald or messenger in "An Imperial Message"—who will carry on striding down stairs, through rooms, and across courtyards for thousands of years after the Emperor himself has died—the sovereign of "The Cares of a Family Man" supposes that Odradek will "always be rolling down the stairs, with ends of thread trailing after him, right before the feet of my children, and my children's children. . . . The idea that he is likely to survive me I find almost painful."⁵²

What, if anything, could thus be said to lie *beyond* Kafka's antechambers in the so-called inner sanctum or chamber of political power? It may be possible to find one more answer to this question in his classic novel of bureaucracy, *The Castle* (*Das Schloss*, 1919). As Olga explains to K., her brother Barnabas, who is employed as a messenger boy by his mysterious boss, Klamm, has a certain, albeit conditional, right of access to the eponymous castle.⁵³ "He's permitted to go into the bureaux or if you prefer, into an antechamber [*Vorraum*]," she reports. "Well let it be an antechamber, it has doors that lead on farther, barriers which can be passed if one has the courage."⁵⁴ To follow Barnabas's convoluted passage as he moves from antechamber to antechamber, what we eventually find is one of the only depictions in the world of Kafka's fiction of the political sanctum sanctorum itself:

> Barnabas has often described it to me, and even sketched the room. He's usually admitted into a large bureau (*ein großes Kanzleizimmer*), but the room isn't Klamm's bureau, nor even the bureau of any particular official. It's a room divided into two by a single reading-desk stretching all its length from wall to wall: one side is so narrow that two people can hardly squeeze past each other, and that's reserved for the officials (*Raum der Beamten*), the other side is spacious, and that's where clients wait (*Raum der Parteien*), spectators, servants, messengers. On the desk there are great books lying open, side by side, and officials stand by, most of them reading. They don't always stick to the same book, yet it isn't the books that they change but their places, and it always astounds Barnabas to see how they have to squeeze past each other when they change places, because there's so little room. In front of the desk and close to it there are small, low tables at which clerks sit ready to write from dictation, whenever the officials wish it.[55]

If Barnabas and (by implication) the reader were ever under the illusion that they have reached the inner sanctum or chamber of the castle, however, this is quickly dispelled by the perverse, indeed almost Borgesian, architectonics of this room, which are worth navigating in a little more detail: Klamm's "bureau" (which is not actually his bureau) is divided into chamber and antechamber by the reading desk (which separates the officials from the messengers), but this chamber is itself subdivided by the low table (which separates the clerks from the officials and the messengers), and, finally, subdivided again by the presence of the "great books, lying open, side by side" to which messengers, clerks, and officials alike all defer. For Kafka, this mythical chamber of power is thus not the ground of an original, absolute and indivisible sovereignty, but something closer to the void of a pure or infinite divisibility of power that goes all the way down: the messengers wait next to the clerks, the clerks "sit ready" for the officials, the officials "stand by" the books, and even the books themselves sit "side by side" with the other books. In a kind of bureaucratic equivalent to the paradox of Zeno's arrow—"A moving object at A," Borges recalls in "Kafka and His Precursors," "cannot reach point B, because it must first cover half the distance between the two points, and before that, half of the half, and before that, half of the half of the half, and so on to infinity"—Kafka's ultimate chamber of power turns out to be nothing but its own antechamber.[56]

SHUVALKIN . . . SHUVALKIN . . . SHUVALKIN . . .

In "Franz Kafka: On the Tenth Anniversary of his Death" (1934), Walter Benjamin retells a story by Alexander Pushkin about Prince Grigory Potemkin, the Russian nobleman, statesman, and military leader, that, he claims, anticipates Kafka's fiction by almost two hundred years. "It is said that Potemkin suffered from states of depression," he begins, during which access to his room was "strictly forbidden." After one particularly long depressive episode, the Russian court officials had become frantic because so many important papers had accumulated in Potemkin's absence that required his signature. Yet, one day, "an unimportant little clerk named Shuvalkin happened to enter the anteroom of the chancellor's palace and found the councilors of state assembled there, moaning and groaning as usual," and, after finding out the reason for their unhappiness, he promptly volunteered to get Potemkin to sign the documents himself. To quote Benjamin's account, Shuvalkin set off through galleries and corridors for Potemkin's bedroom and, like the Marquis of Posa before him, entered without "knocking or even stopping":

> In semidarkness Potemkin was sitting on his bed, in a threadbare nightshirt, biting his nails. Shuvalkin stepped up to the writing desk, dipped a pen in ink, and without saying a word pressed it into Potemkin's hand while putting one of the documents on his knees. Potemkin gave the intruder a vacant stare; then, as though in his sleep, he started to sign—first one paper, then a second, finally all of them. When the last signature had been affixed, Shuvalkin took the papers under his arm and left the room without further ado, just as he had entered it. Waving the papers triumphantly, he stepped into the anteroom.[57]

If Shuvalkin appears to have scored a great diplomatic coup, however, the clerk's moment of triumph is (again like Posa's) short lived, because the reaction of the counsellors of state to the signed papers is nothing more than a stunned silence: "No one spoke a word; the whole group seemed paralyzed." In a state of bewilderment, the solicitous clerk again approaches the counsellors to ask them what the matter is, whereupon, Benjamin concludes, he happens to notice the signature Potemkin has written on the papers: "One document after another was signed Shuvalkin . . . Shuvalkin . . . Shuvalkin . . ."[58]

To close the door upon this chapter, I want to propose that Benjamin's palace comedy or farce is one more *Trauerspiel* of the antechamber: a Machthaber sits in his private chamber signing away his sovereignty piece by piece to a counsellor, but the counsellor, in turn, can no more "hold" or receive this power than the sovereign, and so it subdivides, again, into paralysis. It has been my aim here to track this "long division" of sovereignty in which every unified political body becomes two, then four, and so on. After this bureaucratic death of a thousand cuts, what remains is neither some pure nucleus of power nor even an absolute void or zero so much as the political ontological equivalent of an infinitely recurring remainder in mathematics: Klamm, Odradek, Shuvalkin. If this self-division of sovereign power from prince to counsellor to clerk may appear an exception, contingency, or accident—a Baroque plot, a palace coup, or a trahison des clercs that interrupts the smooth running of the normal order—this chapter has argued it is already underway within the allegedly singular body of the sovereign himself. In the very instant that sovereignty comes into contact with alterity, which is to say the instant that it comes into existence in the first place, it is already dividing itself up both temporally and spatially: the sovereign's own body is only the first of an infinite number of antechambers of power.

If the sovereign is thus already his own first "counsellor," and a counsellor who, indeed, can only betray him, then the whole question of the relationship between sovereignty and its various historical, political or philosophical antechambers (the baroque court; the bicameral parliamentary system; the independent judiciary; Weber's bureaucratic or administrative machine; the soft power of Foucault's "governmentality" and, of course, the quite literal "lobbyists" of special interests, capital, big business) may need to be itself (endlessly) relitigated in that shabby bureaucratic antechamber we call "scholarship." To a certain degree, Geoffrey Bennington's recent deconstructive apology for what he calls "the *politics* of politics" (emphasis mine)—which is to say the grubby business of "politicking" or "playing politics" that constitutes the disavowed but somehow always necessary underbelly of an allegedly purer and more noble "politics"—sets this infinite scholarly labor in motion: "*Politics*," Bennington contends, "*is always already the politics of politics*."[59] In the sense that it is the outworking of an originary divisibility at the heart of sovereignty itself, we might add here that governmentality is always already the "sovereignty" of sovereignty: every Potemkin a Shuvalkin . . . Shuvalkin . . . Shuvalkin.

What exactly, in the end, has Shuvalkin done (or not done) to so upset Potemkin's counsellors of state? It may be, of course, that he has just failed to do his job properly. After all, an official document signed in the name of a humble clerk, rather than a sovereign prince, is worth even less than a blank sheet of paper. Yet, in a paradoxical sense, Shuvalkin's real failure may be that he has actually done his job *too well*: he has not perpetrated a political lie or forgery so much as unwittingly revealed the "truth" of the situation. To conclude this chapter with an unofficial counterreading of Benjamin's parable—a reading that, whatever its ultimate merits, is at least hypothetically possible—I thus want to propose that Shuvalkin's error is that he may just have accidentally stripped away the official fiction of the antechamber's marginal or ancillary status and revealed, to that antechamber's evident horror, its hitherto secret power to the light of day: Potemkin's counsellors of state, who obviously draw up every document that is presented to the sovereign prince for approval, are themselves the real, if unofficial, "signatories" of the official papers all along. If Potemkin signs Shuvalkin's name "as though in his sleep" on one paper after another, in other words, he does not render those documents null and void so much as confirm the nullity of his own "real" power. In his private chamber, this sovereign prince becomes physically in sickness what he might always already have been politically in health: a clerk to his own clerk, a human rubber stamp, a living antechamber.

5

UNDER THE CLOTHES
Montaigne, Kafka, Genet, Agamben

In a high-class brothel called the Grand Balcony, Madam Irma painstakingly choreographs a series of bespoke erotic games for her demanding clientele.[1] To satisfy their desires, this motley collection of plumbers, gasmen, and the like dress up in the finery of a Bishop, a Judge, and a General (which is to say in miters, copes, ornaments, gilded robes, and decorated military uniforms) and, with the assistance of Irma's sex workers, perform highly theatrical sadomasochistic rituals of power: they forgive a penitent sinner, punish a criminal, ride a horse into battle, and so on. However, it quickly becomes clear that, beyond the walls of this bordello, a political revolution is in progress, and real violence is taking place. If the Grand Balcony's clients get their kicks by lovingly impersonating the pillars of the establishment, the real revolutionaries "have it in for the Clergy, for the Army, for the Magistracy" (scene 5) and overthrow them one by one. In order to save the day and restore the status quo, Irma's customers don their theatrical costumes once more and parade in public as the "real" Chief Justice, Bishop, and General to the acclamation of the gathered crowd.

To enter Jean Genet's *The Balcony* (*Le Balcon*, 1956)—and whether we do so as paying customers, audience members, or allegedly disinterested political theorists makes little difference here—we must navigate a libidinal "house of illusions" in which each participant is compelled to choose their cosplay: bishop, judge, general, policeman, scholar.[2] It is not that the brothel's clientele *really* want to have the power of bishops or judges (indeed, Irma carefully builds a fake detail [*détail faux*] into each costume, such as black lace lingerie beneath a nun's habit, to reassure them it is all just a game) so much as to enjoy the symbolic power, the pure performativity, of their roles. As the "Bishop" puts it, what he desires is precisely the glittering *surface* of political theological power—"Miters, lace, gold cloth and glass trinkets [*veroterries*]" (scene 1), which is quite detached from the bare or naked "reality" of that power. If Genet's play seems predicated upon a clear and present ontological difference between appearance and reality (being and function, the naked body of power and the clothed body of ritual), however, *The Balcony* quickly proceeds to deconstruct the boundary between what is inside and outside the brothel before finally revealing that the spectator's own (allegedly neutral, disinterested, or objective) experience of "reality" itself contains a détail faux that betrays its theatricality. In a final coup de théâtre, Madam Irma breaks the fourth wall by informing the audience—us—that the Grand Balcony is now closed for the evening and so we should go home "where everything—you can be quite sure—will be even falser [*encore plus faux*] than here" (scene 9).

If Genet's theater of appearances seems more modern than ever in the epoch of Trump, Putin, and post-truth politics ("It seems to me that power can never do without theatricality," the playwright declares in an interview; "power protects and covers itself by means of theatricality"), I want to suggest that it also belongs to a long scholarly tradition of what we might call the political theology of cosplay, clothing, or *investments* (from the

Latin *vestire*, "to clothe," *vestis*, "robe").³ It may be this historical dimension that Alain Badiou's recent, and unapologetically presentist, reading of the play misses when he criticizes Genet's focus on allegedly outdated or anachronistic figures of power like kings, queens, and bishops rather than celebrities, bankers, or human rights activists.⁴ As Irma proudly recounts, the Grand Balcony's inventory of erotic role-playing games—the "studios"—is actually something close to a secret archive of political theology: her vast repertoire includes Saint Sebastian, "two Kings of France with sacred ceremonies and different rituals," "a missionary dying on the cross" and even "Christ in person" (*Balcony*, scene 5). To view such baroque rituals through the peephole of political theology—and the Grand Balcony's studios are, needless to say, all specially designed to accommodate voyeurs, too—Genet's play thus emerges as an esoteric contribution to a remarkable wave of postwar scholarship documenting the "signifiers" of power (crowns, orbs, scepters, thrones, regalia, robes, and ceremonies) that coincidentally appeared within a very few years of *The Balcony*'s own first production: I am thinking here of such classic works as Percy Ernst Schramm's multivolume magnum opus *The Signs of Power and Symbols of the State* (*Herrschaftszeichen und Staatssymbolik*, 1954–1978); Ernst Kantorowicz's *The King's Two Bodies* (1957); and Norbert Elias's *The Court Society* (*Die höfische Gesellschaft*, 1969).⁵ Perhaps we might even see Madam Irma's exhaustive catalog of sadomasochistic fetishes as a perverse answer to Schramm's famous 1953 call for a "Wissenschaft der Herrschaftszeichen": an objective "science" of the signs of power.⁶ In this scholarly context, the Grand Balcony is revealed as not simply a lucrative business, secular church, media spectacle, or theater (as many critics have already proposed) but a political theological sequel to Richard von Krafft-Ebing's *Psychopathia Sexualis* (1886).

In this chapter, I want to explore some of the virtual political and theological "studios"—where naked bodies become vested and invested in the cosplay of power and glory—that lie both within and without the walls of Genet's house of illusions. It is surprising, for example, that Madame Irma's vast repertory of religious fetishes finds no place for the Fall of Adam and Eve, because not only is it a story full of pornographic possibility, but it is also the first recorded mention of clothing in the Bible: "And the eyes of them both were opened, and they knew that they were naked; and they sewed fig leaves together, and made themselves aprons" (Gen. 3:7). After Genesis 3, of course, we find countless other references to real or metaphorical clothing in the Hebrew Bible and the New Testament: Jacob instructs his household to put on clean clothes prior to making covenant with God (Gen. 35:2); Moses orders the Jews to wash their garments in preparation for the Covenant (Exod. 19:10–14); Aaron and his successors must go through a complex rite of investiture to become High Priests (Exod. 28:41–43, 29:1–9, 21; Lev. 8:30, 16:1–5); Paul draws on clothing as a metaphor for, among other things, the sacrament of baptism (Gal. 3:27); and Revelation's prophecy of the Throne of God contains "four and twenty elders sitting, clothed in white raiment; and they had on their heads crowns of gold" (4:4). To pursue this thread in what follows, this chapter begins to fashion a political theology of investments (e.g., of religio-political investitures; of baptisms, purifications, and glorifications; of travesties, transvestism, disguise, and camouflage; of divestitures, divestments, and the disrobing, defrocking, or denudification of power) whereby clothing becomes the privileged figure of a Christian theological anthropology that traces the itinerary of humanity from prelapsarian innocence, through original sin, to real or possible grace. If political modernity from Rousseau onward seeks to denude humanity of the vestments of this theological anthropology like an outdated suit of clothes—"by stripping [*dépouillant*] this Being, so constituted, of all the supernatural gifts he may have received, and of all the artificial faculties he could only have acquired by prolonged progress," as the former writes in his *Discourse on the Origin and Foundations of Inequality Among Men* (1755), and "considering him, in a word, such as he must have issued from the hands of Nature [*sortir de la nature*]"[7]—I will attempt to show that this classic gesture of denudification is *itself* a form of political theological investiture.[8] In this chapter, I thus analyze a series of different textual corpuses or bodies—Michel de Montaigne's *Essays* (1580), Franz Kafka's *The Trial* (1925), and Giorgio Agamben's "Nudity" (2009)—that all try to recuperate a profane or immanent idea of nudity from its perceived political theological straitjacket but that, as we will see, still find themselves fatally *invested* in political theology. What, if anything, lies underneath the emperor's new clothes?

CLOTHING IS A FORCE

In a note "To the Reader" that introduces his *Essays* (1580), Michel de Montaigne declares himself to be—philosophically speaking, at least—a committed nudist. "I want to be seen in my simple, natural, everyday fashion, without striving or artifice," he tells his reader, because "had I found myself among those peoples who are said still to live under the sweet liberty of Nature's primal laws, I can assure you that I would most willingly have portrayed myself whole, and wholly naked [*je m'y fusse tres-volontiers peint tout entier, et tout nu*]."[9] To reread Montaigne's numerous reflections on nudity, from "On the Custom of Wearing Clothing"

("De l'usage de se vestir") through "On Ancient Customs" ("Des coustumes anciennes") to "On the Cannibals" ("Des Cannibales"), we find what John O'Brien calls a persistent "Montaignian variation" on a classic Renaissance biblical theme: Adam and Eve's clothing (or, rather, lack thereof) in Genesis 3.[10] If a Reformation theologian like John Calvin saw Adam and Eve's nudity as a symptom of original sin, Montaigne's own protocultural anthropology (inspired by explorers' accounts of the "New World" of the Americas) seeks to liberate the naked human body from the vestiges of this classic theological anthropology.[11] What he calls the New World "savage" becomes a kind of anti-Adam—whose nudity is the last remaining shred of our unalienated, shame-free nature—whereas clothing becomes less the marker of "civilized man" than an entirely contingent and superfluous cultural artefact.[12] For Montaigne, nudity is thus synonymous with nature, freedom, and truth in thought and action, whereas clothing (particularly the fine or extravagant dress of the rich and powerful) becomes the signifier of the vicissitudes of culture, artifice, and dissimulation, as well as what we might even call a certain politics of travesty or transvestism: we need only imagine a king or emperor naked, he argues in the essay "On the Inequality There Is Between Us" ("De l'inégalité qui est entre nous"), in order to reveal the real or natural man beneath the robes of power. In Blaise Pascal's response to Montaigne in the *Pensées* (1670), however, this politics of nudity is confronted with an equally powerful political theological defense of clothing that, as we will see, concludes that an entirely shame-free experience of nakedness is, strictly speaking, unimaginable.

To a question provoked by "this chilly season"—do the newly discovered peoples of the Americas go around stark naked purely because of the hot climate or is nakedness the original state of mankind itself?—Montaigne's "On the Custom of Wearing Clothing" gives a clear answer: nudity is our natural condition. It is self-evident to the French philosopher that nature has already furnished us with all the natural "clothing" (his literal expression is the "needle and thread" [*de filet et d'éguille*]) we need to survive in any climate whatsoever: "For this reason nearly all things are clothed with skin," he quotes Lucretius, "or hair, or shells, or bark, or some such thing."[13] Accordingly, the invention of artificial clothing (e.g., leather, wool, cotton) must be the (entirely arbitrary) product of culture, custom or habitus. Yet, over time, this superfluous second cultural skin has increasingly come to conceal our natural or original clothing of skin: "Like those who drown the light of day with artificial light, we have drowned our natural means with borrowed ones [*moyens empruntez*]."[14] For Montaigne, nudity's claim to be the natural state of man is established via a bewildering range of examples, from classical antiquity to modern France, all of which are chosen to demonstrate the sheer cultural relativity or contingency of our clothes: Caesar and Alexander apparently went bareheaded in cold climes; beggars, fools, and pious believers will wear little or nothing no matter the weather; and, notwithstanding the alleged French penchant for colorful clothing, Montaigne himself will "usually wear black and white like my father."[15] If "On the Custom of Wearing Clothing" seeks to flatten or horizontalize the sartorial difference between peoples into more or less arbitrary expressions of their respective cultural identity, Montaigne's "On the Inequality There Is Between Us" performs the same role for social or political difference: what renders us unequal to princes is not natural law or equity but only our different clothes. In the same way that a man who wants to buy a horse must inspect it from top to bottom, we can only know the true value of a king by stripping him naked:

Why do you judge a man when he is all wrapped up and packaged (*tout enveloppé et empacqueté*)? He is letting us see only such attributes as do not belong to him while hiding the only ones which enable us to judge his real worth. You are trying to find out the quality of the sword not of the scabbard: strip it of its sheath and perhaps you would not give twopence (*quatrain*) for it. You must judge him not by his finery but by his own self. As one of the old writers [Seneca] amusingly put it: "Do you know why you think he is so tall? You are including his high-heels!" The plinth is no part of the statue. Measure his height with his stilts off; let him lay aside his wealth and his decorations and show us himself in his undershirt (*qu'il se presente en chemise*). Is his body functioning properly? Is it quick and healthy?[16]

If Montaigne asks us to judge a king without his clothes, however, it is revealing that, as Hans Blumenberg observes, he actually stops a little short of stripping him wholly naked: the king must only, the French philosopher says, "show us himself in his undershirt [*chemise*]."[17] It is precisely this residual reticence or shame at the prospect of what Blumenberg famously calls "the naked truth" that is the subject of Blaise Pascal's critique of Montaigne's politics of nudity in the *Pensées*. As we will see, Pascal basically agrees with Montaigne that a king's clothes are nothing more than a contingent cultural artefact with no foundation in natural law. However, the Catholic theologian draws the exact opposite lesson to his predecessor regarding their political power: what we call the trappings of power must be as rigidly obeyed as naked or unadorned power itself. To refute Montaigne's defense of nature as a first cause of culture, Pascal's Fragment 123 instead valorizes what he famously calls the "reason of effects" (*la raison des effets*), which is to say, the real causal force of the cultural, accidental, and phenomenal:

> This really is admirable: they do not want me to honor a man dressed in brocade, and followed by seven or eight lackeys! What? If I do not salute him, he will give me the stirrups. Clothing is a force (*Cet habit, c'est une force*). It is like a well-harnessed horse in comparison to another. Montaigne is odd (*plaisant*) not to see what a difference there is, to wonder that we find it, and to ask the reason. REALLY, he says, WHERE DOES IT COME FROM, etc.[18]

For Pascal, clothing is a force, not because it possesses any underlying natural cause, foundation, or legitimacy that we may discover rationally, but rather because it performs what he sees as the brute facticity or physics of power in postlapsarian time and space: "justice, like finery, is dictated by fashion," he declares, "and must be obeyed like fashion."[19] Perhaps Montaigne is rationally correct to say that a king with no clothes on looks the same as any other man, but Pascal's reply is that, phenomenologically, we will never encounter him in this state of natural equality: "A very refined reason [*raison bien épurée*] is required to regard as an ordinary man the Grand Turk," he writes elsewhere, "in his superb seraglio, surrounded by forty thousand janissaries."[20] In any dispute between two parties who are naturally or rationally equal in power, Pascal goes on to argue that it will be the—always unequal—distribution of power's sensible appearance that will determine who submits to the other:

> How rightly do we distinguish men by external appearances (*l'extérieur*) rather than by internal qualities! Which of us two shall have precedence? Who will give place to the other? The least clever (*habile*). But I am as clever as he. We should have to fight over this. He has four lackeys, and I have only one. This

can be seen; we have only to count. It falls to me to yield, and I am a fool if I contest the matter. By this means we are at peace, which is the greatest of goods.[21]

In inviting us to "see" a king naked, of course, Montaigne can presumably only mean that we must *imagine* him naked—but this is precisely what Pascal insists the faculty of the imagination prevents us from doing. It is in the celebrated Fragment 78, "Imagination," that the latter fashions the political theological epistemology that will come to clothe what we have seen to be his physics of raw or naked power. As Michael Moriarty argues, Pascal's theory of the imagination wages war upon early modern attempts to found philosophy on reason, nature, or empirical experience by installing an irreducibly deceptive or erroneous dimension within our apprehension of the real.[22] "This superb power, the enemy of reason, who likes to control and dominate it to show how all-powerful she is [*elle peut en toutes choses*], has established in man a second nature."[23] Yet, crucially, this faculty also goes on to establish its own rival empire *over* reality: imagination gives what Pascal calls empirical or physical "force" its irresistible symbolic and normative force.[24] To a degree that even anticipates modern Lacanian or Althusserian theories of "the imaginary," as Moriarty goes on to observe, the Pascalian imagination bestows power, right, or legitimacy upon what would otherwise be purely artifactual political entities: "What but this faculty of imagination dispenses reputation, awards respect and veneration to persons, works, laws, and the great?"[25] For Pascal, a judge, lawyer, or doctor thus obtains their authority in the eyes of society from their external appearance *as* powerful rather than from any essential or objective power they may possess:

> Our magistrates have known this mystery very well. Their red robes, the ermine in which they wrap themselves like furry cats, the courts in which they administer justice, the *fleurs-de-lys*, and all such august apparel (*appareil auguste*) were very necessary. If the physicians had not their cassocks and their mules, if the doctors had not their square caps (*bonnets carrés*) and their robes four times too wide, they would never have duped the world, which cannot resist such an authentic appearance. If magistrates had true justice, and if physicians had the true art of healing, they would have no need for square caps. The majesty of these sciences would be venerable enough in itself. But having only imaginary knowledge, they must employ those vain tools that strike the imagination with which they have to deal. And thereby in fact they attract respect (*ils attirent le respect*).[26]

If Montaigne's anthropological appeal to the naked body of the savage can be read as an attempt to remove or erase the postlapsarian vestments of original sin and reveal a *National Geographic*–style nudity without shame, the Fall of Man remains the foundational event in Pascal's Augustinian philosophical theology: what he calls "imagination" is the weak epistemology of a fallen universe that has become simply unreadable to human beings in natural or rational terms.[27] By critically disrobing or unmasking kings, princes, and gentlemen, Montaigne's reason seeks to reveal the natural equality that lies beneath hierarchies of power, but Pascal's imagination might better be described as the equal or opposite faculty of *dressing up* naked, unadorned power—or, better, of revealing that we can only ever encounter it (at least partially) dressed or *attired* in the first place. In Pascal's revealing phrase, recall, imaginary knowledge is what enables power to "attract" (*attirent*) respect, honor, and glory (*atirer*, from the Old French *a-tirer*, which literally means to negate the act of tearing away; to draw toward; to equip, prepare, and, finally, of course, to *clothe*).

GARMENTS OF SKIN

In a diary entry for June 19, 1916, Franz Kafka recalls the moment in Genesis 3 when God creates clothes out of animal hides for Adam and Eve who, after eating the apple from the Tree of Knowledge, become suddenly ashamed of their nudity: "The Lord God made for Adam and for his wife garments of skins, and clothed them" (3:21).[28] It is thanks to Mark M. Anderson that Kafka's own career-long fascination with the political and religious significance of clothing has come to light. As Anderson documents in his *Kafka's Clothes* (1992), Kafka was himself something of a young dandy, his father ran a clothing accessories store, and his writing is full of unusually precise, curatorial allusions to dress of one kind or another: uniforms, suits, fur coats, nightshirts, leather, hats, scarves, gloves, badges, buckles, belts, and buttons.[29] Yet, as the allusion to Genesis 3:21 suggests, this son of a Prague haberdasher also sees clothing as a mark of Cain that signifies man's originary sin: "clothing, inextricably linked to the realm of his father, serves [Kafka] as the exemplary figure for human existence in history," Anderson writes, "a world of impermanence, false appearances, error, and guilt."[30] To recall the famous opening scene from *The Trial* (*Der Proceß*, 1925), for instance, we find what is only one among many political theological travesties of Genesis 3 in Kafka's body of work: Josef K. is ordered to get dressed by Franz and Willem, the suspiciously well-attired officers of the law who come to arrest him for the unknown crime of which he is accused, so that he can be taken to the police station.[31] If Adam's original sin will be redeemed by Christ's sacrifice, at least according to Christian theology, Kafka's own wretched protagonists will famously endure a state of ineradicable guilt without any atonement: K., symptomatically, will never be able to expunge the invisible vestments of sin that have attached themselves to his body and return to the state of prelapsarian, shame-free nudity that he (at least hypothetically) enjoyed before the novel began. For Kafka, as we will see, human nudity *itself* becomes the fleshly signifier, less of a state of prelapsarian grace, than of our irredeemably postlapsarian guilt or corruption—our nakedness is the guilty "garment of skin," paradoxically, that we can never take off. In the final scene of *The Trial*, which returns us remorselessly to the moment of abject humiliation with which the novel began, K. is stripped naked by his inquisitors and killed "Like a dog!"— but, revealingly, what he cannot remove even here are the vestments of the Adamic shame or guilt he feels at this very nudity: "It was as if the shame would outlive him."[32]

To begin to grasp the counterintuitive idea that human nakedness might itself be our first set of clothes—which is to say the God-given "garment of skin" that both covers and reveals our postlapsarian guilt or shame—we need only recall Kafka's early prose poem "Clothes" ("Kleider," 1912) that directly compares the fragile folds of luxurious clothing to the skin of privileged young women:

> Often when I see clothes with manifold pleats, frills, and appendages which fit so smoothly onto lovely bodies I think they won't keep that smoothness long, but will get creases that can't be ironed out, dust lying so thick in the embroidery that it can't be brushed away, and that no one would want to be so unhappy and so foolish as to wear the same valuable gown every day from early morning till night.

> And yet I see girls who are lovely enough and display attractive muscles and small bones and smooth skin and masses of delicate hair, and nonetheless appear day in, day out, in this same natural fancy dress (*natürliche Maskenanzug*), always propping the same face on the same palms and letting it be reflected from the looking glass.
>
> Only sometimes at night, on coming home late from a party, it seems in the looking glass to be worn out, puffy, dusty, already seen by too many people, and hardly wearable any longer.[33]

If Anderson detects a critique of "feminine *vanitas*" in this Baroque allegory—which leads Kafka to endorse an "aesthetic of simpler, more hygienic forms" over the ornamental clothing of the fin de siècle—what is at stake here seems to be something more fundamental than merely the narcissism of rich young women: it is difficult, after all, to see how the girls in "Clothes" could "wear" anything plainer or simpler than their own naked bodies.[34] They have no choice but to appear in this "natural fancy dress" of muscle, bones, skin, and hair day for the rest of their lives, even when it is "hardly wearable" anymore. For Kafka, "Clothes" does not stage a moment of historical, moral, or aesthetic decadence so much as a kind of originary or ontological decadence that no aesthetic of simplicity can correct. In their private bedrooms, alone and naked, the women must still wear their increasingly worn garments of skin.

If nudity should at least theoretically be a return to the state of grace or innocence we enjoyed before entering the fallen, guilty world of clothing, Kafka's philosophical universe thus, paradoxically, appears to equate nakedness with the unredeemability of guilt. It is striking just how little nudity "reveals" in his corpus: the shivering bare legs of K.'s aged advocate in *The Trial*, for instance, or of the Doctor in "The Country Doctor" (1919) appear to stand for nothing beyond their own abject creatureliness. At other times, nudity is nothing more than the primal scene of ever more extreme acts of arbitrary violence, humiliation, or punishment exacted upon the body by the state apparatus: the condemned man in "The Penal Colony" (1919) is stripped naked, recall, so that his guilt can be written on his body by the Baroque killing machine. To the state's final command to its citizens ("Strip!") Kafka can offer no immunity or exemptions because everyone, including the instruments of that humiliation, is already guilty as charged:[35] Franz and Willem—the two well-dressed warders who arrest Josef K. at the beginning of *The Trial*—are themselves required to "strip quite naked" after the latter's complaint about their behavior to the examining judge, so that they can be whipped.[36] Yet, of course, the examining judge himself cannot escape the shame of nudity, whose guilty truth can always be unveiled by the command to strip, because he is revealed to be the furtive or ashamed consumer of naked bodies via a work of pornography. For Kafka, *The Torments Grete Had to Suffer from Her Husband Hans* (the name of the erotic, presumably sadomasochistic, novel that K. finds concealed inside his examining judge's law books) turns out to be a work of failed or incompetent pornography that inflicts only a kind of pure, gratuitous shame upon the consumer that outlives any compensating possibility of arousal or enjoyment. "K. opened the top book to reveal an indecent picture," the narrator recounts. "A man and a woman were sitting naked on a sofa; the artist's vulgar intention was clear enough, but his incompetence was so great that in fact all that could be seen was a man and a woman projecting their gross physique out of the picture, sitting rigidly upright and, because of false perspective, finding the greatest difficulty in turning towards each other."[37] In this indecent book within a book (within the third book that is *The Trial* itself), Kafka discovers another—indeed, this time, almost gnostic—parody of the book of Genesis: a foolish or capricious demiurge fashions a naked Adam and Eve whose gross and fleshly materiality prevents them from performing the sexual acts for which they were created in the first place.

In order to move beyond this tortuous dialectic of clothing and nudity, guilt and innocence, we perhaps need to turn away from the fallen human body altogether and toward another recurring figure in Kafka's body of work that performs its nudity entirely otherwise: the animal. It is now exhaustively documented by scholars that Kafka's philosophical universe is a radically inhuman, zoomorphic one that is variously populated by insects ("Metamorphosis"); mice ("Josephine the Singer, or the Mouse Folk"); dogs ("Investigations of a Dog"); unnamed burrowing creatures ("The Burrow"); jackals ("Arabs and Jackals"); horses ("A Country Doctor"); leopards ("Leopards in the Temple") and apes ("A Report to the Academy"), among many other animals. As with everything else in his work, Kafka's animals have been relentlessly allegorized as figures of social or religious alienation, dehumanizing political violence, and, most recently, the philosophical problem of anthropocentrism, but such animal skins also belong to the history of human guilt that begins with Genesis 3.[38] To return one last time to *The Trial*, Josef K. constantly finds that it is the *dog*, more than any other animal, that embodies his constant state of abject shame or humiliation: K. seeks to explain away Franz and Willem's screams when they are whipped by saying "it was only a dog howling in the courtyard";[39] he later feels like his "advocate's dog. If the advocate had ordered him to creep into his kennel under the bed and bark from there, he would have done it willingly,"[40] and, finally, of course, he dies, stripped naked, "like a dog!"[41] However, outside of his own anthropomorphizing imaginary, K. can never really be "like a dog" because Kafka's animals live the very life without guilt that is impossible for his human protagonists: a dog may well be able to suffer (as Jeremy Bentham famously proposed), and it can certainly be beaten or killed, but it cannot, strictly speaking, be made to feel *shame*. For Kafka, we can glimpse something close to this species of messianic animal in Kafka's *The Metamorphosis* (*Die Verwandlung*, 1915) where, in yet another profane rendition of Genesis 3, Gregor Samsa seems, albeit briefly, to *enjoy* his new fallen life as a "giant vermin" (*ungeheueres Ungeziefer*):

> He especially enjoyed hanging suspended from the ceiling; it was much better than lying on the floor; one could breathe more freely; one's body swung and rocked lightly; and in the almost blissful absorption induced by this suspension; it could happen to his own surprise that he let go and fell plump on the floor. Yet he now had his body much better under control than formerly, and even such a big fall did him no harm.[42]

If Anderson is correct to say in his own reading of this episode that Gregor's animal carapace is precisely not a form of "clothing", we can go further: Samsa no longer has *any* relation to clothing whatsoever, not even the negative or privative one of pornography, and so belongs to that rare class of creatures that are never, properly speaking, described as "naked" at all such as insects, birds, fish, and, of course, animals.[43] They are the creatures that are "naked without knowing it," as Jacques Derrida writes in his *The Animal That Therefore I Am* (2008), "not being naked therefore, not having knowledge of their nudity, in short, without consciousness of good and evil."[44] By being unclothed without ever being naked—which is to say naked without ever being aware of being naked, naked without any guilt or shame, naked, so to speak, without being nude—Samsa is released, however fleetingly, from his human "garment of skin" and, unlike Adam and Eve, can fall without being harmed.

A THEOLOGY OF CLOTHES

In his essay "Nudity" (2009), Giorgio Agamben claims that "nudity, in our culture, is inseparable from a theological signature."[45] To expand upon this thesis, Agamben goes on to argue that Christian theology (and, in particular, Catholic theology) from Augustine of Hippo to Erik Peterson has effectively reduced human nudity to nothing more than the negation or privation of the original set of "clothes" that is God's glory: "there is no theology of nudity," he claims, "only a theology of clothing."[46] It is only *after* the Fall that human beings became naturally or physically naked for the first time, according to this reading of Catholic theology, because prelapsarian man was in some sense already supernaturally "clothed" in God's grace or glory from the moment of his creation. As Agamben rereads Genesis 3, "Adam and Eve were not naked; rather, they were covered by clothing of grace, which clung to them as a garment of glory," and it was precisely "this supernatural clothing that was stripped from the two after their sin."[47] If Adam and Eve obviously did not wear any physical clothes in Paradise, in other words, they were never, strictly speaking, "nude," either, because they were created in order to be metaphysically clothed in God's grace, and it was precisely the stripping away of the latter that led them, for the first time, to recognize that they were naked: "Man was created without clothes," the German theologian Erik Peterson argues in his "Theology of Clothes," "but he was created with this absence of clothing in order to then be dressed in the supernatural garment of glory."[48] For Agamben, what we call "nudity" thus only exists within the Christian tradition as something like a transitory, intermediate state between the divine or supernatural investiture that we were clothed in before the Fall and will put on again in Heaven: corporeal nakedness is either "a privation of the glory of grace" or "a presaging of the resplendent garment of glory that the blessed will receive in heaven."[49] Finally, and characteristically, Agamben goes on to claim that this theology of clothes (and the classic opposition between nature and grace that underpins it) will persist into an allegedly secular or disenchanted modernity that valorizes nudity as the last remaining signifier of the authentic "real," whether erotically, aesthetically, or politically, but whose concept of the naked body remains fatally enveloped in its ancient theological investiture. In the sense that it still carries the fatal imprint or impression of the light of divine glory, the naked human body can still never appear as "itself" today—not even in those forms of sadomasochistic pornography that seek to capture the body's pure carnality through acts of violence—but only as something like the photographic negative of the glorious theological body it once was.[50]

To liberate the naked human body from the vestments of this theological apparatus, Agamben concludes "Nudity" with his signature call for a pure or immanent nude body, divested of any residue of supernatural grace or natural corruption, which simply is: "*Haecce!* there is nothing other than this."[51] It is possible to suspect, however, that the Italian philosopher's critique of the philosophical fate of "nudity" is somewhat conveniently cut to fit his more celebrated philosophy of *nuda vita*, bare or naked life. After all, Agamben himself draws a (suspiciously neat) parallel between the—apparently original and foundational but, in both cases, violent, reductive, and retroactively produced—"nude life" of theology and the bare life (nuda vita) of biopolitics.[52] Yet the long theological history of the relationship between nature and grace—are they mutually antagonistic or complementary? Is nature ever independent of, or self-sufficient from, grace? Does grace infuse nature from within or must it be superadded to it from without?—is arguably far more complex than this (brief and excessively schematic) history allows. If Agamben claims to liberate a pure human nature from a Christian tradition which has reduced that nature to nothing more than a bare substrate or foundation for grace, there are grounds for suspecting that his biopolitical genealogy of the naked body *invents* the theologeme ("nudity") it claims to reveal. For the *nouvelle théologie* French theologian Henri de Lubac, whose own influential contribution to the nature versus grace debate within modern Catholic theology is absent from Agamben's survey of the field, the very idea of a "pure nature" (*natura pura*), which existed prior to, and independently of, God's grace and to which the latter is merely superadded, is a neo-Scholastic or Renaissance fiction retroactively imposed upon the Church Fathers.[53] In a possible conceptual anachronism of the kind he is fond of exposing in other scholars, Agamben's appeal to a singular or immanent nudity that renders the Christian theology of clothing inoperative may thus be nothing more than an unwitting return to this (entirely modern) Christian theological concept of a "pure nature."

If we focus only on Agamben's own selective reading of the nature versus grace debate in "Nudity," for instance, we will struggle to find in even the most confrontational moments of the Christian tradition the kind of simple dualism or opposition between nature and grace he proposes. To take his commentary upon the debate between Pelagius and Augustine as one example, Agamben speaks of the "irreducible difference" between nature and grace in the Augustinian universe: "Adam and Eve were created with animal rather than spiritual bodies," he glosses Augustine's *De Civitate Dei contra Paganos*, "but their bodies were clothed with grace as if it had been a garment."[54] It is with Augustine's hard opposition between nature and grace, consequently, that the self-styled "theology of clothing" assumes its defining and violent form. According to Agamben's version of Augustine, Adam and Eve's created, animal nature is nothing more than a bare or original placeholder that will inevitably come to be filled by God's grace: what we call the naked human body is at best a kind of dummy or mannequin that exists purely in order to be dressed in glory by its divine tailor. However, this reading risks hardening Augustine's original theology of man's "graceless nature" in his anti-Pelagian tract *De Natura et Gratia* (415)—where man's nature is so corrupted by sin after the Fall that he can only be redeemed from without by God's grace—into what Lubac calls the modern pseudo-Augustinianism of a "pure nature" that exists entirely independently of, and self-sufficiently from, that grace. For Lubac, contra Agamben's strongly naturalist reading, Augustine does not valorize a species of pure, graceless nature that only subsequently and extrinsically assumes the clothing of grace but, rather, proposes a theology of "graced" nature as something that is created by God only in order to receive, share, and participate in his grace. "You made us for yourself," Augustine famously declares to God in the opening of the *Confessions*, "and our hearts find no peace until they rest in you."[55] In his recuperation of Augustine from the doxa of pure nature, Lubac thus reveals a human nature that is already so enveloped in the clothing of grace at the moment of its creation that it becomes impossible to identify any originary state or condition of nudity whatsoever within it—and so that "nudity" can be only be superadded, gratuitously, in a kind of diabolical scholarly travesty of divine grace by the hand of Agamben himself.

In calling into question the very possibility of Agamben's theology of nudity, Lubac's Augustinian theory of "graced nature" also creates the space for a (positive) political theology of clothing in the interstices of Agamben's own reading of the Catholic tradition where it is no longer politically possible to distinguish between the naked and the clothed body. To overcome what he saw as the neo-Eusebian sacralization of temporal power at work in the Weimar Republic, which stretches from Carl Schmitt's *Political Theology* (1922) to contemporary theological attempts to fashion a Reichstheologie out of National Socialism, Erik Peterson's classic essay "Monotheism as a Political Problem" (1935) famously reaffirms the old Augustinian thesis of the two cities—which is to say of the essential separation between temporal and sacred power; the triumph of Trinitarianism over Judeo-Hellenistic divine monarchy, and, with it, the radical asymmetry between God and the secular ruler—in order to reach a singular conclusion: a Christian "political theology" is, strictly speaking, impossible.[56] It is striking, however, that Peterson acknowledges one remarkable exception to the general Augustinian rule of the distinction between church and state: the church only came into existence because, and will only continue to exist for as long as, the Jews, as God's chosen people, have not converted to Christianity. As Agamben acidly observes in *The Kingdom and the Glory* (2011), Peterson's religious anti-Semitism, which mortgages the realization of the Christian kingdom to the disappearance of Judaism, thus could not simply divorce itself from the contemporaneous political anti-Semitism that sought the physical extermination of the Jewish people: "Peterson was probably in Rome," the former recounts, "when, on October 16, 1943, the deportation of a thousand Roman Jews to the extermination camps took place with the conniving silence of Pius XII."[57] Yet, according to Agamben, this rapprochement between Catholicism and National Socialism is—despite or perhaps even because of the German theologian's

Augustinian distaste for the eschatological pretensions of the state—not simply a historical irony, but something closer to a structural condition of Peterson's own anti-political theology. "The attempt to exclude the very possibility of a Christian 'political theology' so as to found in glory the only legitimate political dimension of Christianity," he observes of Ernst Kantorowicz's critique of Peterson's theology of acclamation, "comes dangerously close to the totalitarian" liturgy.[58] If Agamben seems to imply that it is the very exclusion of "nature," recast as a pure haecceity divested of any theological signature, that makes possible Peterson's cryptototalitarian political theology of glory, Lubac again furnishes a very different reading of the relationship between church and state in which it is, ironically, the theology of pure *nature*, not grace, that makes possible the disastrous alliance between Catholicism and Fascism. For Lubac, whose *Surnaturel* (1946) was largely prepared during the Nazi occupation of France, this pseudo-Augustinian split between nature and grace—which is to say the expulsion of grace into the realm of extrinsic divine action and the emergence of nature as a separate and autonomous sphere for human action—was, as Hans Boersma makes clear, precisely what led to the church's cooperation with the Vichy regime: the church concerned itself solely with man's supernatural interests, while the state consequently became theologically free to act in what it deemed to be our natural interests, even if such interests apparently included the deportation of Jews,[59] In a symmetrical reversal of Agamben's verdict upon Peterson's theology of clothes, Lubac thus leads us to wonder whether it is, ironically, Agamben's political theology of *nudity*, a political theology that seeks to subtract from itself any vestige of theological glory and retreat into a pure and inoperative "nature" of its own invention, that here comes "dangerously close" to totalitarianism.

GLORY IN PERSON

In his essay "Comment jouer *Le Balcon*" (How to perform *The Balcony*), Genet offers a crucial, but curiously neglected by its many Marxist and Lacanian critics, instruction on how to stage his play: *The Balcony* is neither a simple political satire nor critical demystification of power, he writes, but rather a *"glorification of the Image and the Reflection [du Reflet],"* and *"its meaning—satirical or not—will appear solely in that case."*[60] To be sure, Genet's play has been read in many ways by philosophers in the more than sixty years since its first performance—as a realist satire of the political passage from sovereignty to bourgeois technocracy (Goldmann); a psychoanalytic exploration of the enjoyment of the symbolic order (Lacan); and, most recently, as a political ontological reflection upon the function of democracy in capitalist modernity (Badiou)—but I want to conclude this chapter by returning to my opening hypothesis that the play is an esoteric dossier upon the political theology of "glory" (*la gloire*).[61] If secular readings of the play tend to dehistoricize the particular theological meaning of this concept, subsuming it under modern categories such as psychoanalytic enjoyment or *jouissance*, the society of the spectacle, and libidinal or commodity fetishism, I thus wish to propose that Genet's *The Balcony* traces the precise political theological lineaments of glorification now famously mapped by figures like Agamben in his *Kingdom and the Glory*. For Agamben, to recall the central thesis of his book, glory is the mysterious field of force that both reveals and conceals the essentially vicarious and empty relation between God the Father and God the Son, the Kingdom and the Government, or sovereignty and governmentality: "Government glorifies the Kingdom, and the Kingdom glorifies Government," he writes, "But the center of the machine is empty, and glory is nothing but the splendor that emanates from this emptiness, the inexhaustible *kabhod* that at once reveals and veils the central vacuity of the machine."[62] In replaying the liturgies of investiture and divestiture in *The Balcony*, I thus want to turn away from what Lacan famously sees as the animating psychoanalytic question of the play—"What can it really mean to enjoy one's state of being a bishop, a judge or a general?" he asks in Seminar 5, *Les formations de l'inconscient*—and turn instead toward the question that animates Agamben's theological genealogy of glory. Why, in short, does Genet's theater of raw or naked power still need to clothe itself in "glory"?

To look underneath the glorious cosplay of sovereignty from Montaigne to Kafka, this chapter has argued that we do not find anything like an unadorned "naked body" of power, whether pristine or dirty, innocent, or shameful, because that nudity itself turns out to be a retroactive work of political theological glorification: the clothing of *no* clothes. It thus refuses every gesture of critical demystification, disrobing or unmasking up to and including Badiou's recent claim that Genet's play enables us to prepare an anti-pornographic "poetic nudity of the present."[63] If denudification is one of the foundational metaphors of political modernity from Rousseau to Badiou, which is to say the divestiture, defrocking, or disenchantment of kings, priests, and politicians to reveal the "real" or immanent political body that lies beneath, I have thus sought to reveal it as a gesture of what we might call *reverse or negative investiture* that inaugurates the modern sovereign, so to speak, into the glorious new office of his own nakedness. For Blumenberg, what political modernity calls the "naked truth" (e.g., Rousseau's natural man, Marx's unalienated labor, even Badiou's nudity) thus turns out to be the site of a new "concealment that must be stripped away in turn if man is at last to be seen for who he really is": our search for "natural nature" thus, he concludes, becomes "interminable."⁶⁴ In Hans Christian Andersen's classic fairy tale "The Emperor's New Clothes" (1837), it is worth recalling that the small child's famous cry as the naked sovereign processes through the town—"But he doesn't have anything on!"—has no discernible political effect whatsoever: the emperor "walked even more proudly, and the two gentlemen of the imperial bedchamber went on carrying the train that wasn't there."⁶⁵

If any reading of Genet's *The Balcony* in the context of a political theology of "glory" may well appear exorbitant at first blush, we need only recall the words of the only philosophical commentator on the play to note its precise theological origins: Genet uses the word "glory," Jacques Derrida observes in *Glas* (1974), "almost as often as the translator of the Gospel, of whom he is in sum the most destructive parodying double."⁶⁶ It (*la gloire* and its various conjugations) is used throughout the play, including no less than eleven times in the final scene: the General, for example, summons his "horse" (a sex worker) to "glory and death" (scene 3); Irma orders Carmen to "glory" in her profession as whore: "Make it shine. Let it illuminate you" (scene 5); and the Queen believes that violently crushing the revolution by killing as many as possible will also "serve my glory" (scene 9). At a more substantive philosophical level, though, Genet's play also rehearses Agamben's bipolar political machine of glory: Kingdom and Government (or, rather, Queen and Court, in this case) participate in an empty or vicarious circle of mutual glorification in which each obtains their presumed legitimacy from the other. To reflect upon the vertiginous mirror play between subject and object, inside and outside, sovereignty and government in Genet's drama, we thus quickly apprehend that glory begins to assume a spectral, detached and autonomous existence of its own as *The Balcony*'s solitary "real" political actor or agent: the Bishop, the Judge, and the General revealingly declare that they have been chosen to defend the political establishment, not by any individual or collective political body, but rather "by Glory in person" (scene 9). Perhaps the most visible symptom of this becoming-glory of the political in Genet's play, however, is the decidedly inglorious figure of Georges, the Chief of Police, who is charged with suppressing the popular uprising in the city. For Genet, in what may be the play's best joke, Georges is not the solitary representative of "real," naked, or unadorned power in this whole house of illusions but rather its most fervent and pathetic worshipper at the altar of the image: what permanently tortures this "sovereign" figure is the fact that the Grand Balcony's clientele, who are all too happy to dress up as inconsequential figures like the Bishop, the Judge, and the General, seemingly have no desire to impersonate someone as genuinely powerful as himself.[67] In Genet's symbolic economy, Georges possesses power without glory—"Glory has given you the cold shoulder [*vous boude*]" Irma crushingly informs him (scene 5)— which means that he ultimately possesses no power at all.

In the play's *denouement* (*dénouer*, to untie), however, the Chief of Police also becomes one last unlikely political theological figure for what we have called the glorious body clothed (*noué*) in its own nudity. It is Georges's deepest desire that he should be represented in the Grand Balcony in an "audacious" image of naked power that befits his elevated political status: "I have been advised," he proudly announces, "to appear in the form of a gigantic phallus" (scene 9). After he succeeds in crushing the revolution, Georges's long-standing dream of taking his place in the brothel's pantheon seem destined to become reality when Roger, the revolution's leader, himself enters the Grand Balcony and becomes the first person ever to ask to perform the role of the Chief of Police. However, in a disturbing gesture that has variously been read by scholars as a symbolic or literal murder, self-sacrifice or suicide, this failed revolutionary does not play by the rules of the game but begins to improvise: "ROGER *takes out a knife*," Genet's stage direction reads, "*and, with his back to the audience, makes the gesture of castrating himself*" (scene 9). To the "real" Police Chief Georges—who has been watching the whole game unfold through a peephole—his archenemy's physical and political self-mutilation appears to provoke a moment of supreme voyeuristic self-gratification: "THE CHIEF OF POLICE: Well played. He thought he had me there [*me posséder*]. (*He places his hand on his fly, very visibly feels his balls and, reassured, gives a sigh*.) Mine are here. So, which of us is fucked [*foutu*]? Him or me? Although my image is castrated in every brothel in the world, I remain intact. Intact, gentlemen" (scene 9; translation modified). If the Chief of Police's reclamation of his physical and political virility from the image of its own symbolic castration has understandably been read in many different ways, I think the most powerful recent reading comes from Alenka Zupančič, who argues that the image of the naked, castrated phallus has, perversely, become nothing less than the "new clothes" that absolute and unaccountable political power assumes today.[68] "The displayed nakedness and castration (vulnerability) of the new masters," she writes, "is designed to prevent us from grabbing their balls to make them answer for what they are doing."[69] By openly parading his alleged "nakedness," the new Emperor secretly accrues (in an exact reversal of Hans Christian Andersen's parable) ever-greater political power to himself: think, for example, of how modern political leaders are all too happy to confess their human, all-too-human weakness in the face of the awesome responsibilities of office even as they continue to wage wars, cut welfare spending for the poor, and so on. Perhaps the *shameless* nudity in which the modern political leader revels, which is the exact opposite and parody, of course, of the shame-free or "innocent" nakedness we allegedly enjoyed before the Fall, is indeed where the postlapsarian political theology of clothes we have been tracing in this chapter ends up, but I think such a conclusion risks prematurely glorifying what is, in fact, a moment of genuine ontological vulnerability in Genet's play: Georges actually grabs *himself* by the balls, recall, and he does so precisely in order to reassure himself, to his obvious relief, that he actually has balls at all. For Genet, the Police Chief's virile boast that he can literally take off or detach the image of his castrated phallus as if it were a set of spare clothes and still be himself ("Though my image is castrated in every brothel in the world, I remain intact") is fatally undermined, indeed emasculated, by an evident anxiety: his "real" phallus is nothing more than an image of an image, the castration of its own castration, the détail faux that gives the game away. What if the first person to cosplay the role of the Chief of Police is not the revolutionary Roger, but Georges *himself*? In the fleeting moment where he is no longer sure if he is naked or not, the new emperor becomes his clothes.

6

INSIDE THE PUPPET THEATER
Cervantes, Hobbes, Benjamin, Derrida

*The story is told of an automaton constructed in such a way that it could play a winning game of chess, answering each move of an opponent with a countermove. A puppet (*Puppe*) in Turkish attire and with a hookah in its mouth sat before a chessboard placed on a large table. A system of mirrors created the illusion that this table was transparent from all sides. Actually, a little hunchback who was an expert chess player sat inside and guided the puppet's hand by means of strings. One can imagine a philosophical counterpart to this device. The puppet called "historical materialism" is to win all the time (*Gewinnen soll immer die Puppe*). It can easily be a match for anyone if it enlists the services of theology, which today, as we know, is wizened and has to keep out of sight.*

—Walter Benjamin, "Theses on the Philosophy of History"

In the First Thesis of Walter Benjamin's "Theses on the Philosophy of History" (1941), we face a political theological opponent seemingly every bit as invincible as the mechanical Turk (*Schachtürke*) it describes. To replay Benjamin's famous act of political checkmate one more time: "historical materialism" can defeat any challenger "all the time," he confidently declares, but only so long as "it enlists the services" of the wizened dwarf called "theology."[1] If Benjamin's cryptic allegory has defeated scholars for almost a century, what makes this prophecy of historical materialism's inevitable—indeed, almost automatic—triumph all the more mysterious is that it also seems to defeat what is generally agreed to be the larger argument of the "Theses on the Philosophy of History" as a whole. For Rebecca Comay, whose reading can be taken here as exemplary in the best sense of the word, Benjamin's elliptical collection of fragments is an attempt to "expose the ultimate illegitimacy of every victory," no matter how "inevitable" that victory may appear, by revealing the trail of destruction they leave, like so many defeated opponents, in their wake.[2] What could it mean, she asks, "to invoke the notion of automatic victory to introduce a text the essential point of which will be, after all, to problematize the very notion of victory, automatic or otherwise, as being the ideology of those on top?"[3] In the First Thesis, nonetheless, we are apparently encouraged for the only time in the "Theses" to identify, not with the losers, but with the winner (*die Gewinner*) in the chess game of history.

To a more streetwise—or, at least, less gullible—audience than the First Thesis's unfortunate victim, Benjamin's peroration on the alleged invincibility of historical materialism may, just like the original Schachtürke itself, appear to be nothing more than an elaborate confidence trick.[4] It is tempting to read it less as a celebration of materialism's triumphant march across the chessboard of time, than as a demystification of the *pseudoautomaticity* of what passes for historical "progress." After all, the mechanical chess player is really only a puppet, whose master is concealed beneath the swathes of the Turk's robes and an elaborate system of mirrors, and the chess game itself nothing but a cheap and tawdry puppet show. If we were to read the chess-playing automaton less as an avatar of historical materialism than of German social democracy, and the geometric black-and-white squares of the chess board as equivalent to the "homogenous, empty time" that the latter notoriously occupies, then Benjamin's task could thus once again be to reveal the human cost of this remorseless winning "machine."[5] In the hidden recesses of every great puppet, underneath all the robes, mirrors, and curtains, there is a wizened human being who is pulling the strings all along.

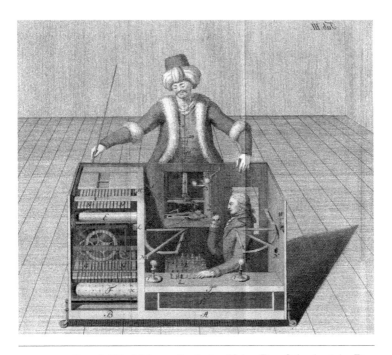

FIGURE 6.1 Joseph Friedrich von Racknitz, Ueber Den Schachspieler Des Herrn Von Kempelen Und Dessen Nachbildung: mit seiben Kupfertafein. Leipzig [u.a.]: Breitkopf, 1789. Print. Taf.: III. Humboldt-Universität zu Berlin. Public Domain.

If any human challenger is foolish enough to think they have defeated it, though, Benjamin's political theological machine arguably has one last surprise—one final knight's move—up its sleeve. It is often observed by scholars that this famous thought experiment actually performs a surreal reversal of the power relation between the puppet and the dwarf imagined by Wolfgang von Kempelen's original chess-playing machine.[6] After all, Kempelen's original design famously contains a concealed human operator who quite literally pulls the strings of the mechanical puppet. Yet Benjamin's own allegory of the chess-playing automaton short-circuits the original Schachtürke in a way that defeats any critical attempt to expose a hidden prime mover or efficient cause that lies inside the mechanical prosthesis or apparatus. For Benjamin, on the contrary, historical materialism "enlists the services" of theology, rather than the other way around: the historical materialist puppet consequently becomes the master of the theological dwarf who is thus reduced to nothing more than the puppet of his own puppet. In the secret interiority of the Schachtürke, we do not find an Aristotelian first cause or a Cartesian homunculus but something closer to a Russian Matryoshka doll that is only full of ever smaller versions of itself.

In Benjamin's First Thesis—a parable about puppets, dwarves, masters, slaves, kings, queens, knights, and pawns—I want to contend that we encounter one scene in what we might call a larger *marionettentheater* of sovereignty.[7] It is possible to argue, of course, that the philosopher and the puppeteer, the *theatricum philosophicum* and the puppet theater, share a common thaumaturgical origin. As Jessica Lightfoot is only the most recent scholar to remind us, Greek philosophy begins in *thauma* ("wonder," marvel," "astonishment," as well as "puppetry"), and the comparison between philosophy and puppetry will famously be pursued by Plato, Aristotle, René Descartes, Thomas Hobbes, Heinrich von Kleist, Sigmund Freud, Walter Benjamin, and Jacques Derrida, among others.[8] However, at the same time, the puppet theater is also a theater of the political whose dramatis personae extend from Ernst Kantorowicz's wax effigies signifying royal dignitas at the funeral rites of medieval French kings,[9] through Thomas Hobbes's mighty "Artificiall man" called the Leviathan,[10] up to what Michel Foucault calls Frederick the Great's clockwork or automatic "puppet" armies.[11] To enter the Benjaminian puppet theater, a thaumaturgical world peopled by children's dolls, waxwork dummies, automata, and marionettes who may be more or less than alive, I want to argue that we are faced not simply with a Kleistian drama about a mechanical sovereignty that is even more powerful than its human equivalent but with a kind of toyland *Trauerspiel* in which the master themselves is reduced to a puppet on a string. For Benjamin, what takes place in this miniature theater of sovereignty is the tragicomic spectacle of a creaturely sovereign master who constantly finds themselves to be the slave of mysterious uncreaturely forces at work inside their own body: an internal uprising, a coup d'état, or a revolution. If Benjamin's sovereign puppet master is revealed to himself be a puppet, we will also see that his response to this immanent insurrection is frequently an act of (self-) destructive violence in which he seeks, tragically or farcically, to kill the puppet within himself once and for all. In what follows, I rehearse three different scenes from the political puppet theater—Miguel Cervantes's puppet show, Thomas Hobbes's Leviathan, Jacques Derrida's marionettes—that all stage, in their different ways, what we might call this Benjaminian "becoming-master" of the puppet. Who or what, then, pulls the strings of the puppet master?

MASTER PEDRO'S PUPPET SHOW

In chapter 26 of part 2 of Miguel Cervantes's epic novel *Don Quixote* (1605–1615), Alonso Quixano—the deluded nobleman who reimagines himself as the heroic knight-errant Don Quixote de la Mancha—destroys a puppet show. To recall the events leading up to this act of tragicomic vandalism, Don Quixote and Sancho Panza are invited by a renowned puppeteer, Master Pedro, to attend his performance of a chivalric romance, "The Liberation of Melisendra from the Moors." It depicts the travails of a knight, Señor Don Gaiferos, who rescues his wife, Melisendra (who also happens to be the daughter of the Emperor Charlemagne), from captivity in the independent Muslim state of Sansueña (Saragossa). After the couple are shown escaping the clutches of the Moorish king Marsilio, though, the watching Don Quixote becomes vocally critical of the show's lack of historical accuracy: "No, that is wrong!" he says when the King raises the alarm by ringing the bells of the city's mosques. "Master Pedro is incorrect in the matter of the bells, for the Moors do not use bells but drums."[12] However, straight after attacking the play's verisimilitude, the novel's protagonist is so overcome by the image of the army of Moors giving chase that the show apparently comes to life. For Don Quixote, whose heroic identity is famously predicated on his inability to distinguish between courtly romance and real life, Master Pedro's puppet show suddenly becomes a stage upon which he can not only passively watch, but actively *perform*, the role of chivalrous knight-errant: "And taking action, he unsheathed his sword, leaped next to the stage, and with swift and never before seen fury began to rain down blows on the crowd of Moorish puppets, knocking down some, beheading others, ruining this one, destroying that one."[13] If Master Pedro frantically seeks to remind him that the enemy are just papier mâché puppets—"Your grace must stop, Señor Don Quixote, and realize that the ones you are overthrowing, destroying, and killing are not real Moors but only pasteboard figures!"—this literally self-made Knight carries on until he lays waste to the entire cast of Christians and Muslims alike: "But this did not keep Don Quixote from raining down slashes, two-handed blows, thrusts, and backstrokes. In short, in less time than it takes to tell about it, he knocked the puppet theater to the floor, all its scenery and figures cut and broken to pieces."[14] In surveying the destruction he has wrought all around him, though, Don Quixote sees only the indestructibility of the chivalric ideal he lives by: "Long live knight-errantry, over and above everything in the world today!"[15]

To return to the ruins of Cervantes's puppet show after reading Benjamin's First Thesis, we might at first blush be tempted to find here a comic reversal of the fable of the chess-playing puppet who wins all the time: Don Quixote heroically refuses to lose to the seemingly indomitable figure of the Schachtürke but vanquishes the massed ranks of the Moorish enemy and saves the knight and his lady. It is actually, of course, an absurdly Pyrrhic "victory" by a serial loser who is defeated throughout the novel by proto-Benjaminian puppets masquerading as real people. After all, Quixote will later be fooled once again by Don Antonio's "Enchanted Head" (*cabeza encantada*), a supposedly supernatural prognosticating statue that, like the chess-playing Turk, turns out to be a smoke-and-mirrors mechanism controlled by a hidden human operator.[16] If Quixote is every bit as much a loser as Benjamin's hapless chess player, it is not only because he accidentally checkmates his own king—the puppet of the Christian Emperor Charlemagne revealingly ends up with "his head and crown ... split in two" on the floor alongside that of the Muslim king Marsilio—but because he commits the human chess-player's fatal error of taking the puppet theater for reality in the first place.[17] In Benjamin's famous con trick, the house always wins, and here, too, the loser must admit defeat and pay his debts. "I wish to sentence myself to pay the costs," the apparently chastened Quixote admits to Sancho Panza when he realizes what he has done, "let Master Pedro decide what he wants for the damaged puppets, for I offer to pay it at him immediately in good, standard Castilian coin."[18]

If Cervantes scholars have read Master Pedro's puppet show in many different ways, it is most frequently interpreted today as an early modern experiment in historical metafiction that exposes the medieval political theological theater of chivalry, and, arguably, even the genre of theater itself, as little more than a cheap circus act presided over by a cynical huckster.[19] It is thus only a matter for we—self-professedly streetwise—modern critics of revealing who or what is pulling the puppets' strings. According to this demystifying reading, Master Pedro would of course be the prime suspect for the role of the wizened Benjaminian dwarf. "Go on, boy," he tells his young assistant after Quixote criticizes the play's historical accuracy, "let them say what they will, for as long as I fill my purse, there can be more errors than atoms in the sun."[20] To excuse his wanton destruction of the puppet show, Don Quixote himself even resorts to the ingenious metafictional defense that he was not in control of his actions but had become a "puppet" whose strings were being pulled by some diabolical external actor. "Now I believe," he ruefully confesses, "what I have believed on many other occasions: the enchanters who pursue me simply place figures as they really are before my eyes, and then change and alter them into whatever they wish."[21] For Cervantes, whose magnum opus is generally seen as narrating not only the birth of political modernity but of the novel itself as modernity's own privileged aesthetic form, Quixote's demolition of the marionettentheater ("he knocked the puppet theater to the floor, all its scenery and figures cut and broken to pieces") would thus appear to constitute a fictional laying bare of the (literally and aesthetically) bankrupt theatrical device of medieval noblesse together with an attempt to construct a new and more prosaic mercantile foundation for an early modern Spanish empire that was already in political and economic crisis by the early seventeenth century. In this disenchanted bourgeois world, Don Quixote's only reliable way of righting wrongs is no longer the heroic or chivalrous deeds of knight-errancy but the more commonplace remedy of civil financial compensation—"good, standard Castilian coin."[22]

In uncanny anticipation of Benjamin's First Thesis, though, Cervantes's novel goes on to reveal that the prosaic (in every sense of the word) form of sovereignty called "bourgeois modernity" is every bit as much of a puppet show as its predecessor. It is worth recalling here that Benjamin himself reads Don Quixote as a novel about the messianic *reversal* of life and literature, master and slave, puppeteer and puppet. As he recounts in his essay "Franz Kafka: On the Tenth Anniversary of His Death" (1934), Kafka identifies Quixote's long-suffering servant as the novel's secret "master": "Sancho Panza, a sedate fool and a clumsy assistant, sent his rider [Don Quixote] on ahead."[23] Yet, arguably, the real reversal of life and literature, of puppet and master, in the novel can be found, not in the external relation between Panza and Quixote, but in the immanent relationship between the far more foolish Alonso Quixano and his own mythological heroic persona, Don Quixote de la Manche. To any savvy modern critic who claims that the puppet show scene unmasks the "reality" behind the fantasy of knight-errancy, we may reply that, on the contrary, the supposedly real, flesh-and-blood Alonso Quixano who remerges at the end is simply a performing dummy controlled by the persona of Don Quixote and the former's apology to Master Pedro nothing more than an act of lip service or ventriloquism to bourgeois values: Quixote even manages to negotiate a reduction in the compensation he owes Pedro via the surreal argument that he could not possibly have destroyed the puppet of Gaiferos's wife, Melisendra, because she had already escaped to France by the time he arrived on the scene.[24] If our professedly streetwise scholar is still tempted to dismiss Quixote's protestations of innocence as just another symptom of his boundless capacity for self-delusion, Cervantes's novel affords us another, less self-congratulatory, interpretation of Master Pedro's puppet show: we modern cynical readers may be the real dupes in this drama because, unlike Quixote, we do not realize that the realist novel called modernity is just another marionettentheater. For Cervantes, recall, Master Pedro's melodramatic tale of good Christian heroes and villainous Turks does actually contain a *real* pantomime villain unbeknownst to any modern hermeneutic of suspicion: "Master Pedro" himself is later revealed to be none other than Gines de Pasamonte, a galley slave whom Quixote had freed earlier in the book, but who repaid the knight's charity by stealing Sancho Panza's donkey and embarking on a new career as a confidence trickster. By reading the play so disastrously wrongly and mistaking theater for real life, Quixote thus perversely turns out be the only one among us who reads it *right*. In his destruction of Master Pedro's puppet show—and, with it, Pasamonte's lucrative career as a con artist—Alonso Quixano ironically succeeds for the first time in performing the role of the chivalrous Don Quixote de la Mancha: "Long live knight-errantry, over and above everything in the world today!"

MR. HOBBES'S ARTIFICIAL MAN

In the opening to his *Leviathan: Or The Matter, Forme, and Power of a Commonwealth Ecclesiasticall and Civil* (1651), Thomas Hobbes asks one of the most famous questions in early modern political theory: "For seeing life is but a motion of Limbs, the beginning whereof is in some principall part within, why may we not say, that all *Automata* (Engines that move themselves by springs and wheeles as doth a watch) have an artificiall life?"[25] It is not, of course, that Hobbes is the first philosopher to compare the human body to a machine or automaton. As René Descartes had already written a decade earlier in his *Meditations* (1641), "I might consider the body of a man as a kind of machine equipped with and made up of bones, nerves, muscles, veins, blood and skin in such a way that, even if there were no mind in it, it would still perform all the same movements as it now does in those cases where movement is not under the control of the will."[26] To reread Hobbes's classic anatomy of his "Artificiall Man" in the introduction to *Leviathan*, however, we might argue that the English philosopher is nonetheless the first to construct an explicit political theory of the puppet: the Hobbesian Commonwealth becomes, for the first time, a rationally calculable, predictable, controllable and reproducible form of political life.[27] For Hobbes, Descartes's philosophical anthropological question—does the body require an animating soul or mind to pull its strings?—will thus become the modern political question of whether an artificial body politic can function entirely autonomously of its animating sovereign demon or homunculus. If Hobbes appears to insist that the figure of the sovereign remains the "Artificiall Soul" of his body politic, giving "life and motion to the whole body" in the manner of the Benjaminian puppeteer, I want to argue that this new Hobbesian sovereign will, in spite or because of all the philosophical differences between them, gradually succumb to the same fate as the Benjaminian dwarf of theology: what should animate or control the machine is revealed, as Carl Schmitt will observe in his 1938 requiem for the absolutist Hobbes, to be simply one more cog in the machine.[28] In Hobbes's *Leviathan*, the sovereign puppeteer becomes just another puppet.

To the question of who or what might pull the strings of Hobbes's vast Artificiall Man, Carl Schmitt seems to give an emphatic answer in his *Political Theology* (1922): a person. It is Hobbes, more than anyone else, who embodies the German jurist's philosophy of sovereign personalism or decisionism: "The classical representative of the decisionist type," he writes, "is Thomas Hobbes."[29] Almost immediately, though, Schmitt also begins to wonder whether there might be something radically inhuman—indeed, mechanistic—inside this sovereign person: Hobbes's political personalism comes into conflict with his philosophical materialism, which leads to the "reduction of the individual to an atom."[30] For the later Schmitt of his *Leviathan in the State Theory of Thomas Hobbes* (1938), revealingly, Hobbes's fatal decision to choose the divisive biblical figure of the Leviathan to symbolize his Commonwealth will transform the last great hero of sovereign personalism into the unwitting quixotic progenitor of the liberal and rational depoliticization of the state: what the English philosopher intended to be the signifier of unified, absolute, and incontestable state power instead became "the symbol of a monstrosity" that only succeeded in uniting its enemies against it.[31] If the Jews of the Old Testament feared the sea monster as a symbol of hostile pagan forces, Schmitt (whose anti-liberalism and anti-Semitism begin to merge at this point) notoriously argues that modern "liberal Jews" like Spinoza and Mendelssohn were equally suspicious of the absolute power of the Hobbesian state: Spinoza exploits Hobbes's concession that the religious subject possesses freedom of conscience to turn the private individual into the authentic source of public sovereignty. In political modernity, Hobbes's mighty Artificiall Man has been emptied of all authority to the point where it has become little more than a massive state bureaucracy administering for private men—an empty sovereign puppet controlled by myriad liberal dwarves.[32]

If Schmitt's reading of Hobbes's *Leviathan* is principally a work of political theological esotericism, which seeks to decode what he sees as the hidden significance of the mythic sea monster, it is rarely observed that the German jurist offers another, and significantly less hermetic, account of the text that, rather than returning to the Hebrew Bible, situates *Leviathan* within its absolutely contemporary Cartesian context. It argues that Hobbes's theory of the state is not merely based on the ancient political mythopoeia of the biblical Leviathan, but on the radically new philosophical anthropology produced by mechanical philosophy. According to Schmitt—whose own text was written to mark the three-hundredth anniversary of the publication of Descartes's *Meditations*—"Hobbes transfers . . . the Cartesian conception of man as a mechanism with a soul onto the 'huge man,' the state, made by him into a machine animated by the sovereign-representative person."[33] To read it in this contemporary context, Hobbes's philosophy is less a work of political theological mythography than a species of political Cartesianism that projects Descartes's dualist theory of man, where the human is said to be composed of mechanical matter and immaterial mind, into a dualist theory of the state as something composed of a mechanical body and a sovereign personalist "soul." Yet, revealingly, Hobbes's political theory outstrips even Descartes's philosophical anthropology in Schmitt's verdict, because in the end his state is not dualist at all, but monist: what Descartes had insisted remained entirely immaterial—which is to say the mind or soul of man—will become just one more part of the mechanism in Hobbes. For Schmitt, Hobbes's "sovereign-representative person," who once pulled the strings of the state, is no longer a metaphysical sovereign person like a Baroque absolutist prince but simply a cog in the new machine of political representation. "The sovereign-representative person is only the soul of the 'huge man' state," the German jurist writes. "The process of mechanization is not, however, arrested but completed by this personification. This personalistic element too is drawn into the mechanization process and becomes absorbed by it. As a totality, the state is body and soul, a *homo artificialis*, and, as such, a machine."[34] In Schmitt's verdict, Hobbes's theory of the sovereign person thus ironically ends up setting in motion the first wholly artificial and depersonalized entity that is capable of running entirely by itself: Leviathan is "the first product of the age of technology," he argues, "the first modern mechanism in a grand style, as a *machina machinarum*."[35]

In his extended political obituary for Hobbes's thought experiment on absolute sovereignty, though, Schmitt is oddly ambivalent about the real cause of death of the mighty Leviathan in liberal modernity: Is it suicide, say, murder, or death by misadventure? It is tempting to read this account of the fate of Hobbes's great invention as a political theological tragedy that casts the philosopher as an early modern Prometheus who arrives too early upon the stage of history, or, perhaps better still, an Epimetheus who arrives too late. After all, Schmitt will himself embrace the fate of this latter mythical figure—who is Prometheus's brother, whose name literally means "afterthought," and whose impetuousness will set in motion the course of events that will lead to the opening of Pandora's box—in his own postwar internment.[36]

However, in another sense, Hobbes's fatal error is not recklessly building a machine that contains a design flaw or structural weakness—which is to say the "barely visible crack in the theoretical justification of the sovereign state" called "freedom of conscience" that liberalism would exploit to break that state in two—but perhaps building a machine in the first place, because Schmitt's essay is really a study of the artificial life of the puppet itself, which continues long after the puppet master's demise.[37] To jump ahead almost twenty years forward to his "Dialogue on Power and Access to the Holder of Power" (1954), in which he returns to the modern fate of the Hobbesian sovereign person once more in the radically new epoch of the atomic bomb, game theory, and the cybernetic revolution, Schmitt even appears to argue that the English philosopher's great *machina machinarum* does not exceed its maker's original intentions because it is badly made or ill used but precisely because *it works too well*: "In this sense the well-functioning European state of the early modern period was the first modern machine and simultaneously the concrete presupposition of all further technological machines. It was the machine of machines, the *machina machinarum*, a Super-Human [*Über-Mensch*] compiled of humans gathered together, which comes into existence via human consensus and yet, in the moment that it is present, exceeds all human consensus."[38] For the later Schmitt, Hobbes's machina machinarum (quite literally a machinating machine, a machine of machines, or metamachine), may well be the product of the social contract, but, once it is set in motion, it immediately breaks that contract and "exceeds all human consensus." If Hobbes is renowned as one of the first great early modern theorists of political poiesis, which is to say the classic idea that statecraft consists of the making or fabrication of an artefact whose workings will always remain intrinsically knowable to, and predictable by, its maker,[39] what Schmitt seems to be proposing in his own genealogy of the birth of the rational or technocratic state here is ironically something closer to what the evolutionary and systems biologists Humberto Maturana and Francisco Varela will call, less than twenty years after Schmitt's own essay, call the theory of autopoiesis: we can never know what we have made or constructed ourselves because what we have made remakes itself—reproduces itself through itself—and in ways that will inevitably escape and resist our knowing.[40] In showing how "power has slipped out of human hands even more than has technology," Schmitt reveals that the Hobbesian puppet ultimately outlives its puppet master.[41]

MONSIEUR TESTE KILLS HIS PUPPET

In "Learning to Live Finally" ("Apprendre à vivre enfin," 2004), his last interview with Jean Birnbaum for *Le Monde*, Jacques Derrida poignantly describes his own writing as an uncanny kind of shadow play or puppet theater: "*A fortiori*, when one writes a very general book, one does not know whom one is talking to, " he says, "you invent and create silhouettes, but in the end it no longer belongs to you. Spoken or written, all these gestures leave us and begin to act independently of us. Like machines or, better, like marionettes."[42] To reread the later Derrida in the light of this fascinating (conceptually and almost literally postmortem) remark, we quickly find marionettes everywhere: they appear in *Specters of Marx* (1991), "Faith and Knowledge" (1995), *Paper Machine* (2005), and the *Beast and Sovereign* seminars (2009), among other texts. If Derrida's puppets are clearly an avatar for a set of classic themes in his philosophy more generally—whether it be arche-writing (*arche-écriture*), the phallus, the fetish, the question of technology (*la technique*) or the prosthesis or, massively, the aporetic relationship between life/death (*La vie/la mort*)—it is seldom remarked that they are also situated within an explicitly political context that stretches from Hobbes's *Leviathan* (1651), through the French Revolution and Marx's *Capital* (1867), up to Paul Valéry's "Question of Dictatorship" (1934). In Derrida's first seminar on *The Beast and the Sovereign*, whose pedagogical moves strangely recall both Benjamin and Schmitt's *Puppenphilosophie* at key moments, what we have seen to be the classic philosophical anthropological question of who or what pulls the strings of the marionette in the Cartesian theater of consciousness again quickly becomes the political question of who or what has power over life and death in the Hobbesian theater of sovereignty. "It's difficult to know what a marionette is," he speculates. "Is it something of the order of the mechanical and inanimate thing," or is it "already of the human order, and thereby able to emancipate itself, to respond autonomously, as it were, and to take hold prosthetically, proth-statically, of a sovereign power"?[43]

To pursue our guiding Benjaminian theme of the tragicomic "becoming-puppet" of the master into Derrida's own marionettentheater, I thus finally want to turn to the later Derrida's reading of Paul Valéry's quasi-autobiographical story about a solitary, self-absorbed intellectual, "The Evening with Monsieur Teste" ("La soirée avec Monsieur Teste," 1896).[44] It is the study of another quixotic, all-knowing talking head (*teste* is the Old French word for "head") who, as we will see, turns out to be yet another puppet on a string. For Valéry's narrator, Monsieur Teste has dedicated his life to becoming the "master of his thought" by divesting himself of everything—which is to say bodily appetites, physical states and even ritualized social behavior—inside him that is not under his strict rational control:[45]

He was a man absorbed in his own variations, one who becomes his own system, who surrenders himself entirely (*qui se livre tout entier*) to the frightening discipline of the free spirit, and who kills his joys with his joys, the stronger killing the weaker—the sweetest, the transitory (*temporelle*), the pleasure of the moment and the hour just begun, destroyed by the fundamental—by the hope for the fundamental (*l'espoir de la fondamentale*).[46]

In Valéry's novella, as Derrida goes on to observe in his *Beast and the Sovereign* seminar, Monsieur Teste's attempt to kill off the transitory joys within him once and for all revealingly takes the symbolic form of an act of puppet "murder." "M. Teste was perhaps forty years old," Valéry's narrator says. "His speech was extraordinarily rapid, and his voice low. Everything about him was unobstrusive [*Tout s'effaçait en lui*], his eyes, his hands. Yet his shoulders were military and his step had an astonishing regularity. When he spoke he never lifted an arm or a finger; he had *killed his puppet* [*il avait tué la marionnette*]. He never smiled, nor said good morning or goodnight; he seemed not to hear a 'How are you?'"[47]

If Monsieur Teste seeks to kill off the puppet within himself—which here takes the form of the obligatory and almost automatic gestures of everyday politesse expected of a gentleman—and live a pure life of the mind, Valéry's story makes clear that this grand Cartesian act of puppet murder is really just another act of Quixotic self-harm.[48] To set in motion his own reading of the novella, Derrida begins by noting the obvious performative contradiction of Monsieur Teste attempting to kill something that is, by definition, never actually "alive" in the first place: "Is a marionette that one wishes to kill still a marionette?" he asks. "Is a marionette of which one can only rid oneself by condemning it to death, by removing its life, still a marionette?"[49] It is perversely the very act of attempted puppet-killing, in other words, that confirms the uncanny artificial *life* of the puppet. As Valéry's narrator observes in the above scene, the self-absorbed Monsieur Teste seeks to kill the puppet within himself by refusing to raise even "an arm or a finger" in greeting to the people he meets in the street because he is utterly contemptuous of such banal acts of reflexive, mechanical etiquette. Yet, as the narrator's own description of the protagonist already reveals, Teste's resistance to such cultural automatism in the name of the "free spirit" is itself a curiously automatic gesture: we are told he has "military" shoulders, for instance, an astonishingly "regular" step, and everything "alive," animated, or spontaneous within him has apparently already been subsumed into his system (*Tout s'effaçait en lui*). For Valéry, to recall the narrator's own later verdict, Teste thus ironically strives to kill what we might call his "weak" or creaturely automatism, not in the name of some freedom of spirit, but rather by submitting himself to an even stronger, indeed almost algorithmic, form of cognitive automatism: "He watched for the repetition of certain ideas," the narrator recounts. "He sprinkled them with numbers. This served to make the application of his conscious studies in the end mechanical. He even sought to summarize this labor. He would often say: 'Maturare!'"[50] By seeking to kill the puppet within his own body, an automatism that is inseparable from his being and without which that being could not survive, Monsieur Teste's act of marionette murder might thus better be described as an act of puppet *suicide*.[51]

In his discussion of "La soirée avec Monsieur Teste" from the *Beast and the Sovereign* seminars, Derrida re-poses the old Schmittian question of who is the "boss, the author, the creator or the sovereign, the manipulator and the puppeteer" of the marionette, and his answer will now be familiar: the sovereign master is *themselves* a puppet.[52] To reveal what he elsewhere calls the "originary technicity" of the human (which does not tragically or culpably befall us from without, as we saw in the case of Schmitt's version of Hobbes, but is always already at work within us from the beginning) in this determinedly political context, Derrida stages a new kind of Benjaminian puppet palace coup or revolution—indeed, perhaps even a kind of puppet *regicide*—against their despised sovereign master.[53] It is revealing, for instance, that his discussion of the figure of the marionette in this seminar begins with Hobbes's *Leviathan*, which, recalling Schmitt, he variously describes as a "robot," a "gigantic prosthesis" and as a "dead machine, or even a machine of death,"[54] before going on to describe Valéry's scrupulously a-political "La soirée avec Monsieur Teste," as an exercise in "quasi-Cartesian politics."[55] As Derrida observes, Teste's attempt to kill the marionette within himself is nothing less than a classic Cartesian or Hobbesian act of body politics that asserts the free and proper sovereignty of the head (the *teste* or *tête*) over the merely mechanical or automatic body. However, as we have already glimpsed, Valéry's story refutes its own epigraph that "Vita Cartesii res est simplicissima" (Cartesian life is the simplest thing): a marionette that has to be killed must already be as vital as its "sovereign" executioner, who is, in turn, inevitably rendered less sovereign, less alive. For the later Derrida, as his seminars on the *Death Penalty* (2013) also make clear, what we have called this becoming-master of the puppet is again revealingly figured as a kind of anti-Cartesian coup d'état or popular revolution in which the mechanical body begins to "take hold, prosthetically, prosthstatically, of a sovereign power," with literally fatal results for the sovereign.[56] If we remain in any doubt about whether Derrida's own textual marionettes really "come to life" or not—which is to say whether this elegant Kleistian ballet of masters and puppets, kings and revolutionaries, and life and death has any real political existence of its own, independently (as he puts it in the interview with *Le Monde*) of his spoken or written words—then the *Death Penalty* seminars also remind us that, almost exactly one hundred years before Valéry's "La soirée avec Monsieur Teste," the Jacobin leader Maximilien de Robespierre had described the trial and execution of Louis XVI as an early Valéryan exercise in killing the puppet: what we call a "king" is less a living, breathing human being, Robespierre declares in a contemporary speech, than a "crowned automaton" (*l'automate couronné*).[57] In decapitating their own puppet king (the soi-disant "Citoyen Capet") the Jacobins had already found a somewhat literal, if undeniably efficient, way of fulfilling Monsieur Teste's Cartesian dream of becoming a head without a body.

(UN)CREATURELY SOVEREIGNTY

In his essay "Hope in the Past: On Walter Benjamin" (1978), Peter Szondi recalls that Benjamin was apparently inspired to write his famous essay on *The Origin of German Tragic Drama* (1928) by looking at the figure of "a king in a puppet theater whose hat sat crookedly on his head."[58] To return to Benjamin's classic study of baroque creaturely sovereignty in this context, we arguably find ourselves confronted once again by the uncanny reversal of puppet and master with which we began: Benjamin's model for the human, all too human prince of early modern Trauerspiel turns out to not actually be a human being at all, but a broken puppet king. For Benjamin—who reportedly had his own puppet theater when he was a child that he reused to stage a puppet show for children during Hanukkah in 1926—this political "becoming-master" of the puppet is a recurring trope or figure in his recreations of the lost childhood world of toys, games, role-play, and storytelling.[59] If "a proper puppeteer is a despot . . . that makes the Tsar seem like a petty gendarme," as he argues in his radio talk for children "Berlin Puppet Theater" (1929), Benjamin revealingly goes on to add that, even in the case of puppet masters, *le roi règne mais il ne gouverne pas*: "He has to get along with his puppets, because for him they're alive. All great puppeteers maintain that the secret of the trade is actually to let the puppet have its way, to yield to it."[60] In becoming their own masters so easily, the puppets in this miniature theater end up miniaturizing the "real" political masters in the audience: "They take the greatest of men and mimic them, as if to say 'What man can do, so can any puppet.' In old Austria, for example, they ridiculed the tyrants."[61]

To become the masters that they so evidently are, however, this chapter has argued that Benjamin's puppets do not simply "come alive," like political versions of Heinrich von Kleist's marionettes, so much as reveal that the old human masters they served so faithfully were themselves nothing but puppets on a string all along. It is the *masters*, perversely, who now imitate the greatest of puppets as if to say, "What puppets can do, so can any man." After all, the puppet king with a crooked hat who inspired the creaturely sovereign of *The Origin of German Tragic Drama* will reappear as the—crooked in every sense of the word—sovereign from Thesis 1 of the "Theses on the Philosophy of History" with whom we began: "A little hunchback who was an expert chess player sat inside and guided the puppet's hand by means of strings." If Benjamin's political theological dwarf claims to pull the strings of his historical materialist puppet, however, this chapter has argued that he ends up enduring the same tragicomic fate as those other crooked sovereigns, Cervantes's Don Quixote, Hobbes's Leviathan, and Valéry's

Monsieur Teste: each becomes the puppet of their own supposed puppets. For Benjamin, what we call sovereignty's allegedly immaterial soul or head, which is assumed to transcend and preside over its material, mechanical or machine-like body, constantly finds itself doubled back into, or onto, a body that thus becomes sovereign over sovereignty itself. In Benjamin's marionettentheater, we thus find a radically anti-naturalist, tragicomic variation upon Trauerspiel that even contains its own metaphysical pathos: a sovereign is as *uncreaturely* as any toy, doll, or puppet.[62]

If Benjamin seems to describe an infinite political regress of puppets inside puppets, what remains to be seen here is whether there is any exit or way out from this miniature theater of sovereignty. To the inevitable question of whether we can apply the emergency brake on the runaway political theological winning machine that is the Schachtürke, I think Benjamin's answer is finally ambivalent, but one intriguingly utopian solution proposed in his 1928 *Frankfurter Zeitung* review of an exhibition of children's toys at the Märkisches Museum in Berlin is a species of puppet "communism."[63] It is in the allegedly prepolitical space of the children's playroom—with its assortment of tin soldiers, wax dolls, and marionettes—that Benjamin find yet another stage upon which political history is played out. As he contends elsewhere, a child is no miniature Robinson Crusoe living on a politics-free island, because they always "belong to the nation and the class they came from": "Their toys cannot bear witness to any autonomous separate existence, but rather are a silent signifying dialogue between them and their nation."[64] Yet the small child at play is not simply a passive puppet either—whether of their parents, their class and nation, or the age of mechanical reproduction in which their toys are produced—because their play is "always liberating."[65] For Benjamin, as Giorgio Agamben recognizes in his essay "In Praise of Profanation,"⁶⁶ children's play always consists of a certain emancipation of any object from its functional fate or identity so that anything whatsoever can become a toy: "A child wants to pull something, and so he becomes a horse; he wants to play with sand, and so he turns into a baker; he wants to hide, and so he turns into a robber or a policeman."⁶⁷ In the profane hands of that rogue puppet called the child, Benjamin even imagines that the broken puppet sovereign can perhaps be put back together and returned to the common use (and communism) that is play: "Once mislaid, broken, and repaired, even the most princely doll becomes a capable proletarian comrade in the children's play commune."⁶⁸

In closing, though, I want to consider one final and more somber mise-en-scène from our Benjaminian political puppet theater that represents a curious kind of dress rehearsal for the First Thesis: "Rastelli's Story" (1935). To quickly unpack the narrative of this short essay, Benjamin recalls a tale apparently told to him by the famous twentieth-century juggler, Enrico Rastelli, about another juggler in ancient times who achieved worldwide fame because of the incredible tricks he could perform with a large ball.⁶⁹ It is revealed by Rastelli, however, that the juggler's amazing tricks were actually another ingenious confidence trick performed by another homunculus: a "boy dwarf," hidden inside the ball, manipulated it on his master's behalf.⁷⁰ At a special command performance in front of the "imperious, even cruel" Turkish sultan, Mohammad Ali Bey, the juggler performed his pièce de resistance by seeming to make the ball dance in time to music.⁷¹ "The flutist blew more strongly," the narrator recounts, and the ball's "bounces gradually became higher. Meanwhile the master began raising his arm, until, having calmly brought it shoulder high, he stretched out his little finger—keeping up the music as he did—and the ball, obeying a last, long trill, settled on his fingertip with a single bound."[72] Yet this very familiar fable of a puppet, a dwarf, a Turk, and a trick contains a surprising denouement, because, unbeknownst to the juggler, his boy had fallen ill before the royal performance and has thus been unable to play his customary role. For Benjamin's Rastelli, what this means is that the confidence trickster, quite unintentionally, ended up becoming a genuine artist for the first time ever: he really performed his amazing feats all by himself, just as he has always falsely claimed, because for once there was no one hiding inside the ball pulling its strings. If "Rastelli's Story" is sometimes seen as holding out the possibility of a different ending to the celebrated chess game in the First Thesis—which is to say an endgame where historical materialism can apparently defeat sovereign princes without resorting to surreptitious acts of dialectical string-pulling—I want to conclude that what we have called the marionettentheater of sovereignty makes possible another, albeit somewhat less redemptive, interpretation of Benjamin's fable: the juggler may well have been able to "beat the Turk" all by himself but, of course, he could only really do so because he still, more or less automatically, *believed* that the boy dwarf was helping him all along.[73] What if the juggler had merely replaced the *real* dwarf inside the ball, who controlled the latter's movements, with an *imaginary* dwarf inside his head who controlled his own actions? In Benjamin's puppet theater, the puppet master apparently still sees himself as a puppet—even when there is no one left to pull his strings.

7

IN THE CROWD
Jarry, Le Bon, Kelsen, Foucault

In the first scene of Alfred Jarry's *Ubu roi* (*King Ubu*), which opened on December 10, 1896, at the Théâtre de l'Oeuvre in Paris, a fat man brandishing a toilet brush enters the stage and utters a single word: *"Merdre"* ("Shit" pronounced wrongly).[1] It apparently took fifteen minutes for the play to resume as outraged members of the audience screamed abuse—including *"Mang're!"* (presumably "Eat [shit]!," also pronounced wrongly)— back at the actor.[2] After the curtain fell on opening night, which would also turn out to be closing night, a full-blown riot broke out with the crowd splitting into angry pro- and anti-Ubu factions who fought one another. To recall the plot of Jarry's play, which is today seen by scholars as a revolutionary theatrical event that paved the way for modernism, Dadaism and the Theater of the Absurd, *Ubu roi* is a burlesque parody of Shakespeare's *Macbeth* in which the obese, vulgar, and scatological Père Ubu leads a palace coup in his native Poland: Ubu kills the reigning King Wenceslas and installs himself as a tyrant before he is successively assailed by a popular counterrevolution, a Russian invasion led by the Tsar, and even a bear, before finally escaping with his wife to France. If *Ubu roi*'s premiere variously attracted praise and censure from such renowned literary figures as

FIGURE 7.1 Alfred Jarry, Program for *King Ubu* (*Ubu roi*) from *The Beraldi Album of Theatre Programs*, 1896. One from an album of fifty lithographs, sheet: 9 11/16 x 12 11/16 in. (24.6 x 32.3 cm). Publisher: Théâtre de l'Oeuvre, Paris. Edition: varies. Johanna and Leslie J. Garfield Fund, Mary Ellen Oldenburg Fund, and Sharon P. Rockefeller Fund. Acc. no.: 289.2008.38. Museum of Modern Art (MoMA), New York, USA. Public Domain.

Catulle Mendès, Stephane Mallarmé, and Arthur Symons, it was a young Irish poet who understood virtually nothing of what was taking place on stage—he spoke little French—who seemed, nonetheless, to best comprehend the historical enormity of this theatrical moment. In his memoir *The Trembling of the Veil* (1922), written almost twenty-five years later, W. B. Yeats remembered how his initial sense of artistic solidarity with Jarry against the baying crowd ("Feeling bound to support the most spirited party, we have shouted for the play") later gave way to a foreboding that the grotesque figure of Ubu was an apocalyptic messenger of not simply the fin de siècle but the end of civilization: "After Stephane Mallarmé," Yeats famously asks, "after Paul Verlaine, after Gustave Moreau, after Puvis de Chavannes, after our own verse, after all our subtle colour and nervous rhythm, after the faint mixed tints of Conder, what more is possible?" before answering his own question by declaring, "After us the Savage God."[3]

To return to the scene of the first performance of Jarry's play at the Théâtre de l'Oeuvre after 120 years, we—impeccably polite, well-behaved, and unshockable—spectators may wonder why *Ubu roi* provoked such a violent response from its original audience: Who or what, exactly, was the "Savage God"? It is now common among critics, of course, to see *Ubu roi* as an anarcho-theatrical "bomb" whose purpose was to outrage the delicate bourgeois sensibilities of the late-nineteenth-century Parisian theatergoer.[4] As Jarry subsequently wrote in his essay "Questions de théâtre," a crowd "is an inert and uncomprehending [*incompréhensive*] and passive mass that must be hit [*frapper*] from time to time."[5] Yet, in fact, what took place in the aftermath of the play's production was in no way a spontaneous, unpredictable, and self-organized uprising, but an entirely controlled theatrical explosion. For Jarry, Père Ubu was quite literally an agent provocateur whose theatrical task was to stage a riot: Georges Rémond, a friend of the playwright, even claimed that a group had been planted in the audience with the instruction to "provoke uproar" by "uttering cries of rage" if the audience applauded and letting out cries of "admiration and ecstasy" if there was booing.[6] If any self-respecting bourgeois member of the audience sought to break up or interrupt the play on the grounds of offending public decency, in other words, they thus found themselves effectively becoming just another player in a mise-en-scène that, appropriately enough, concludes with the main character being chased from the stage by an angry mob. In Jarry's theatrical laboratory, we might argue that the crowd itself is put onstage for the first time: Yeats's "Savage God" is us.[7]

If Jarry's Ubu has often been seen as a prototype of modern populist sovereignty from Mussolini to Trump, it is also possible to read the play—together with the angry response it provoked—as the dramatization of that classic nineteenth-century collective political subject without whom what we now call "populism" would be unimaginable: the crowd. It is an intriguing historical coincidence that, just one year before the opening night of *Ubu roi*, the French polymath Gustave Le Bon first raised the question of why an allegedly rational, responsible, and self-interested individual behaves so very differently when they become part of a group in his *The Crowd* (*Psychologie des foules*, 1895). Against this backdrop, we may thus be tempted to read Jarry's own theatrical experiment in crowd theory as an attempt to put Le Bon's thesis to the test in a "natural" environment: "crowd psychology" is a pathology, the latter argues, whose (distinctly Ubu-esque) symptoms include "impulsiveness, irritability, incapacity to reason, the absence of judgement and of the critical spirit, the exaggeration of the sentiments."[8] However, what really unites the very different figures of Le Bon and Jarry—the political reactionary and the theatrical anarchist—is a particular elitist contempt for the *passivity* of the crowd, its suggestibility to, or malleability by, external stimuli. To introduce Le Bon's larger argument, which we will unpack in more detail momentarily, what makes a crowd so dangerous socially and politically is that (like Jarry's own audience) it is not the spontaneous explosion of chaos or anarchy it appears to be but is rather a curiously herdlike beast that follows rather than leads. "A certain number of living beings [who] are gathered together, whether they be animals or men," the crowd theorist asserts, "place themselves instinctively under the authority of a chief."⁹ For the political conservative Le Bon, a crowd's pathological search for anyone or anything to lead them anywhere will thus inevitably result in the overthrow of civilized representative authority and a return to primitivism, barbarism, and even a cult of "the leader": enter, once again, Yeats's "Savage God." In the same way, Jarry's own (allegedly liberatory) attempt to turn the passive and bourgeois crowd into a real and conscious political actor in its own right by abolishing the divide between audience and stage arguably vindicates the critique that Jacques Rancière will famously level against the playwright's theatrical heirs Bertolt Brecht and Antonin Artaud more than one hundred years later: every attempt to theatrically "emancipate the spectator" only ends up demonstrating how fatally *unemancipated* the crowd really is.¹⁰

In this final chapter, I want to argue that Jarry's *Ubu roi* perhaps also represents the beginning of a modern political *Massentheater*—which is to say both a theater of the crowd and the crowd *as* a form of theater—that extends from Gustave Le Bon's crowd psychology to Michel Foucault's disciplinary society. It will be my aim in what follows to read the opening night of Jarry's play, where an apparently free, spontaneous, and self-organizing uprising against "theater" turns out to have been entirely rehearsed, staged, and performed by (both literal and figurative) "bad actors," as a dramatic microcosm for the political fate of the crowd over the next century. As many scholars have observed, Jarry's attempt to put the crowd itself "onstage" was quickly taken up and exploited by a new wave of political leaders in the epoch of mass or populist politics: Benito Mussolini, who was himself an enthusiastic reader of Le Bon, would go on to argue in a 1933 speech for a new "mass theater" (*teatro di masse*) that would be able to cater for no less than fifteen thousand or twenty thousand spectators.¹¹ To enter the (all too crowded) field of crowd theory from Le Bon to Foucault, this chapter contends that what we really confront is a theory of the *audience*: a crowd is an audience that does not know that it is an audience and so fatally begins to take or mistake theater or fiction for "real life." For crowd theorists like Le Bon, what we call "the social" is a nineteenth-century form of social media whose own viral pile-ons, witch hunts, and shitstorms turn out to be every bit as choreographed by invisible laws or algorithms as its modern technological equivalent. If a set of random individuals apparently naturally or spontaneously begin to see themselves as a crowd—that is, as a real collective political entity, subject, or person such as a divine elect, a chosen people, or a master race—then the task of crowd theory will be to reverse-engineer what it sees as nothing more than an individual pathology. In a reading of Gustave Le Bon's crowd psychology, Hans Kelsen's neo-Kantian legal formalism and Michel Foucault's disciplinary society, I will argue that crowd theory constitutes a political attempt to *theatricalize*—to deessentialize, depersonalize, and, of course, politically delegitimize—this "becoming-crowd" of the individual. Finally, though, I will return to the lonely figure of Yeats at the opening of Jarry's *Ubu roi* to propose that crowd theory also betrays a similar fear—or perhaps even desire—concerning the fate of the crowd theorist themselves under the rule of Ubu: Hal Foster's essay "Père Trump" (2020) explores precisely the dilemma of what we might call the "out-trumped" critic. What if the paradigmatically individual figure of the *critic* (i.e., the poet, scholar, or crowd theorist) turns out to be just one of the crowd?

THE UNEMANCIPATED SPECTATOR

In the introduction to his classic *The Crowd*, Gustave Le Bon surveys the popular revolutions of the preceding century from the French Terror, through the Paris Commune, to the rise of universal suffrage, and concludes that there is one "last surviving sovereign force" in modernity—"the power of crowds."[12] To become a member of a crowd, we participate in the making of a new collective subject that is more than the sum or aggregate of its individual parts and can even be said to have a group or hive "mind" of its own: a "psychological crowd," he writes, "forms a single being, and is subject to the *law of the mental unity of crowds*."[13] It is Le Bon's objective in his work of popular social theory to articulate this unwritten, indeed unconscious, "law" to which the (purportedly sovereign) crowd remains pathologically subject. As many scholars have documented, Le Bon deploys a number of analogies (political, chemical, viral) to explain the fatal capture of the crowd by its own unconscious, but it has rarely been observed that his privileged metaphor is theatrical: what we confront in the fin-de-siècle "crowd"—which is allegedly spontaneous, unpredictable, collective, impatient of any delay in its gratification, and immediately prone to excessive or transgressive action—is, perversely, a kind of displaced and misrecognized theatrical *audience*. If Le Bon was by no means the first nor the last thinker to fashion a dialectic between the political crowd and the theatrical audience (a gesture that goes as far back as Plato's theatrocracy and as far forward as Rancière's emancipated spectator), I want to propose here that the French social theorist's analogy between these two—absolutely contemporaneous yet apparently rival or antagonistic—forms of nineteenth-century popular subjectivity can be seen as part and parcel of a larger contemporary political attempt to, for better or worse, "theatricalize" the crowd. For Kimberly Jannarone, who is one of the few scholars to explore the relationship between the crowd and the audience in this period, a series of material, social, and economic transformations in the production of the theatrical space combined to create a new kind of audience by the end of the nineteenth century whose sole unifying law, in apparently diametrical opposition to that of the crowd, was to *behave*. "Activities such as talking to one another or to the performers during the show, eating, arguing, arriving late, leaving early, moving around, booing, hissing, stamping," Jannarone observes, "vanished under the combined internal and external pressures of manners and their enforcement by uniformed ushers, mandated silence, late-seating policies, and the removal of rowdy elements from the auditorium."[14]. In the same way, Le Bon's crowd psychology seeks to construct a new theoretical space in which the apparently anarchic crowd can be produced as, and divided into, a polite and well-behaved audience.

To subject themselves to the law of the crowd, Le Bon argues that an individual must surrender their critical or rational faculty to the faculty of the imagination: "A crowd thinks in images, and the image itself immediately calls up a series of other images, having no logical connection with the first," he observes, "Our reason shows us the incoherence there is in these images, but a crowd hardly sees it, and what its distorting imagination [*imagination déformante*] adds to the real event it will confuse with reality itself."[15] It is this crude form of collective *Vortsellung* or picture-thinking, among many other pathologies, that leads Le Bon to draw a series of analogies between the two allegedly very different groups or collectives called the crowd and the audience. As he goes on to elaborate in a remarkable conceit, what we call "the crowd"—which remains fatally subject to the random generating power of the imagination to superimpose itself upon reality—becomes equivalent to an audience at a popular nineteenth-picture show that is dazzled by the projection of one image after another upon a screen. "These imagelike ideas are not connected by any logical bond of analogy or succession," he writes, "and may take each other's place like the slides of a magic-lantern which the operator withdraws from the groove in which they were placed one above the other."[16] If Le Bon's analogy obviously invites us to see a crowd as a kind of passive theatrical audience, it must be added that this tableau also contains a third party—namely, the mysterious figure of the "operator" of the magic-lantern spectacle who projects images onto the screen of the real in order to dazzle their unemancipated spectators. For Le Bon, real-life political and historical "operators" such as Napoleon Bonaparte will assume the role of mediator of the image for the masses and, consequently, become the leader that the crowd was looking for all along: "To know the art of impressing the imagination of crowds is to know at the same time the art of governing them [*l'art de les gouverner*]."[17] In Le Bon's Massentheater, a crowd is thus what we might call an *unemancipated* spectator whose arrival as an allegedly new and radical collective political actor upon the stage of history in the nineteenth century does not represent a liberation from the subject position of passive consumer of theatrical spectacle so much as an even more fundamental mode of capture by that spectacle that leads it to misrecognize theater as reality.

If we want to observe how a crowd behaves in its "natural" environment, Le Bon consistently argues that we should thus look neither to the city street nor the public square but to the theatrical stage. To enter into the allegedly make-believe world of the theater and watch a play—such as one of the "bread and circus" (*panem et circenses*) spectacles designed to appease the Roman plebs—Le Bon argues, a crowd of people does not so much leave the real world behind as become the theatrical audience it already virtually was and begin to observe what is, strictly speaking, nothing more than the play *within* the play it calls "reality."[18] "Crowds being only capable of thinking in images are only to be impressed by images," he contends, which means that "theatrical representations, in which the image is shown in its most clearly visible shape, always have an enormous influence on crowds."[19] It thus becomes the political objective of *The Crowd* to put the unruly crowd back into the (literal and figurative) box from which it first emerged: the theater. As Le Bon goes on to explain, a theatrical audience differs from the political crowd because it freely and voluntarily, rather than involuntarily and pathologically, subjects itself to the spectacle by engaging in what Samuel Taylor Coleridge famously calls a "willing suspension of disbelief": "the most unconscious spectator cannot ignore that he is the victim of illusions," the French scholar observes, "and that he has laughed or wept over imaginary adventures."[20] For Le Bon, what we might call the "voluntary" or "self-unemancipating" spectator that is the audience only metabolizes into the involuntary, indeed unconscious, unemancipated spectator called the crowd if or when it suspends its own suspension of disbelief and begins to believe that what is taking place onstage is real: "The story has often been told of the manager of a popular theatre," he revealingly recalls, who was "obliged to have the actor who took the part of the traitor protected on his leaving the theatre, to defend him against the violence of the spectators, indignant at the crimes, imaginary though they were, which the traitor had committed."[21] In the year after the publication of *The Crowd*, of course, a new theatrical manager would pursue this theory of the becoming-crowd of the audience to its logical political conclusion: Jarry actively provoked his own audience to express their revulsion at the central character in his play—another traitor called Père Ubu—by turning itself into a social or political crowd and revolting against the actor, company, and even "theater" itself.

In Le Bon's Massentheater, however, we can paradoxically find one more unemancipated spectator besides the unthinking or uncritical crowd who will reappear in different forms throughout crowd theory: the critic. It is already well documented that the author of *The Crowd*—who personally witnessed the destruction wrought by the Paris Commune in 1871 and even considered such impeccably liberal democratic institutions as trial-by-jury, elections, and parliaments to be examples of "crowds"—was an unapologetic political elitist who viewed the rule of *la foule* with undisguised horror. As he chronicles the inexorable rise of the crowd to political power, Le Bon thus also eulogizes the demise of the "small intellectual aristocracy" (*un petite aristocratie intellectuelle*) that he deems solely responsible for the world-historical task of creating and sustaining historical civilizations: "A civilization involves fixed rules, discipline, a passing from the instinctive to the rational state, forethought for the future [*prévoyance*], an elevated degree of culture—all of them conditions that crowds, left to themselves, have invariably shown themselves incapable of realizing."[22] Yet, once again, this political dialectic between the intellectual aristocracy and the crowd is expressed by means of a theatrical analogy—namely, the relation between the theater critic or reviewer and the audience. To metonymize the slow death of the intellectual aristocracy at the hands of the crowd, for instance, Le Bon laments the fate of the theater critic or reviewer, who was once the sole arbiter of mass culture, but whose expert judgement has now been rendered completely redundant by the "wisdom" of the crowd:

> Even the critics have ceased to be able to assure the success of a book or a play. The papers are so conscious of the uselessness (*l'inutilité*) of everything in the shape of criticism or personal opinion, that they have reached the point of suppressing literary criticism, confining themselves to citing the title of a book, and appending a "puff" (*réclame*) of two or three lines. In twenty years'

time the same fate will probably have overtaken theatrical criticism.²³

By passively following the instincts of the crowd, rather than leading them, the theater critic effectively becomes a member of that crowd themselves: a follower of the followers. For Le Bon, what should be the "intellectual aristocracy" has likewise lost the very power of critical foresight or *prévoyance* that distinguished them from the crowd in the first place and enabled them to mitigate the latter's desire for instant gratification: "We must submit to the reign of the crowd, since improvident hands [*mains imprévoyantes*] have successively overthrown all the barriers that might have kept the crowd in check."²⁴ Perhaps we can best observe this inexorable becoming-crowd of the intellectual aristocracy in another celebrated work of crowd theory where, once again, the critic finds themselves in the audience, rather than on the stage, of history: I am thinking here of José Ortega y Gasset's *The Revolt of the Masses* (*La rebelión de las masa*, 1930). In a work that begins by lamenting the fact that the political explosion of the crowd in the twentieth century means that there are no more seats to be had at the theater—"people anxious to use them are left standing outside"²⁵—Gasset continues by, imaginatively at least, taking his own seat as just one more paying member of the audience to watch the new spectacle that is the crowd itself: "Now, ticket in hand, I can cheerfully enter into my subject, see the show [*espectáculo*] from inside."²⁶

POLITICAL THEOLOGY OF THE AS-IF

In an unpublished 1953 interview that is held in the Library of Congress Freud archive, the renowned Austrian legal theorist Hans Kelsen recalled that his first personal encounter with

Sigmund Freud thirty years earlier concerned a curious *Traumdeutung*: a dream interpretation.[27] It appears that Kelsen had a colleague—a professor of economics—who had recently had a nightmare about the death of his children. As he happened to be meeting Freud the next morning, Kelsen volunteered to ask the author of *The Interpretation of Dreams* (*Die Traumdeutung* 1899) for an explanation of its meaning. To recount the dream's manifest content, the professor dreamt he was told his sons had died, but that he had received the terrible news with total indifference and responded only with the brusque command "Well, put them in the icebox!" ("*Gut, legen Sie sie in den Eiskasten!*").[28] For Freud, this—apparently "typical"—dream actually had a very simple latent content that he immediately described to Kelsen: the professor wanted to divorce his wife in real life, but felt he had to stay in the marriage for the sake of his children, and so the dream was really an expression of his own unconscious death wish (*Todeswunsch*).[29] If Kelsen's account is to be believed, it was at this precise moment that he became a convert to psychoanalysis, because he privately knew that his colleague was having an affair with his secretary and did indeed want to leave his wife, but that divorce was impossible because of his children.[30]. In his little-known early essay "The Conception of the State and Social Psychology, with Special Reference to Freud's Group Theory" ("Der Begriff die Staats und die Sozialpsychologie. Mit besonderer Berücksichtigung vons Freuds Theorie der Masse," 1922), which he would prepare immediately after this encounter with Freud, Kelsen would thus go on to incorporate Freud's group psychology (*Massenpsychologie*) into his own celebrated neo-Kantian attempt to construct a theory of the state ruled, not by an arbitrary sovereign person like Ubu, but by rules themselves.[31]

To briefly revisit Kelsen and Freud's postwar interpretation of a dream in which fathers and sons symbolically kill one another, but no one actually dies, and everyone ends up just carrying on following the rules as before, I want to propose that this Traumdeutung is also a particular interpretation of political theology at the very moment of its inauguration as a modern academic discipline: a "political theology of the as-if." It is possible, after all, to read the professor's dream about a tyrannical father whose pursuit of sexual ownership of women requires the submission of his sons as a polite bourgeois restaging of the famous Freudian origin myth of the *Urvater* or primal father, which first appeared in *Totem and Taboo* (*Totem und Tabu*, 1913) and resurfaced, coincidentally, right around the time of the psychoanalyst's first meeting with Kelsen, in *Group Psychology and the Analysis of the Ego* (*Massenpsychologie und Ich-Analyse*, 1921). As Freud's own (reassuringly normalizing) interpretation of the dream reveals, Kelsen will find in psychoanalysis a kind of therapeutic prophylaxis that can protect his own theory of the liberal, rules-based, democratic state against such archaic political theological fantasies of origin: what is significant about Freud's dream interpretation is that the modern primal father ends up settling down in domestic peace with the primal mother, they have hordes of primal children, and everyone lives unhappily ever after. However, my own aim in what follows will be to situate the Freud-Kelsen debate in the context of a now obscure reading of Immanuel Kant's theory of practical reason by Hans Vaihinger in his *The Philosophy of "As If"* (*Die Philosophie des Als Ob*, 1911), which controversially argues that Kant's ideas of pure reason from the *Critique of Pure Reason* (1781), such as God, the soul, and the will, should properly be understood as self-conscious *fictions* that, nonetheless, possess a certain theoretical and practical utility.[32] For Kelsen, whose early work explicitly seeks to translate Vaihinger's philosophy of fiction into the realm of legal theory, we can likewise construct what we might call a *Politische Theologie des als-ob*, a political theology of the as-if, that converts the kind of archaic political theological dreams of origin in which fathers kill sons and sons kill fathers into useful legal fictions that protect rather than destroy the rule-based liberal democratic state.[33] If Kelsen found one dimension of the father's dream about killing his sons particularly compelling, revealingly, it was this professor of economics' businesslike instruction to put their dead bodies in the icebox as if they could be cryogenically suspended and brought back to life later. "I'll take them out again later," is how Kelsen later interprets this request, "and then I'll use them again!" (Später werd' ich sie wieder herausnehmen, werd "ich dann wieder vonn Ihnen Gebrauch machen!"][34] In his own theater of sovereignty, Kelsen will, so to speak, seek to preserve political theology's corpse in the icebox of fiction, so that he can use it again for his own purposes.

If Kelsen's postwar political theology of the as-if can be encapsulated in a single project, it is the attempt to redescribe the political theological persons of God, leader, and state as nothing more than heuristic fictional devices that enable the citizen to better navigate what is, in his own neo-Kantian jurisprudence, the wholly impersonal, freestanding, and self-referential complex of norms that make up the legal state: God still has a role to play in the new liberal state, in Kelsen's verdict, so long as no one actually believes in Him. It will be the special task of Freud's Massenpsychologie to inoculate this new fictional political theology against the very real threat of what Vaihinger, following Kant's famous discussion of the paralogisms of pure reason in the First Critique, calls "hypostasis": "man's natural tendency," he writes, "is to take his thought for the direct expression of reality and to see in the forms of thought forms of existence."[35] As Kant famously argues, our ideas of pure reason (God, soul, will) are permanently at risk of being erroneously hypostatized into real persons or entities, and Kelsen will extend the very same classic critique of the transcental illusions of metaphysics into legal theory: what begin as nothing more than innocent legal fiction, which tautologically repeat or redouble a norm in the form of an imaginary empirical object like a person, are all too easily hypostatized into real empirical entities that are taken to exist independently of, and to predetermine, the norm. To turn in more detail to his "Conception of the State and Social Psychology," for example, Kelsen contends that Gustave Le Bon's original crowd theory falls into the cardinal error of hypostatizing "the crowd," which is nothing more than the sum or aggregate of the individual psychologies that comprise it, into a real entity with a group mind or psyche of its own. Yet what attracts Kelsen to Freud's *Massenpsychologie* in his recently published *Group Psychology and the Analysis of the Ego* is that "the phenomena of the so-called group mind" are revealed, contra Le Bon, to be nothing more than "manifestations of the individual mind."[36] By returning this collective psychological fantasy of the state to its primal scene in individual psychology, Kelsen argues, Freud "rends the veil of the hypostatized 'collective psyche.' "[37] For Kelsen, Freud's *Massenpsychologie* reverse-engineers the hypostases endemic to contemporary theories of state formation from Le Bon to Durkheim, which are all deemed guilty of presupposing some kind of real psychological or sociological entity like the crowd or society to be the organic "cause" of the legal order, back into what the former calls "makeshift" fictions that have been created solely "for purposes of illustration and simplification (abbreviation)."[38] In the final sentence of his essay, Kelsen thus assigns Freud the propaedeutic task of preparing the ground for his own *Staatsbegriffe*: "Freud's psychological analysis has rendered an inestimable preparatory service" to his own pure theory of law, he concludes, "by resolving into their individual psychological elements the hypostatizations of God, society and the state, equipped as they are with all the magic of their centuries-old terminology."[39]

In the aftermath of his philosophical encounter with Freud, however, Kelsen's political theology of the as-if would ironically find *itself* accused of magically becoming a real political theology in the very text that defines the field for the first time: Carl Schmitt's *Political Theology: Four Essays on Sovereignty* (*Politische Theologie. Vier Kapitel zur Lehre von der Souveränität*, 1922). It is well known that Schmitt's essay, which was published in the same year as Kelsen's own "God and the State" ("Gott und Staat," 1922), poses what we might call a neo-Hegelian challenge to the neo-Kantian theory of the state: Schmitt claims that Kelsen's pure theory of law is nothing more than an empty formalism (as Hegel had once famously claimed of Kant's *Moralität*) which requires a sovereign political decision to give it concrete actuality. At the same time, however, I do not think it has been properly recognized until now that the German jurist (who had himself written a positive review of Vaihinger's *Die Philosophie des Als Ob* in the *Deutsche Juristen-Zeitung* almost ten years earlier) is also presenting an obscure immanent critique of the Austrian legal theorist's neo-Kantianism, which, ironically, accuses it of not being Kantian *enough*: Kelsen fails to learn the very lesson he seeks to teach by confusing political theological fiction for reality.[40] To realize the normative legal unity of the state in the world without appealing to any preexisting real ground in psychology or sociology, Schmitt contends that Kelsen's political theology of the as-if is effectively left with no other option than to perform an act of *self-hypostatization* that turns the norm itself into a really-existing unity. "As if speaking time and time again of uninterrupted unity and order would make them the most obvious things in the world," Schmitt ironically parrots the Vaihingerian language of the "as if" back at Kelsen, "as if a fixed harmony existed between the result of free juristic knowledge and the complex that only in political reality constitutes a unity."[41] For Schmitt, Kelsen's rational jurist—who allegedly does nothing more than perceive the objective unity of the law from without— thus ironically becomes a secret personal sovereign who is always taking a series of arbitrary political decisions in the name of a hypostatized unity that does not really exist: "Unity and purity are easily attained, when the basic difficulty is emphatically ignored and when, for formal reasons, everything that contradicts the system is excluded as impure."[42] If Schmitt's *Political Theology* claims that any formal theory of legal unity needs to be grounded in a real and preexisting political unity in order to become law, Freud intriguingly goes on to rehearse a very similar Hegelian critique of Kelsen's pure theory of law from his own vantage point in *The Ego and the Id* (*Das Ich und das Es*, 1923).[43] Freud's theory of the superego (*das Über-Ich*) establishes an unconscious psychic "tribunal" inside the subject, Étienne Balibar has compellingly argued, that allows Kelsen's otherwise empty system of legal norms to be concretized or actualized.[44] Perhaps most importantly, however, Balibar goes on to contend that Freud's superego does not thus finally supply the pure theory of law with the—real or fictional—ground it always required to exist in the world but rather exposes that theory to a radical and antinomian *groundlessness*: what Kelsen sees as the ideal Kantian figure of the rational jurist who disinterestedly describes the law from outside, and Schmitt describes as the personalist sovereign creating law via their decisions, is now reimagined by Freud as the notoriously cruel and despotic figure of the superego issuing contradictory and unfulfillable commandments (You ought to be like your father! You mustn't be like your father!) that can never be realized by the subject as law. Finally, Kelsen is once again left with no alternative but to embrace an arbitrary act of sovereign self-hypostatization if he wishes to realize his allegedly "pure" theory of law in the world. "What this signifies, I think, is that the juridical order envisaged from a psychoanalytic perspective is, strictly speaking, 'groundless,'" Balibar concludes, "and that one can really no longer act 'as if' it had a ground, unless one were to *believe in a fiction* or to 'realize' this fiction, which is indeed a form of myth or of illusion."[45] In Freud's Massentheater, where bad dreams come true, fictional fathers become real ones, and the political theology of the as-if becomes just another violent political theology, Kelsen's theory of a state ruled by nothing but the rules themselves ironically ends up becoming indistinguishable from a state ruled by a capricious, greedy, personal sovereign: Ubu.[46]

UBU-ESQUE

In the opening session of his 1974–1975 lecture course at the Collège de France, Abnormal (2003), Michel Foucault speaks briefly of something he calls "Ubu-esque" sovereignty.[47] It goes without saying, of course, that Foucault is one of the most persistent modern theorists of the theatricality of power. As many scholars have observed, he deploys the stage, spectacle or mise-en-scène as a privileged metaphor for everything from the public execution of the regicide Robert-François Damiens in *Discipline and Punish* (1975) to the theatrical practice of raison d'état in *Security, Territory, Population* (2008). Yet, in contrast to his readings of Shakespeare, say, Foucault's brief and elliptical comments on Jarry have attracted little attention. To call someone or something "Ubu-esque," Foucault observes, we are not simply indulging in puerile name-calling (the term has entered French dictionaries as a synonym for "ludicrous") but rather naming "a precise category of historico-political analysis."⁴⁸ "Political power," he says, "can give itself, and has actually given itself, the possibility of conveying its effects and, even more, of finding their source, in a place that is manifestly, explicitly, and readily discredited as odious, despicable, or ridiculous."⁴⁹ For Foucault, the Ubu effect seems to consist precisely in a hyperbolization of the theatrical *effect* or effects of power at the expense of the diminishment of the person of the sovereign who is the alleged real "cause" of that power: "Ubu-esque terror, grotesque sovereignty," he contends, is "the maximization of effects of power on the basis of the disqualification of the one who produces them."⁵⁰ If the proper name "Ubu" may well appear to signify a grotesque malfunction or inoperativity in the smooth-running machinery of power, Foucault argues (and his metaphor is not coincidental) that it is an integral cog in that machine whose working can be traced from Pierre Clastres's anthropological studies of tribal societies in South America, through Shakespearean royal tragedies, all the way back to figures like Nero or Marcus Aurelius Antoninus in ancient Rome. In a lecture course delivered the year before he will begin to map the historical transition from sovereignty to governmentality in *Society Must Be Defended*, however, Foucault goes on to observe that *Ubu roi* also captures something of the peculiar theatricality of *modern* political power.

To pursue the "-esque" of Foucault's own Ubu-esque a little further, what is modern about this political theatrical gesture is less the delegitimization of power—via the revelation of the utter inadequacy of the sovereign—so much as power's depersonalization and automatization into a system that operates entirely independently of its holder. "I do not think that explicitly showing power to be abject, despicable, Ubu-esque or simply ridiculous is a way of limiting its effects and of magically dethroning the person to whom one gives the crown," he contends, but is rather "a way of giving a striking form of expression to the unavoidability, the inevitability of power, which can function in its full rigor and at the extreme point of its rationality even when in the hands of someone who is effectively discredited."[51] It is thus perfectly possible to see the Ubu-esque—for all its pseudo-Shakespearean trappings—as a symptom of the broader historical transition from premodern absolutist sovereignty to modern liberal constitutional sovereignty in which the monarch becomes a mere placeholder. After all, nothing could dramatize the liberal constitutional difference between the person and the office more clearly than a manifestly unfit person who, nonetheless, becomes a legitimate leader. If the Ubu-esque is an essential cog in the machine of sovereignty, it is thus because it reveals that modern power is *itself* a machine whose privileged representative is neither the capricious Roman emperor, nor even the dutiful constitutional monarch, but the faceless bureaucrat or functionary who is tasked with keeping the wheels of power turning: "Since the nineteenth century," Foucault observes, "an essential feature of big Western bureaucracies has been that the administrative machine, with its unavoidable effects of power, works by using the mediocre, useless, imbecilic, superficial, ridiculous, worn-out, poor and powerless functionary."[52] In Foucault's verdict, Ubu's omnipresent toilet brush is thus less a parody of a royal scepter than of a bureaucrat's pen: "Ubu the 'pen-pusher' is a functional component of modern administration, just as being in the hands of a mad charlatan was a functional feature of Roman imperial power."[53]

If Foucault's modern sovereign thus appears to be the faceless bureaucratic gatekeeper who protects the alleged majesty of the law from the unwashed masses who vainly seek access to it, however, it is possible to argue that this figure is more Kafkaesque than genuinely Ubu-esque: what I want to propose here instead is that Jarry's play anticipates Foucault's later work on governmentality by exploring what happens when the crowd is actually admitted *through* the juridico-political gate, so to speak, and becomes a population to be biopolitically managed. It is in this later body of work that Foucault—who is obviously no "crowd theorist" in the tradition we have been describing here—begins to diagnose another pathological species of *Massenpolitik* at work in the nineteenth century state, namely, the "swarming" (*l'essaimage*) of disciplinary mechanisms.[54] As with Freud's group psychology and Kelsen's legal formalism, Foucault's theory of the disciplinary society describes an attempt to politically—and, in this case, biopolitically—disaggregate the allegedly monolithic entity or substance called "the crowd" into its constituent parts. To recall his classic discussion of Jeremy Bentham's panopticon in *Discipline and Punish* (1975), a text that was published in the same year he delivered the Abnormal lectures, Foucault revealingly describes Bentham's theoretical prison as an impersonal and automatic institutional machine for molecularizing the collective entity or subject called a crowd into a set of individual, or rather biopolitically *individualized*, subjects. "The crowd [*la foule*], a compact mass, a locus of multiple exchanges, individualities merging together, a collective effect," he observes, "is abolished for the benefit of a collection of separated individualities."[55] Yet what is more remarkable here is that despite Foucault's own claim that the disciplinary society is very different from the classical theater of sovereignty—"our society is one not of spectacle, but of surveillance," he famously writes, "we are neither in the amphitheatre, nor on the stage, but in the panoptic machine"—Bentham's panopticon is recognizably a modern political Massentheater.[56] For Foucault, Bentham's theoretical prison—whose cells are like "so many small theatres [*petits théâtres*], in which each actor [*acteur*] is alone, perfectly individualized and constantly visible"—presides, once again, over the modern theatrical "becoming-audience" of an early modern crowd that is thereby reduced to a silent, docile and obedient series of numbered individuals whose sole vocation is to watch over or surveil their own individuality.[57] In the miniature theater that is Foucault's surveillance society, every subject is both performer and spectator in the one-man show that is themselves.

In yet another curious admission of the critic's defeat in the face of the power of the crowd, Foucault confesses to his audience at the Collège de France that "I have neither the strength, nor the courage" to devote the entire lecture course to the theme of Ubu-esque or grotesque sovereignty, but, of course, this only begs the question of what form such a "strong" reading might take.[58] To be sure, Jarry's play has most frequently been read as a grotesque parody of a classic tyrant who (quite literally) tests the theory of absolute sovereignty to destruction: Père Ubu's reign of terror begins with the wanton annihilation of the entire machinery of government (nobles, magistrates, and bankers), which leaves the new king in the absurd position of having to collect the crown's taxes from the people all by himself. It is equally possible, of course, to see the play as a satire upon popular sovereignty because the vulgar, greedy, and scatological Ubu is recognizably a kind of Demogorgon: a "people-monster." As Nicole Jerr astutely observes, Jarry's antihero—who personally embodies almost every symptom that Le Bon pathologized under the category of the group "mind" just one year earlier—can plausibly be read as a representation of the playwright's own elitist fears of mob rule: Ubu is a kind of one-man crowd.[59] However, I want to briefly propose here that that we can also read Jarry's play not as a Grand Guignol of (absolute or popular) "sovereignty" at all, but of an (equally, if not more, grotesque) governmentality: *Ubu roi* describes a recognizably modern world in which, as unlikely as it may appear, the sober nineteenth century science of political economy trumps the florid excesses of medieval political theology. For the new King of Poland, whose preferred title out of the many he accumulates is "Maître des Financiers," sovereignty immediately takes the economic form of producing a credible "tax and spend" fiscal policy to balance the books. "I want to get rich," Ubu declares upon assuming the throne, but his adviser replies that "if you don't make any distributions, the people won't want to pay their taxes," and so the monarch reluctantly agrees to "assemble three million people and cook a hundred and fifty cows and sheep" (2.6). If Jerr is right to say that "Jarry is not calling attention to the dangers of tyranny but rather pointing to the dangers of a lack of self-governance,"[60] Ubu's response to his own spiraling sovereign debt crisis—"we must be thrifty [*économe*]" (3.1)—is, ironically, that of self-professed "belt-tightening" governments everywhere: a fiscal policy of socialism for the rich (i.e., bailouts for the king and his cronies) and capitalism for the poor in the form of spending cuts and tax rises that effectively impose what Elettra Stimilli calls a "debt of the living" upon his subjects.[61] Perhaps we can already see something of the performative cruelty of neoliberal "austerity" in Ubu's idea that his largesse should not be distributed equally amongst the people but that they should be seen to compete for it in a "beau spectacle": the new king stages a literal race to the bottom amongst the assembled three million in which a single winner takes the lion's share of the money (*Ubu roi*, 2.7). In a final confirmation of Foucault's theory that grotesque sovereignty operates wholly independently of the figure of the sovereign himself, Ubu is eventually forced to flee Poland, but

Jarry's play concludes with him cheerfully planning to export his model of grotesque governmentality to the rest of the continent in what looks like the beginning of an Ubu-esque "European Union": "I'm going to rename myself Master of Finance in Paris" (5.4).

TRUMP(ED)

In drawing this chapter (and this book) to a close, however, I want to return to the opening night of *Ubu roi* and to the lonely figure of W. B. Yeats, standing in the middle of the angry crowd, watching what he believed to be the manifestation of a "Savage God." To recall his own recollection of the event almost twenty-five years later in *The Trembling of the Veil* (1922) once more, Yeats describes himself as a simultaneously awestruck and horrified witness to something that uncannily resembles the "rough beast" slouching toward Bethlehem to be born that he had recently prophesized at the end of his poem "The Second Coming" (1920).[62] If the poet's response to the rough beast in the latter poem is famously ambivalent—does he fear or welcome its imminent messianic judgement?—it is possible to detect something of the same ambivalence in his reaction to the return of Jarry's "Savage God" as well: Yeats's lifelong cultural elitism and contempt for "the mob" would notoriously petrify over the 1920s and 1930s into a valorization of the authoritarian figure of "the leader," admiration for Mussolini as well as support for quasi-fascist groups like the Irish nationalist Blueshirts.[63] In Yeats's conflicted reaction to Jarry's play, we can perhaps detect not only an aesthete's horror at a philistine crowd baying for blood but a political excitement that he may *himself* be one of that crowd—and that he may even share the pathological crowd psychology that Freud had already begun to diagnose just one year earlier in his *Group Psychology and the Analysis of the Ego* (1921). What if Yeats, like all the other members of the crowd, really *wants* to be led by a Savage God?

To enter into what crowd theory calls "the crowd," this chapter has argued that we do not become part of a real organic social or political entity that is bigger than ourselves so much as pass through a theoretical mincing machine that is designed to politically miniaturize or molecularize us: group psychology is an exercise in the production or subjectivation (*assujettissement*), not of the crowd, but that other classic nineteenth century political entity called "the individual". It is the theatrical audience—which is to say a crowd that has been taught that it is *not* a crowd, that knows what it is watching is a fiction, and that (above all) knows how to behave—that becomes crowd theory's privileged model for the political assemblage of free rational individuals in modernity. Yet the story of the becoming-audience of the crowd is not quite the classic liberal narrative in which the collective is superseded by the individual, violent coercion by peaceful consent, and the real presence of a sovereign god or father by the polite fictions of representative democracy. If crowd theory is really a kind of *anti*-crowd theory, which seeks to reverse engineer the collective fantasy called a "crowd" and lay bare the myriad individual psychological energies that create it, this chapter has sought to show that it also betrays the fear or desire that this pathological becoming-crowd of the individual may be irreversible—and may even consume the critical imaginary that seeks to diagnose it. In a tragic or farcical repetition of Yeats's position at the opening of *Ubu roi*, crowd theory's own privileged critical persona—whether it takes the form of Le Bon's theater reviewer, who ends up following mass taste instead of leading it; Kelsen's jurist, who succumbs to the hypostatizations that he is allegedly capable of seeing through; or even Foucault's melancholy genealogist, who lacks the optimism of the will necessary to take on a grotesque sovereignty that is just not funny anymore—finds itself becoming just one more member of the crowd.

If Yeats's response to Jarry reveals the secret anxiety of every critic of so-called mass or popular culture—what if the crowd might, after all, be *right?*—it is possible to find an uncanny echo of this anxiety almost one hundred years later in the art critic Hal Foster's essay "Père Trump" (2020), which explores the dilemma of another critic, in the middle of another angry crowd, in front of another Ubu-esque sovereign.[64] It is hardly surprising, of course, that an "Ubu Trump" meme went viral after the arrival of what many took to be another vulgar, childlike, and obscenity-spouting sovereign upon the political stage to, so to speak, thunderous applause from the stalls and howls of disapproval from the balcony. Yet what distinguishes Foster's essay from the crowd is that it is not actually a meditation on Donald Trump himself, nor even on his legions of die-hard followers, but rather upon the beleaguered figure of the Trump(ed) *critic*. To recall Foster's own very Yeatsian hypothesis in his collection *What Comes After Farce?* (2020), what the aspiring critic of the post-Trumpian world order must address today is the dispiriting fact that we do not simply live in a post-truth epoch but in a *post-shame* one that has completely destroyed the moral and intellectual high ground traditionally occupied by critique itself. "How to demystify a hegemonic order that dismisses its own contradictions?" he asks. "How to belittle a political elite that cannot be embarrassed, or to mock party leaders who thrive on the absurd? How to out-dada a president whose prototype seems to be the child monster Père Ubu of Alfred Jarry?"[65] In order to explain Trump's seemingly indestructible popularity in the face of critique, Foster revealingly even returns to Freud's own explorations of *Massenpsychologie* and, in particular, to the primal horde's desire for its primal father: "And so, we have a celebrity president ('when you're a star you can do anything') as throwback primal father (the bully-in-chief), and there are legions of white guys who want to be his apprentices."[66]

In the age of Trump, though, I want to conclude by proposing that the critic *himself* (who is demographically still more likely than not, lest we forget, to belong to "the legions of white guys" described by Foster) perhaps also cannot help but become one of the primal father's psychic apprentices—even or especially when they want to kill him. It is sobering to recall here that the opening night of *Ubu roi* was not in fact the play's premiere at all but its *répétition générale*, dress rehearsal and press night—and so the rioting crowd consisted predominantly of newspaper reviewers and other theater industry professionals.[67] As this audience of critics would have seen, Jarry's play is not just a parody of the tyrannical sovereign but of the crowds of independent authorities or experts (lawyers, economists and, yes, critics) who allegedly possess the privilege to speak truth to power but whose positions are all simply commandeered by Ubu himself: "See, that's what I call erudition!" is how Ubu's wife, Mère Ubu, replies to one of her husband's many absurd pseudointellectual boasts of scholarly expertise (5.4). To answer the question of why Trump and his fellow Ubu-esque sovereigns—who themselves, needless to say, often have a professional background in the media, television or newspaper industries—appear to be so impenetrable to critique, I thus want to end by hypothesizing that, in addition to the many other reasons with which we are overfamiliar, it is because they have put, not just the crowd, but the *critic* "onstage" as part of their act. For Trump and company, just as we saw in the case of Jarry, we spectators are free to cheer or boo, laugh or scorn, praise or blame in equal measure—so long as we continue to pay unemancipated attention. If Foster's lament seems to be that critique has no effect whatsoever upon the grotesque spectacle of the Ubu-esque, for instance, the situation is arguably even more grotesque than he claims: the mainstream American media's (pathological?) inability *to stop talking about Trump*, to stop talking about his unfitness for office, stop talking about his moral culpability or alleged criminality, even stop talking about why it should stop talking about him and "move on" to something better or higher instead, is now generally recognized to have been itself a decisive factor in his rise to popularity. Perhaps more disturbingly, though, we might speculate that the American media's very commitment

FIGURE 7.2 Mr. Fish, "Reign of Idiots" (2017). Photomontage. © the artist.

to "critique" itself—which is to say to, among other things, an ethic of balance, impartiality, and the reporting of "both sides" of the argument—plays into the hands of someone who was not simply the first "post-truth" or "post-shame" but (with apologies to Rita Felski) also arguably the first *post-critical* president.[68] What need is there for the media establishment's earnest cult of "bothsidesism," after all, when Trump himself is able to go one better (or rather worse) by declaring that "there are some very fine people on both sides" during the standoff between white supremacists and antifascists at Charlottesville in 2017?[69] In the figure of the fatally trumped critic, whose very claim to critical emancipation from the spectacle turns out to be the purest form of unemancipated spectatorship, we may thus find the logical conclusion of Jarry's century-old attempt to put the crowd on stage: every spectator in the Massentheater, even or especially the theater critic themselves, will be absorbed into what Jean Baudrillard once called "the system's claim to perfect sphericity (Ubu Roi's belly)."[70]

CONCLUSION
In the Empty Space

I can take any empty space and call it a bare stage. A man walks across this empty space whilst someone else is watching him, and this is all that is needed for an act of theatre to be engaged. Yet when we talk about theatre this is not quite what we mean.
—Peter Brook, *The Empty Space*

In his classic book *The Empty Space* (1968), the renowned director Peter Brook offers what has, for better or worse, become our single most influential modern definition of "theater." To briefly recall the opening of this famous manifesto, Brook reimagines the play space as a radical theatrical tabula rasa where, apparently, any place in which any human being does anything whatsoever can instantly become a "stage." If postwar English commercial theater of the 1950s and 1960s existed on a decadent and cluttered stage of "red curtains, spotlights, blank verse, laughter, darkness," as the director disdainfully recalls, Brook's own ideal stage is, by contrast, a kind of stripped-down modernist antitheater that is reminiscent of the blank, abstract, or minimalist tableau of, say, a Samuel Beckett drama, a Mark Rothko painting, or a John Cage composition.[1]

In this empty space—which is nothing in itself, because it must be re-created and re-invented each time in every performance—we encounter nothing less than the "truth" of theater: "Truth in the theatre is always on the move," Brook concludes. "In the theatre the slate is wiped clean all the time."[2]

To draw this book to a close, I want to propose that Brook's celebrated theory of the theater may well constitute something like the modern equivalent to Plato's allegory of the cave with which we began: what the former calls the "empty space" of the modernist theater is nothing less than modernity's own theater of sovereignty. If this book has had a governing hypothesis, after all, it is that the story of modern political theory is the story of the progressive kenosis or emptying out of the space of power: Claude Lefort famously concludes, as we saw in the introduction, that modern liberal democracy is the only political system to have represented power as an "empty place" (*lieu vide*).[3] In many ways, Brook's own antitheatrical theory of theater represents an aesthetic equivalent to this antitheatrical theory of the political: what he calls the "empty space" is nowhere, belongs to no one, and thus can be occupied by anyone.

If post-Hobbesian political thought frequently presents or represents itself as a kind of political antitheater that strips away the old metaphysical architecture of premodern politics from the stage of history like so much superfluous clutter, this book has nonetheless tried to contend that the allegedly empty space of modern political theory remains a kind of theater—or metatheater—of sovereignty. To supersede the old, restricted economy of representation, which circulated around the apparently real political theological presence of the sovereign person, I have sought to demonstrate that modern political theory instead institutes, whether by accident or design, its own new general economy of political representation in which a pure or empty machine of representability itself increasingly becomes "sovereign."[4] In Brook's theory of theater, recall, an empty space is not really an "antitheater" at all, but the single most theatrical space imaginable, because it can represent anything whatsoever.

In this conclusion, I thus want to argue that Brook's own apparently transparent, horizontal, and democratic antitheater also remains a theater of sovereignty, which, like its political equivalent, contains its own obscure violence. To the naked eye, what Brook calls the "empty space" may well seem to be a Lefortian democratic empty space, which can be occupied by anyone whatsoever because it belongs to no one, but it can equally be seen as a kind of open field or playground for the exercise of a personal sovereign power. It is, after all, verbally summoned into being ex nihilo by a sovereign or performative speech act that is equivalent to the voice of God in Genesis 1:3: "*I can take* any empty space and *call it* a bare stage" (emphasis mine). At the same time, this performative gesture is predicated upon the precarious assumption that the empty space is indeed completely empty—which is to say devoid of any indigenous, autochthonic people, history, or tradition of its own—before the theatrical sovereign arrives on the scene to perform his magic. For Brook, of course, what really matters in this mise-en-scène is not what the empty space is, was, or may have been in the past, but rather what we can make and re-make it into in a seemingly infinite future—namely, a "bare stage." In the closing pages of his book, Brook even argues that this revolutionary call to "make it new" is itself inevitably becoming out-of-date from the very moment it is put into writing, but despite or rather because of its planned disposability or obsolescence, I suspect that what he calls the "empty space" may, in fact, be more politically timely than ever. What if this modernist manifesto for a creative and destructive power which can transform any real space into a virtual site of inexhaustible fungibility, performativity, or productivity has ironically become a panegyric for the *theatrum politicum* of postmodern neoliberalism?

IN THE MARKETPLACE

In order to explore why Brook's antitheater becomes a new theater of sovereignty, we need only explore the theatrical fate of the "empty space" itself over the last fifty years. To start with, of course, Brook's apparently simple idea that "I can take any empty space and call it a bare stage" led the director to a succession of groundbreaking modernist productions in the postwar era that reinvented Shakespeare, among others, as a contemporary of Artaud, Beckett, and Ionesco: Brook's *Romeo and Juliet* (1947) and *King Lear* (1962) were performed on largely bare or open stages, devoid of elaborate props, scenery, or costumes, whereas his famous *A Midsummer Night's Dream* (1970) was staged, not within some pastoral idyll, but inside a simple white cube or box. If Brook's dramaturgy undoubtedly revolutionized theater for generations of practitioners around the world, its apparently innocent claim that we can turn any empty space into a bare stage has increasingly met with criticism that it reproduces the classic colonial logic whereby every space is assumed to be physically, culturally, or politically empty unless or until the colonist comes to occupy it. In the aftermath of his 1985 production of the Sanskrit epic the *Mahabharata*, as we will see momentarily, Brook's theory of the empty space was effectively accused of presiding over an act of political and economic *emptying-out*—which is to say of cultural amnesia, erasure, or even neoliberal creative destruction—that produced the very tabula rasa it claimed to innocently discover.

To explore the political fate of the empty space, we might next turn to Ngũgĩ wa Thiong'o's play *I Will Marry When I Want* (*Ngaahika Ndeenda*, 1977, cowritten with Ngũgĩ wa Mirii) which was first performed to an audience of some ten thousand people at a newly built open-air theater in the Kamĩrĩĩthũ Community Education and Cultural Centre in Kenya in 1977. It is now well documented that Ngũgĩ's objective in staging this play was to begin the work of liberating indigenous Kenyan theater from the bourgeois theatrical conventions imposed by British colonial rule and reestablishing links with traditional ritual and ceremony but, intriguingly, he also narrates its performance as an attempt to reoccupy a precolonial "empty space." As Ngũgĩ makes clear in his classic *Decolonising the Mind* (1986), indigenous Kenyan theater consisted of collective popular rituals and ceremonies that could "take place anywhere—wherever there was an 'empty space,' to borrow the phrase from Peter Brook."[5] For Ngũgĩ, British colonial rule in Kenya contrastingly attempted "to destroy the concept of the 'empty space' among the people by trying to capture it within government-supervised urban community halls, schoolhalls, church buildings, and in actual theatre buildings with the proscenium stage."[6] By building a new open-air community theater that could accommodate some ten thousand people in the village of Kamĩrĩĩthũ, Ngũgĩ and his creative collaborators were thus both literally and symbolically seeking to return to the "empty space" of Kenyan indigenous theater: "For instance, there was an actual empty space at Kamĩrĩĩthũ [where the theater could be built]."[7]

If Ngũgĩ sees his own anticolonial theatrical project as an attempt to operationalize Brook's own theory of theater—which also defined itself in opposition to an established bourgeois, private, and, indeed, "English" theatrical status quo—it is clear, however, that that he means something very different from the latter when he speaks of indigenous Kenyan theater as an "empty space." To take an empty space and call it a "bare stage" in Kenya, as he literally did when he built the Kamĩrĩĩthũ Community Education and Cultural Centre, Ngũgĩ was not attempting "to start again" with something radically new, like Brook, but rather to reoccupy what he saw as a living, if oppressed, national tradition:

> Kamĩrĩĩthũ then was not an aberration, but an attempt at reconnection with the broken roots of African civilization and its traditions of theater. In its very location in a village within the kind of social classes described above, Kamĩrĩĩthũ was the answer to the question of the real substance of a national theater. Theater is not a building. People make theater. Their life is the very stuff of drama. Indeed Kamĩrĩĩthũ reconnected itself to the national tradition of the empty space, of language, of content and of form.[8]

For Ngũgĩ, what defines the empty space of Kenyan national theater is thus not Brook's formless and contentless antitheater, but something closer to the excess or overflowing of a living theater that cannot be contained within any single institution or organization. In "Enactments of Power: The Politics of Performance Space" (1997), an essay published some twenty years after the original performance of *Ngaahika Ndeenda*, Ngũgĩ finally delivers a negative verdict upon Brook's theory, in which the latter is implicitly criticized for emptying out the performance space into a kind of ahistorical vacuum. "Is a performance site ever empty, as in the title of Brook's book?" he asks, before answering: "The performance space is never empty. Bare, yes, open, yes, but never empty. It is always the site of physical, social and psychic forces in society."[9]

In his 1997 critique of Brook's empty place, Ngũgĩ was participating in a growing critical reaction against the former's work that, as I have already suggested, came to a head with his theater company's controversial adaptation of the *Mahabharata* (1985). To quickly rehearse this famous or notorious episode in his career, Brook's nine-hour production of the Sanskrit epic sought to capture what in a contemporary interview with Georges Banu he called a certain "universality" in the original text that, he believed, transcended its original cultural and historical context: "We are telling a story which, on the one hand, is universal, but, on the other, would never have existed without India. To tell this story, we had to avoid allowing the suggestion of India to be so strong as to inhibit human identification to too great an extent, while at the same time telling it as a story with its roots in the earth of India."[10] It will be no surprise to learn, though, that Brook's "universal" version of the *Mahabharata*—which was performed on a largely bare stage; cut or condensed significant scenes, dialogue, and characters from the original text; and entirely omitted the Hindu philosophy without which the narrative scarcely makes sense—almost immediately faced charges of orientalism. According to the Indian theater scholar Rustom Bharucha, who saw the play on Broadway, Brook's interpretation of the *Mahabharata* was predicated upon a false opposition between universalism and particularity that risked depriving indigenous Indians their own right to identify as universally "human." "One cannot agree with the premise that, 'The *Mahabharata* is Indian but it is universal,'" Bharucha writes. "The 'but' is misleading. The *Mahabharata*, I would counter, is universal *because* it is Indian."[11] If Brook rejected the criticism that his theater only enacted or performed a very particular "Western" concept of universality, it is thus all the more surprising to see him turn to another—highly overdetermined—universal metaphor for his theatrical universe in which people, labor, goods, and services circulate freely: "Theatre is not a lecture, theatre is not a religious ritual, theatre is not a sermon," he tells David Britton in a contemporary interview, *"Theater is something happening in the market place."*[12] For Brook, what began as a theater of the empty space this ironically ends up becoming (as Bharucha once again notes of the Broadway playhouse in which the *Mahabharata* production was staged) a theater of the free market in every sense of the term:

> This "natural" vista is framed within the elaborate proscenium of the Majestic Theater, an 84-year-old vaudeville and opera house, which was abandoned many years ago and then remodelled for the *Mahabharata* production. Millions of dollars were spent not just to renovate the theater, but to retain its omnipotence of decay. Chloe Obolensky's ambitious design extends to the entire auditorium, where artistically preserved disfigurements and patches of brick on the wall enhance the antique aura on stage.[13]

In a kind of theatrical equivalent to what Joseph Schumpeter famously calls capitalism's logic of "creative destruction" (*schöpferische Zerstörung*), Brook's *Mahabharata* thus does not simply empty out a preexisting historical space, but even goes to the length of painstakingly restoring that space to its former glory, purely so that it can then be transformed into an empty space.[14] "Only the "West' could afford to renovate a theatre," Bharucha concludes, "and then spend more money to make it look old again."[15]

IN THE SOVEREIGNTY OF THEATER

In this book, I have sought to describe the passage from what we might call a "theater of sovereignty," in which a real or personal sovereign is the first or principal political representative, to a "sovereignty of theater" in which the allegedly pure or empty space of representability itself takes center stage. To stage this political drama, chapter 1 began by mapping out the democratic kenosis or emptying-out of the (already empty) throne of Christ; chapter 2 tracked how holy oil becomes the elixir of a pure, contentless, and all-purpose performativity that bestows legitimacy on any surface it touches; chapter 3 teased out the baroque inexplicability (i.e., the impossibility of being unfolded) of the curtain that veils the political sanctum sanctorum; chapter 4 performed the political long division of the sovereign's chamber of power into an infinite series of antechambers; chapter 5 exposed the fact that there is nothing, not even the naked body, underneath the emperor's new clothes; and chapter 6 staged the uncreaturely becoming-puppet or marionette of the allegedly sovereign creature. Finally, chapter 7 explored the transformation of the popular crowd into a kind of misplaced or free-floating theatrical audience that had mistaken the play for real life. In Peter Brook's theory of theater, where nothing is represented but representation itself, what I have called the sovereignty of theater assumes its definitive—empty—form.

To rehearse each of these—apparently singular, contingent, and improvised—scenes one last time, we witness something like the same script playing itself out differently: a privileged "prop" or property, which bespeaks of a specific political lifeworld (e.g., thrones, veils, holy oil, regalia, chambers), is progressively converted into a fungible token of universal equivalence; a particular political theological medium of making-present (Greek or Christian natural law theory, divine right, or popular sovereignty, sovereign personalism et al.) is absorbed into an entirely generalized representational economy that ultimately represents nothing but itself; and, finally, a real and historical stage (which was originally occupied by gods, kings, or peoples) is transformed into the empty space of a pure or absolute performativity. In this very modern form of political thaumaturgy, all that is solid melts into theater.

If we ask what exactly this new theater of sovereignty might still hide or obscure from us—its principal political players—then modern political theory's answer from Hobbes to Lefort would, of course, be "nothing." To enter the brilliantly lit empty space called "political modernity," we leave behind forever the shadowy Platonic cave in which tyrannical puppet masters had imprisoned us in order to prevent us seeing the light of truth and apparently submit to nothing more coercive or violent than the bare antitheatrical or metatheatrical representation of representability. However, it is precisely this new general economy of representation, in which there is nothing to see but seeing itself, that may be the real political violence hiding in plain sight here. In the empty space of modern neoliberal democracy, what remains fundamentally obscure is the simple fact *that there is no such thing as an empty space*: every apparently empty space has been emptied, more or less violently, of its original occupants.

In its own final scene, what I have called the "theater of sovereignty" is thus revealed to be a modern political equivalent to Antonin Artaud's Theatre of Cruelty, albeit without any of the latter's compensatory possibility of catharsis.[16] To turn the allegedly empty space of history into the gloriously bare stage of political modernity, recall, this theater presides over a bloody Grand-Guignol climax in which everyone and everything must die. If the theater of sovereignty we have observed in this book is the story of the becoming-empty of politics, after all, it has also been the story of royal and republican decapitations, beheadings or executions (Shakespeare, Milton, Cervantes, Jarry, Valéry); governmental or bureaucratic deaths of a thousand cuts (Schiller, Benjamin, Foucault); political theological sadism, masochism, and torture (Kafka, Genet, Bacon); ecological extraction, evisceration, and disembowelment (Melville, Ionesco); ontological shame, abjection, or abasement (Benjamin, Kafka); existential laying-waste, devastation, and apocalypse (Cervantes, Jarry, Ionesco); libidinal suicide, castration, and self-mutilation (Melville, Valéry, Genet) and, finally, neoliberal creative destruction (Brook). In the theater of sovereignty, the peace of the empty space is the peace of the grave.

NOTES

INTRODUCTION

This epigraph is taken from Plato, *The Republic*, book 7, trans. Paul Shorey, in *The Collected Dialogues*, ed. Edith Hamilton and Huntington Cairns, 575–845, 514c (Princeton, N.J.: Princeton University Press, 1961).

1. See Jean Przyluski, "Le Théâtre d'Ombres et la Caverne de Platon," *Byzantion: Revue Internationale des Études Byzantines* 13 (1938): 595–603; Asli Gocer, "The Puppet Theater in Plato's Parable of the Cave," *Classical Journal* 95, no. 2 (December 1999—January 2000): 119–29; and Chiara Cappelletto, "The Puppet's Paradox: An Organic Prosthesis," *RES* 59–60 (Spring–Autumn, 2011): 325–36 for readings of Plato's allegory of the cave to which I am indebted.
2. Plato, *Republic*, 514a3.
3. Plato, 514a3.515c.
4. Plato, 601b.
5. Plato, *Laws*, trans. A. E. Taylor, in *The Collected Dialogues*, ed. Edith Hamilton and Huntington Cairns, 1225–516, 701a (Princeton, N.J.: Princeton University Press, 1961).
6. See Jessica Lightfoot, *Wonders and the Marvellous from Homer to the Hellenistic World* (Cambridge: Cambridge University Press, 2021) for a discussion of Plato and *thauma*.
7. Plato, *Theaetetus*, trans. F. M. Cornford, in *The Collected Dialogues*, ed. Edith Hamilton and Huntington Cairns, 845–919, 155d (Princeton, N.J.: Princeton University Press, 1961).

8. See Philippe Lacoue-Labarthe, "Typography," trans. Eduardo Cadava, in *Typography: Mimesis, Philosophy, Politics*, ed. Christopher Fynsk and intr. Jacques Derrida (Stanford, Calif.: Stanford University Press, 1998), 43–138, 92. In Lacoue-Labarthe's words, *"The theoretical itself is placed 'en abyme'"* (emphasis in original).
9. See Martin Heidegger, *The Essence of Truth: On Plato's Cave Allegory and Theaetetus*, trans. Ted Sadler (London: Bloomsbury, 2013) for arguably the most influential modern reading of Plato's allegory of the cave that offers a theory of truth as not the contemplation of fixed and unchanging Forms but as a process of unconcealment or *aletheia*.
10. Simon Critchley, *Tragedy, the Greeks, and Us* (New York: Profile, 2019), 6. See also Christian Meier, *The Greek Discovery of Politics*, trans. David McLintock (Cambridge, Mass.: Harvard University Press, 1990); Jean-Pierre Vernant and Pierre Vidal-Naquet, *Myth and Tragedy in Ancient Greece*, trans. Janet Lloyd (New York: Zone, 1990); and J. Peter Euben, *The Tragedy of Political Theory: The Road Not Taken* (Princeton, N.J.: Princeton University Press, 1990) for influential discussions of the relation between Greek tragedy and Greek politics.
11. To be sure, a very large secondary literature now exists on the intimate proximity between sovereignty and theatricality whether by political theorists, philosophers, historians, anthropologists, or literary critics. See the following for a range of influential modern and contemporary perspectives to which I am indebted: Stephen Greenblatt, *Renaissance Self-Fashioning: From More to Shakespeare* (Chicago: University of Chicago Press, 1980); Victor Turner, *From Ritual to Theater: The Human Seriousness of Play* (New York: PAJ, 1982); Louis Marin, *Portrait of the King*, trans. Martha M. Houle, foreword by Tom Conley (London: Macmillan, 1988); Peter Burke, *The Fabrication of Louis XIV* (New Haven, Conn.: Yale University Press, 1992); Jacques Taminiaux, *Le Théâtre des philosophes: La tragédie, l'être, l'action* (Grenoble: Jérôme Millon 1995); Jacques Rancière, "From Archipolitics to Metapolitics," in *Disagreement: Politics and Philosophy*, trans. Julie Rose (Minneapolis: University of Minnesota Press, 1998), 61–94; Paul Friedland, *Political Actors: Representative Bodies and Theatricality in the French Revolution* (Ithaca, N.Y.: Cornell University Press, 2002); Samuel Weber, *Theatricality as Medium* (New York: Fordham University Press, 2004);

Eric L. Santner, *The Royal Remains: The People's Two Bodies and the Endgames of Sovereignty* (Chicago: University of Chicago Press, 2011); Zvi Ben-Dor Benite, Stefanos Geroulanos and Nicole Jerr, eds., *The Scaffolding of Sovereignty: Global and Aesthetic Perspectives on the History of a Concept* (New York: Columbia University Press, 2017); and Jason Frank, *The Democratic Sublime: On Aesthetics and Popular Assembly* (Cambridge: Cambridge University Press, 2021).

12. See here Marc Bloch's classic *The Royal Touch* [*Les rois thaumaturges. Étude sur le caractère surnaturel attribué à la puissance royale particulièrement en France et en Angleterre*] (London: Routledge and Kegan Paul, 1973).

13. Jonas Barish, *The Anti-Theatrical Prejudice* (Berkeley: University of California Press, 1981).

14. Paul A. Kottman, *A Politics of the Scene* (Stanford, Calif.: Stanford University Press, 2008). In what follows, I am indebted to Kottman's reading of Hobbes.

15. "September 1642: Order for Stage-Plays to Cease," in *Acts and Ordinances of the Interregnum, 1642–1660*, ed. C. H. Firth and R. S. Rait (London: n.p., 1911), 26–27.

16. Hannah Arendt, *The Human Condition* (Chicago: University of Chicago Press, 1958), 188.

17. Thomas Hobbes, *Leviathan: Or The Matter, Forme, and Power of a Common Wealth Ecclesiasticall and Civil* (Cambridge: Cambridge University Press, 1996), 112.

18. Kottman, *Politics of the Scene*, 55.

19. See Christopher Pye, "The Sovereign, the Theater, and the Kingdome of Darknesse: Hobbes and the Spectacle of Power," *Representations* 8 (1984): 84–106; David Runciman, *Pluralism and the Personality of the State* (Cambridge: Cambridge University Press, 1997); and Mónica Brito Vieira, *The Elements of Representation in Hobbes: Aesthetics, Theater, Law, and Theology in the Construction of Hobbes's Theory of the State* (Leiden: Brill, 2009) for readings of Hobbes and theatrical representation to which I am indebted.

20. Kottman, *Politics of the Scene*, 64. In acknowledging the heuristic or fictional status of Hobbes's state of nature, Kottman is placing himself within a reading of Hobbes that goes back to at least Jean-Jacques

Rousseau's "Discourse on the Origin and Foundations of Inequality Amongst Men," in *The Discourses and Other Early Political Writings*, ed. Victor Gourevitch (Cambridge: Cambridge University Press, 1997), 1:111–231.

21. Thomas Hobbes, *The Citizen* in *Man and Citizen [De Homine and De Cive]*, ed. Bernard Gert (Indianapolis: Hackett, 1991), 98–99; emphasis mine. In his reading of this scene, Giorgio Agamben also argues that the Hobbesian state of nature is not chronologically or ontologically antecedent to society but a principle internal to the Commonwealth: "Exteriority—the law of nature and the principle of the preservation of one's own life—is truly the innermost center of the system." See Giorgio Agamben, *Homo Sacer: Sovereign Power and Bare Life*, trans. Daniel Heller-Roazen (Stanford, Calif.: Stanford University Press, 1998), 36.

22. See Carl Schmitt, *Romanticism and Political Form*, trans. Gary L. Ulman (Westport, Conn.: Greenwood, 1996) for the classic study of this theory of representation.

23. See here William Egginton, *How the World Became a Stage: Presence, Theatricality, and the Question of Modernity* (Albany: State University of New York Press, 2002) for a powerful account of the passage from a premodern Christian and incarnationalist theatricality to a modern, neutral, and theoretical theatrical space which culminates with what Heidegger famously calls the age of the "world-picture [*Weltbildes*]."

24. James VI and I, *Basilikon Doron* in *Political Writings*, ed. J. P. Sommerville (Cambridge: Cambridge University Press, 1994), 49.

25. Carl Schmitt, *The Leviathan in the State Theory of Thomas Hobbes: Meaning and Failure of a Political Symbol*, trans. George Schwab and Erna Hilfstein (Chicago: University of Chicago Press, 2008), 34.

26. Hobbes, *Leviathan*, chapter 16, 111. In his *Politics of the Scene*, Kottman astutely diagnoses Hobbes's revolutionary theory of political representation, whereby singular human beings become nothing more than "infinitely substitutable bodies" (70) that can represent and be represented by anything else, but my claim here is that the allegedly real body of the sovereign person also falls victim to this logic of infinite substitutability.

27. Jean-Jacques Rousseau, *Letter to Monsieur D'Alembert on the Theater*, intr. and trans. Allan Bloom (Ithaca, N.Y.: Cornell University Press, 1968).
28. Jacques Derrida, "The Theorem and the Theater," in *Of Grammatology*, intr. and trans. Gayatri Chakravorty Spivak (Baltimore, Md.: Johns Hopkins University Press, 1976), 302–13, 304.
29. Jacques Rancière, "The Paradoxes of Political Art," in *Dissensus: On Politics and Aesthetics*, intr. and trans. Steven Corcoran (London: Bloomsbury, 2010), 142–59, 144.
30. Rousseau, *Letter to d'Alembert*, 116; translation modified.
31. Rousseau, 125; translation modified.
32. Rousseau, 125.
33. See, for example, Ngũgĩ wa Thiong'o, *Decolonising the Mind: The Politics of Language in African Literature* (London: James Currey, 1986), 34–63. In his 1977 play, *Ngaahika Ndeenda* [*I Will Marry When I Want*] Ngũgĩ wa Thiong'o famously sought to reconstruct an indigenous tradition of Kenyan popular theater that would break with the bourgeois conventions of colonial theater: *Ngaahika Ndeenda* was written and performed in Kikuyu, drew upon traditional elements like song, dance, and mime and was staged in a purpose-built open-air theater for some ten thousand people in the village of Kamĩrĩĩthũ.
34. Rousseau, *Letter to d'Alembert*, 126.
35. Rousseau, 126.
36. Rousseau, 111.
37. Derrida, *Of Grammatology*, 309.
38. Rousseau, *Letter to d'Alembert*, 126; translation modified.
39. Jean Starobinski, *Jean-Jacques Rousseau: La transparence et l'obstacle* (Paris: Gallimard, 1971).
40. If we recall some of the real historical attempts to stage the kind of republican spectacle Rousseau had in mind—such as the various French revolutionary festivals—it is perhaps symptomatic that we do not find anything remotely like his minimal, nonrepresentational performance of pure popular sovereignty but, rather, an explosion of increasingly baroque, elaborate, and eccentric theatrical tableaux. In the case of the Festival of the Supreme Being organized by Jacques-Louis David, for example, the political space took the form of an enormous artificial

mountain, topped by an "Altar of the Nation" and a Tree of Liberty, that was erected on the Champs de Mars. See Mona Ozouf, *Festivals and the French Revolution* (Cambridge, Mass.: Harvard University Press, 1988).

41. See Bernard Flynn, *The Philosophy of Claude Lefort: Interpreting the Political* (Evanston, Ill.: Northwestern University Press, 2005); Daniel Steinmetz-Jenkins, "Claude Lefort and the Illegitimacy of Modernity," *Journal for Cultural and Religious Theory* 10, no. 1 (Winter 2009): 102–17; and Stathis Gourgouris, "The Void Occupied Unconcealed," in *Lessons in Secular Criticism* (New York: Fordham University Press, 2013), 120–44 for readings of Lefort's essay to which I am indebted.

42. Claude Lefort, "The Permanence of the Theologico-Political?," in *Democracy and Political Theory*, trans. David Macey (Minneapolis: University of Minnesota Press, 1988), 213–55, 225.

43. Lefort, "Permanence of the Theologico-Political," 225.

44. Lefort, 218–19.

45. Lefort, 222–23; translation modified.

46. Benite et al., *Scaffolding of Sovereignty*, 20.

47. In arguing that there is no such thing as a "view from nowhere," though, I am painfully aware that my own selection of authors, texts, and figures in this book could nonetheless be seen as historically, politically, and geographically limited: a view from the "somewhere" called Europe. To be sure, I work in a field—political theology—that remains dominated by certain privileged signatures (Thomas Hobbes, Carl Schmitt, and Walter Benjamin); historical spaces (the post-Westphalian European nation state); and religious traditions (Judaism, Christianity), and this is reflected in many of the chapters that follow. In this book, I do also seek to introduce diverse and minoritized voices into the political theological debate where possible.

48. See Bruno Latour, "From *Realpolitik* to *Dingpolitik* or How to Make Things Public," in *Making Things Public: Atmospheres of Democracy*, ed. Bruno Latour and Peter Weibel (Cambridge, Mass.: MIT Press, 2005), 14–41; Jane Bennett, *Vibrant Matter: A Political Ecology of Things* (Durham, N.C.: Duke University Press, 2010); and Diana Coole and Samantha Frost, eds., *New Materialisms: Ontology, Agency, and Politics* (Durham, N.C.: Duke University Press, 2010)

for a range of examples of the "materialist" turn in contemporary political theory.
49. Andrew Sofer, *The Stage Life of Props* (Ann Arbor: University of Michigan Press, 2010).

1. IN THE CHAIR

1. Eugène Ionesco, *Les Chaises*, ed. Michel Lioure (Paris: Gallimard, 1996); translation mine.
2. Ionesco, *Les Chaises*, 76.
3. See Kenneth Tynan, *Curtains* (New York: Athenaeum, 1961), 177. In Tynan's memorable verdict, Ionesco's play describes an absurd universe in which "truth is a tale told without words to people who cannot hear it."
4. Kenneth Tynan, "Ionesco, Man of Destiny?," *Observer*, June 22, 1958, 15; emphasis in original.
5. Tynan, "Ionesco, Man of Destiny?"
6. Eugène Ionesco, "'Le Coeur n'est pas sur la main," in *Notes et contre-notes* (Paris: Gallimard, 1966), 152–61, 155.
7. Eugène Ionesco, "Propos sur mon théâtre et sur les propos des autres," in *Notes et contre-notes* (Paris: Gallimard, 1966), 101–28, 111.
8. Charles Picard, "Le Trône vide d'Alexandre dans la Cérémonie de Cyinda et le culte du Trône vide à travers le monde Gréco-Romain," *Cahiers Archéologiques Fin de l'Antiquité et Moyen Age* 7 (1954): 1–17.
9. Jacques Le Goff, "A Coronation Program for the Age of Saint Louis: The Ordo of 1250," in *Coronations: Medieval and Early Modern Monarchic Ritual*, ed. János M. Bak (Berkeley: University of California Press, 1990), 46–57, 53.
10. To be clear, Agamben is generally skeptical of what he calls "regal" readings of the empty throne. See Giorgio Agamben, *The Kingdom and the Glory: For a Theological Genealogy of Economy and Government*, trans. Lorenzo Chiesa and Matteo Mandarini (Stanford, Calif.: Stanford University Press, 2011), 243–45.
11. Julia Reinhard Lupton, "The Renaissance *Res Publica* of Furniture," in *Animal, Vegetable, Mineral: Ethics and Objects*, ed. Jeffrey Jerome Cohen (New York: Punctum, 2011), 211–36, 225. In what follows, I am greatly indebted to Lupton's reading of *Macbeth*, notwithstanding any

differences of interpretation, for drawing my attention to the ambiguity between stools and thrones in the play.
12. Julian Bourg, "Translator's Foreword," in Claude Lefort, *Complications: Communism and the Dilemmas of Democracy*, intr. and trans. Julian Bourg (New York: Columbia University Press, 2007), 1–20, 15.
13. Claude Lefort, "The Permanence of the Theologico-Political?," in *Democracy and Political Theory*, trans. David Macey (Minneapolis: University of Minnesota Press, 1988), 213–55, 225.
14. Lefort, "Permanence of the Theologico-Political," 225.
15. Eugène Ionesco, "Sur la crise du théâtre," in *Notes et contre-notes* (Paris: Gallimard, 1966), 308; emphasis mine.
16. William Shakespeare, *Macbeth*, the Arden Shakespeare, ed. Sandra Clark and Pamela Mason (London: Bloomsbury, 2015), 3.4.1; all further references will be given in the text by act, scene, and line number.
17. J. P. Dyson, "The Structural Function of the Banquet Scene in *Macbeth*," *Shakespeare Quarterly* 14, no. 4 (Autumn 1963): 369–78, 371.
18. Simon Forman, *The Bocke of Plaies and Notes therof p formans for Common Pollicie*, quoted in William Shakespeare, *Macbeth*, ed. Kenneth Muir (London: Methuen, 1972), xvi. In "The Renaissance *Res Publica* of Furniture," Lupton draws attention to this very early account of the play that dates from around five years after its first performance.
19. See here Dyson, "Structural Function of the Banquet Scene," 374, as well as Lupton, "The Renaissance *Res Publica* of Furniture," 228. In Dyson's view, Macbeth's association of the chair with the stool is a "metaphysical" claim about his loss of status as a man rather than as a king, whereas Lupton argues that "Macbeth's violations of hospitality have permanently cost him his place at life's great feast, and a haunted stool, not a haunted chair, may be the most appropriate seat to bear this void."
20. Lupton, "Renaissance *Res Publica* of Furniture," 229.
21. Eugène Ionesco, *Macbett* (Paris: Gallimard, 1972); emphasis mine.
22. For some contemporary journalists, academics and political opponents in the aftermath of the Iraq War, British prime minister Tony Blair's administrations were seen as pursuing a style of "sofa government" in which key decisions were allegedly taken informally by an unofficial group of advisors and formal governmental structures like cabinet were marginalized.

23. See Arthur Bradley, *Unbearable Life: A Genealogy of Political Erasure* (New York: Columbia University Press, 2019), 85.
24. Lefort, "Permanence of the Theologico-Political," 225.
25. Immanuel Kant, *The Conflict of the Faculties* [*Der Streit der Fakultäten*], trans. Mary J. Gregor (New York: Abaris, 1979), 27–29.
26. Kant, *Conflict of the Faculties*, 27n2.
27. In the post-1688 English constitutional settlement, the king increasingly presides as a ceremonial (i.e., symbolic or empty) head of state, while the real seat of sovereignty becomes Parliament itself and, specifically, the "lower" house.
28. Reinhard Brandt, "Zum 'Streit der Fakultäten,'" in *Kant Forschungen*, vol. 1, *Neue Autographen und Dokumente zu Kants Leben, Schriften und Vorlesungen*, ed. R. Brandt and Werner Stark (Hamburg: Felix Meiner, 1987), 31–72, 31; quoted in Hent de Vries, *Religion and Violence: Philosophical Perspectives from Kant to Derrida* (Baltimore, Md.: Johns Hopkins University Press, 2001), 48.
29. Kant, *Conflict of the Faculties*, 59.
30. De Vries, *Religion and Violence*, 40–41.
31. Jacques Derrida, "Vacant Chair: Censorship, Mastery, Magisteriality," trans. Jan Plug, in *Eyes of the University: Right to Philosophy 2*, (Stanford, Calif.: Stanford University Press, 2004), 43–63. In Derrida's corpus, this essay is, of course, only one of a series of reflections on Kant's text that includes the earlier "Mochlos, or The Conflict of the Faculties."
32. Derrida, "Vacant Chair," 50.
33. Derrida, 54–55.
34. Derrida, 60–63.
35. Derrida, 56.
36. Derrida, 58.
37. Immanuel Kant, *Critique of Judgment*, ed. and trans. Werner S. Pluhar (Indianapolis: Hackett, 1987), 408n27. In "Vacant Chair," Derrida also reads *The Conflict of the Faculties* in the light of the critique of teleological reason in the third *Critique*.
38. De Vries, *Religion and Violence*, 41.
39. Francis Bacon, *Catalogue Raisonné*, ed. Martin Harrison, 5 vols. (London: The Estate of Francis Bacon, 2016).

40. Gilles Deleuze, *Francis Bacon: The Logic of Sensation*, trans. Daniel W. Smith (London: Continuum, 2003), x.
41. David Sylvester, *Interviews with Francis Bacon: The Brutality of Fact* (London: Thames and Hudson, 2008), 26; emphasis mine.
42. Deleuze, *Francis Bacon*, 36.
43. Deleuze, 38.
44. Deleuze, 45.
45. Deleuze, 59.
46. Deleuze, 38.
47. Deleuze, xi.
48. Deleuze, 41.
49. Eric L. Santner, *The Royal Remains: The People's Two Bodies and the Endgames of Sovereignty* (Chicago: University of Chicago Press, 2011). In this section, I am greatly indebted to Santner's reading of the Screaming Popes.
50. David Sylvester, *Looking Back at Francis Bacon* (London: Thames and Hudson, 2022), 29–30.
51. Deleuze, *Francis Bacon*, 36.
52. Sylvester, *Interviews with Francis Bacon*, 26.
53. Deleuze, *Francis Bacon*, 53.
54. Deleuze, 53.
55. Deleuze, 53–54.
56. Ionesco, *Les Chaises*, 92–93.
57. Eugène Ionesco, "Sur *Les Chaises*: Lettre au premier metteur en scène," in *Notes et contre-notes* (Paris: Gallimard, 1966), 257–62, 261.
58. Eugène Ionesco, "Lettre à un metteur en scène" (January 1952), in *Notes et contre-notes* (Paris: Gallimard, 1966), 262–63, 262.
59. Slavoj Žižek, *For They Know Not What They Do* (London: Verso, 2008), 267.
60. Hans Urs von Balthasar, "Excursus on Brecht and Ionesco," in *Theo-Drama: Theological Dramatic Theory, Vol. 1: Prolegomena*, trans. Graham Harrison (San Francisco: Ignatius, 1988).
61. Nicole Jerr, "Exit the King? Modern Theater and the Revolution," in *The Scaffolding of Sovereignty: Global and Aesthetic Perspectives on the History of a Concept*, ed. Zvi Ben-Dor Benite, Stefanos Geroulanos, and Nicole Jerr (New York: Columbia University Press, 2017), 340–63, 343.

62. Ionesco, *Les Chaises*, 33.
63. Ionesco, "Le Coeur n'est pas sur la main," 156; emphasis mine.
64. Claude Shannon, *The Mathematical Theory of Communication* (Evanston: University of Illinois Press, 1949).

2. ANOINTED WITH OIL

This epigraph is taken from Anglican Liturgical Library, *The Form and Order of the Service That Is to Be Performed and the Ceremonies That Are to Be Observed in the Coronation of Her Majesty Queen Elizabeth II in the Abbey Church of St Peter Westminster on Tuesday the Second Day of June 1953* (London: Eyre and Spottiswoode, 1953), 18.

1. See Percy Ernst Schramm, *A History of the English Coronation*, trans. Leopold G. Wickham Legg (New York: Oxford University Press, 1937).
2. To recall Sergio Bertelli's verdict here: "One must keep in mind that a royal coronation, with the Hebraic symbolism of anointing at its apex, was, in many aspects, an embalming. Thanks to this rite the king became *Christos kuriou*, the Messiah Yahweh, the 'Son of God' ('this day have I begotten thee'; Psalm 2:7). To underscore his new status, his transformation into a sacred person, the king even changed his name (or added a numeral to it). Once anointed, he became a sacred person: '*Nolite tangere christos meos!*' (Do not touch my anointed ones). Access to the sacrament of anointing also made him similar to a priest." See Sergio Bertelli, *The King's Body: Sacred Rituals of Power in Medieval and Early Modern Europe*, trans. R. Burr Litchfield (University Park: Penn State University Press, 2001), 21–2.
3. Joseph Canning, *A History of Medieval Political Thought, 300–1450* (London: Routledge, 1996).
4. Marc Bloch, *The Royal Touch: Sacred Monarchy and Scrofula in England and France* trans. J. E. Anderson (London: Routledge and Kegan Paul, 1973).
5. Ernst Kantorowicz, *The King's Two Bodies: A Study in Medieval Political Theology* (Princeton, N.J.: Princeton University Press, 1957), 46.
6. H. E. J. Cowdray, *Pope Gregory VII, 1073–1085* (Oxford: Oxford University Press, 1988), 76. In Catholic sacramental theology, the key distinction is between those sacraments that are deemed to confer

"character" and so cannot be revoked or repeated—ordination, baptism, and confirmation—and those that do not: confession, communion, and extreme unction.

7. Thomas Cranmer, "The Archbishop's Speech at the Coronation of King Edward V, February 20th, 1547," in *Miscellaneous Writings and Letters*, ed. John Edmund Cox (Cambridge: Cambridge University Press, 1846), 126–27, 126.
8. Walter Benjamin, letter to Gerhard Scholem, September 16, 1924, in *The Correspondence of Walter Benjamin, 1910–1940*, ed. Gershom Scholem and Theodor Adorno, trans. Manfred R. Jacobson and Evelyn M. Jacobson (Chicago: University of Chicago Press, 1994), 246–51, 246.
9. Zygmunt Bauman, *Liquid Modernity* (London: Polity, 2000).
10. William Mazzarella, Eric. L. Santner, and Aaron Schuster, *Sovereignty, Inc.: Three Enquiries in Politics and Enjoyment* (Chicago: University of Chicago Press, 2020).
11. William Shakespeare, *King Richard II*, the Arden Shakespeare, ed. James R. Siemon, (London: Bloomsbury, 2009), 3.2.54–57; all further references to the plays will be given in the text by act, scene, and line number.
12. Kantorowicz, *King's Two Bodies*, 36n22. In Kantorowicz's view, the very question of "sacramental kingship"—and whether it conferred a *character indelibilis* upon the monarch—was already an anachronism by the reign of Richard II: "The notion of the 'sacramental character' was developed only at the time when the royal (imperial) consecrations were excluded from the number of the seven sacraments."
13. William Shakespeare, *King Henry IV, Part 1*, the Arden Shakespeare. ed. David Scott Kastan, (London: Thomson 2002), 4.3.40.
14. William Shakespeare, *Richard III*, the Arden Shakespeare, ed. James R. Siemon, (London: Bloomsbury, 2009), 5.3.124–25.
15. William Shakespeare, *King Lear*, the Arden Shakespeare, ed. R. A. Foakes (London: Thomson, 1997), 3.7.57.
16. William Shakespeare, *Macbeth*, the Arden Shakespeare, ed. Sandra Clark and Pamela Mason (London: Bloomsbury, 2015), 2.3.67–68.
17. William Shakespeare, *King Henry VI, Part 3*, the Arden Shakespeare, ed. John D. Cox and Eric Rasmussen (London: Thomson, 2001), 3.1.16–17.

18. See Bloch, *The Royal Touch*, for a discussion of the relationship between the ritual of anointment and the royal thaumaturgic touch or benediction. In Bertelli's summary, "The formula repeated when touching those sick with scrofula—'*Le roi te touche, Dieu te guerisse*' (The king touches you, God cures you)—recalled the sacrament of anointing" (*King's Body*, 26).
19. Samuel Johnson, "Miscellaneous Observations on the Tragedy of *Macbeth*" (1745), in *Selections from Johnson on Shakespeare*, ed. Bertrand H. Bronson with Jean M. O'Meara (New Haven, Conn.: Yale University Press, 1986), 1:259–60. In Johnson's words, "The reading [in one of the folio editions] is 'Anoint thee,' in a sense very consistent with the common accounts of witches, who are related to perform many supernatural acts by the means of unguents, and particularly to fly through the air to the places where they meet at their hellish festivals. In this sense 'anoint thee, Witch,' will mean, 'Away, Witch, to your infernal assembly.'"
20. Chris Laoutaris, *Shakespearean Maternities: Crises of Conception in Early Modern England* (Edinburgh: Edinburgh University Press, 2008), 195.
21. Kantorowicz, *King's Two Bodies*, 27.
22. Victoria Kahn, *The Future of Illusion: Political Theology and Early Modern Texts* (Chicago: University of Chicago Press, 2014), 6.
23. Kantorowicz, *King's Two Bodies*, 35.
24. Philip Lorenz, *Tears of Sovereignty: Perspectives of Power in Renaissance Drama* (New York: Fordham University Press 2013).
25. John Milton, *A Defence of the People of England* [*Defensio pro Populo Anglicano*], in *Political Writings*, ed. Martin Dzelzainis and trans. Claire Gruzelier (Cambridge: Cambridge University Press, 1991), 51–254, 132.
26. Lancelot Andrewes, "A Sermon Preached before his Majestie, on Sunday the Fifth of August Last, at Holdenbie, ANNO DOM. 1610," in *Selected Sermons and Lectures*, ed. Peter McCullough (Oxford: Oxford University Press, 2005), 178–206, 189–91.
27. John Donne, "Number 13: Preached at St Paul's, upon Christmas Day. 1628. Lord, Who Hath Beleeved Our Report? *Domine, quis credidit auditui nostro?*," in *The Sermons of John Donne*, ed. Evelyn M. Simpson and George R. Potter (Berkeley: University of California Press, 1962), 8:292–311, 297; emphasis mine.

28. Jim Daems and Holly Faith Nelson, eds., *Eikon Basilike with Selections from John Milton's* Eikonoklastes (Calgary: Broadview, 2005), 87.
29. John Milton, *Second Defence of the English People [Defensio Secunda]*, in *Complete Poems and Major Prose*, ed. Meritt Y. Hughes (Indianapolis: Hackett, 2003), 817–38, 824. In response to Moulin's claim that he has a "spare, shrivelled, and bloodless form," Milton says: "My face, which is said to indicate a total privation of blood, is of a complexion entirely opposite to the pale and the cadaverous."
30. Daems and Faith, *Eikon Basilike*, 32.
31. John Milton, *Eikonoklastes*, in *Complete Prose Works of John Milton, Vol. 3, 1648–1649*, ed. Merrit Y. Hughes (New Haven, Conn.: Yale University Press, 1963), 439.
32. Milton, *Defence of the People of England*, 156.
33. Gil Anidjar, *Blood: A Critique of Christianity* (New York: Columbia University Press, 2014).
34. Milton, *Defence of the People of England*, 132.
35. Milton, 132.
36. Milton, *Eikonoklastes*, 595.
37. John Milton, "The Tenure of Kings and Magistrates," in *Political Writings*, ed. Martin Dzelzainis, trans. Claire Gruzelier (Cambridge: Cambridge University Press, 1991), 3–50, 8.
38. Herman Melville, *Moby-Dick*, ed. Hershel Parker. Norton Critical Edition (New York: Norton, 2018), 95–96.
39. Carl Schmitt, letter to Ernst Jünger, July 4, 1941, in Ernst Jünger and Carl Schmitt, *Briefe 1930–83*, ed. Helmuth Kiesel (Stuttgart: Klett-Cotta, 2012), 121. In Schmitt's words, "*Moby-Dick*, as an epic of the sea, can only be compared to the *Odyssey*."
40. Anidjar, *Blood*.
41. Jason Frank, "Pathologies of Freedom in Melville's America," in *Radical Future Pasts: Untimely Political Theory*, ed. Roman Coles, Mark Reinhardt, and George Shulman (Lexington: University of Kentucky Press, 2014), 435–58; Bonnie Honig, "Charged: Debt, Power, and the Politics of the Flesh in Shakespeare's *Merchant*, Melville's *Moby-Dick*, and Santner's *The Weight of all Flesh*," in Eric Santner, *The Weight of all Flesh: On the Subject-Matter of Political Economy* (New York: Oxford University Press, 2016), 131–82.

42. Honig, "Charged," 138.
43. Melville, *Moby-Dick*, 49.
44. Melville, 261.
45. Melville, 276.
46. Melville, 309.
47. Melville, 356.
48. Frank, "Pathologies of Freedom," 452.
49. Ernst Jünger, letter to Carl Schmitt, August 28, 1941, in Ernst Jünger and Carl Schmitt, *Briefe, 1930–83*, ed. Helmuth Kiesel (Stuttgart: Klett-Cotta, 2012), 127.
50. Melville, *Moby-Dick*, 309.
51. Melville, 261.
52. Honig, "Charged," 153.
53. Melville, *Moby-Dick*, 95, 76.
54. Heidi Scott, "Whale Oil Culture, Consumerism, and Modern Conservation," in *Oil Culture*, ed. Ross Barrett and Daniel Worden (Minneapolis: University of Minnesota Press, 2014), 3–18.
55. Melville, *Moby-Dick*, 95.
56. Melville, 309.
57. Melville, 261.
58. For Bauman, postmodernity or late capitalism is famously reanointed as a "liquid modernity" that is characterized by capital's power to dissolve or liquidate previously "solid" social bonds that bind the individual and the collective together: "The 'melting of solids,' the permanent feature of modernity, has therefore acquired a new meaning, and above all has been redirected to a new target—one of the paramount effects of that redirection being the dissolution of forces which could keep the question of order and system on the political agenda. The solids whose turn has come to be thrown into the melting pot and which are in the process of being melted at the present time, the time of fluid modernity, are the bonds which interlock individual choices in collective projects and actions—the patterns of communication and co-ordination between individually conducted life policies on the one hand and political actions of human collectivities on the other" (*Liquid Modernity*, 6).
59. See Sean Coughlan, "Sacred Coronation Oil Will Be Animal-Cruelty Free," BBC, March 3, 2023, https://www.bbc.co.uk/news/uk-64836101.

60. In "The Rebranding of Sovereignty in the Age of Trump: Towards a Critique of Manatheism," Eric Santner deploys Noam Yuran's claim that the brand name itself has become a bearer of surplus value in a way that forces us to rethink the original Marxian analysis of production (*Sovereignty, Inc.*, 29–32).
61. *The Coronation of Their Majesties King Charles III and Queen Camilla* (London: Barnard and Westwood, 2023), 4.
62. Melville, *Moby-Dick*, 95.

3. BEHIND THE CURTAIN

1. Thomas Hobbes, *Leviathan: Or The Matter, Forme, and Power of a Common Wealth Ecclesiasticall and Civil*, ed. Richard Tuck (Cambridge: Cambridge University Press, 1996).
2. Horst Bredekamp, *Leviathan: Body Politic as Visual Strategy in the Work of Thomas Hobbes*, ed. and trans. Elizabeth Clegg (Boston: De Gruyter, 2020), 6.
3. See Arthur Bradley, *Unbearable Life: A Genealogy of Political Erasure* (New York: Columbia University Press, 2019), 95–118 for a discussion of Hobbes and the political theology of sacrifice.
4. Carl Schmitt, entry for November 12, 1947, *Glossarium: Aufzeichnungen aus den Jahren 1947–51*, ed. Eberhard Freiherr von Medem (Berlin: Duncker and Humblot, 1991), 39–42; translation mine. I am indebted to Antonio Cerella for drawing this reference to my attention.
5. Carl Schmitt, *The Leviathan in the State Theory of Thomas Hobbes: Meaning and Failure of a Political Symbol*, trans. George Schwab and Erna Hilfstein (Chicago: University of Chicago Press, 2008).
6. Jean Seltz, "An Experiment by Walter Benjamin," trans. Maria Louise Ascher, in Walter Benjamin, *On Hashish*, ed. Howard Eiland (Cambridge, Mass.: Belknap Press of Harvard University Press, 2006), 147–55, 151–52.
7. See, for example, Hans Blumenberg, "Metaphorics of the 'Naked' Truth," in *Paradigms for a Metaphorology*, trans. Robert Savage (Ithaca, N.Y.: Cornell University Press, 2010), 40–51; Hélène Cixous and Jacques Derrida, *Veils*, trans. Geoffrey Bennington (Stanford, Calif.: Stanford University Press, 2001); and Pierre Hadot, *The Veil of Isis: An Essay on*

the *History of the Idea of Nature*, trans. Michael Chase (Cambridge, Mass.: Belknap Press of Harvard University Press, 2006).
8. Carl, Schmitt, *Political Theology: Four Chapters on the Concept of Sovereignty*, trans. George Schwab (Cambridge, Mass.: MIT Press, 1985), 36. In Schmitt's famous thesis, "All significant concepts of the modern theory of the state are secularized theological concepts."
9. Jacques Derrida, "A Silkworm of One's Own (Points of View Stitched on the Other Veil)," in *Acts of Religion*, ed. Gil Anidjar (New York: Routledge, 2002), 309–55, 315–16.
10. Walter Benjamin, Letter to Greta Karplus, ca. May 26, 1933, in *Gesammelte Briefe*, ed. Christophe Gödde and Henri Lonitz (Frankfurt: Suhrkamp 1995–2000), 4:216–20.
11. Walter Benjamin, *Berlin Childhood Around 1900*, trans. Howard Eiland (Cambridge, Mass.: Belknap Press of Harvard University Press, 2006), 99.
12. Benjamin, *Berlin Childhood Around 1900*, 101.
13. Walter Benjamin, *Arcades Project*, trans. Howard Eiland and Kevin McLaughlin (Cambridge, Mass.: Belknap Press of Harvard University Press, 1999), I2, 6.
14. To consult what survives from the archive of Benjamin's drug writings, see Walter Benjamin, *On Hashish*, ed. Howard Eiland, trans. Howard Eiland and others (Cambridge, Mass.: Belknap Press of Harvard University Press, 2006). In a letter to Scholem, Benjamin spoke of completing a "truly exceptional" study of hashish ("Translator's Foreword," in *On Hashish*, xiii) but apparently all that remains are the essays, protocols, and other fragments collected in this posthumous volume.
15. Walter Benjamin, "Main Features of my Second Impression of Hashish," in *On Hashish*, ed. Howard Eiland, trans. Howard Eiland and others (Cambridge, Mass.: Belknap Press of Harvard University Press, 2006), 23–30, 24.
16. Benjamin, *Arcades Project*, I2, 6.
17. Walter Benjamin, "Crock Notes," in *On Hashish*, ed. Howard Eiland, trans. Howard Eiland and others (Cambridge, Mass.: Belknap Press of Harvard University Press, 2006), 81–5, 82. In Benjamin's writing on drugs, "crock" is his code word for opium.
18. Benjamin, "Crock Notes," 82.

19. See Howard Caygill, *Walter Benjamin: The Colour of Experience* (London: Routledge, 1995) for an excellent account of Benjamin's experimental synthesis of Kantian and Hegelian, transcendental and speculative, theories of experience.
20. Selz, "Experiment by Walter Benjamin," 151–52; emphasis in original.
21. Walter Benjamin, "Surrealism: The Last Snapshot of the European Intelligentsia," in *Reflections: Essays, Aphorisms, Autobiographical Writings*, ed. and intr. Peter Demetz, trans. Edmund Jephcott (New York: Harcourt Brace 1978), 177–92, 179; emphasis in original.
22. Benjamin, "Letter to Greta Karplus," 216–20.
23. Gilles Deleuze, *The Fold: Leibniz and the Baroque*, trans. Tom Conley (London: Athlone, 1993).
24. Alain Badiou, "Gilles Deleuze, the Fold: Leibniz and the Baroque," in *Gilles Deleuze and the Theater of Philosophy*, ed. Constantin V. Boundas and Dorothea Olkowski (London: Routledge, 1994), 51–69, 52.
25. Gilles Deleuze, *Foucault*, trans. Sean Hand (London: Continuum, 1999), 81.
26. Deleuze, *Fold*, 35.
27. Deleuze, 34.
28. Gilles Deleuze, *Negotiations, 1972–90*, trans. Martin Joughin (New York: Columbia University Press, 1990), 157.
29. Deleuze, *Fold*, 32–33.
30. Gottfried Leibniz, "A New System of the Nature and Communication of Substances, and also of the Union That Exists Between the Soul and the Body," trans. Jonathan Bennett, Early Modern Texts, https://www.earlymoderntexts.com/assets/pdfs/leibniz1695c.pdf (accessed May 6, 2024), 1–8, 6.
31. Deleuze, *Fold*, 29.
32. Deleuze, 35.
33. Deleuze, 125.
34. Deleuze, 93.
35. Deleuze, 24.
36. Peter Sloterdijk, *In the World Interior of Capital* (London: Polity, 2013).
37. Deleuze, *Fold*, 28.
38. Deleuze, 100.
39. Deleuze, 110.

40. Deleuze, 119.
41. Deleuze, 119.
42. Deleuze, 110.
43. Jacques Derrida, *Glas*, trans. John P. Leavey Jr. and Richard Rand (Lincoln: University of Nebraska Press, 1986), 68b.
44. Derrida, "Silkworm of One's Own," 314.
45. G. W. F. Hegel, "The Spirit of Christianity and Its Fate," in *Early Theological Writings*, trans. T. M. Knox (Chicago: University of Chicago Press, 1948), 182–301, 192.
46. Derrida, *Glas*, 49a.
47. Derrida, 1a.
48. Derrida, 33–34a.
49. G. W. F. Hegel, *Phenomenology of Spirit*, trans. A. V. Miller (Oxford: Oxford University Press, 1977), 103.
50. Derrida, "Silkworm of One's Own," 317. See also Arthur Bradley, *Negative Theology and Modern French Philosophy* (London: Routledge, 2004) for an extended discussion of Derrida's philosophy of religion.
51. Derrida, "Silkworm of One's Own," 317.
52. Derrida, 326.
53. Derrida, 326.
54. Derrida, 326.
55. Derrida, 338.
56. Derrida, 327.
57. Pliny, *Natural History Books*, trans. H. Rackham (London: William Heinemann, 1952), 6:65, 308–10. See also Kathryn Murphy, "Drawing the Curtain," Apollo, August 15, 2015, https://www.apollo-magazine.com/drawing-the-curtain/, for a discussion of representations of the curtain in art from Pliny to the present to which I am indebted.
58. See also Quentin Skinner, "Hobbes on Representation," *European Journal of Philosophy*, 13: 2 (2005): 155–84 for a reading of Hobbes on representation in the light of Pliny.
59. In his *Leviathan: Body Politic as Visual Strategy in the Work of Thomas Hobbes*, Horst Bredekamp is only the latest scholar to observe that the philosopher's scientific interest in optics, lenses and anamorphosis feed directly into his original political concepts of representation, personation and the passions (74–80).

60. Giorgio Agamben, *Homo Sacer: Sovereign Power and Bare Life*, trans. Daniel Heller-Roazen (Stanford, Calif..: Stanford University Press, 1998), 106.
61. Agamben, *Homo Sacer*, 35.

4. IN THE ANTECHAMBER

This epigraph is taken from Dante Alighieri, *Inferno*, in *The Divine Comedy*, intr. and trans. Allen Mandelbaum (Berkeley: University of California Press, 1980), canto 3, lines 31–42.

1. Roland Barthes, *On Racine*, trans. Richard Howard (New York: Hill and Wang, 1964), 4.
2. William Shakespeare, *Hamlet*, the Arden Shakespeare, ed. Anne Thompson and Neil Taylor (London: Bloomsbury, 2016).
3. Franz Kafka, "Before the Law," in *Complete Short Stories*, ed. Nahum Glatzer, trans. Willa and Edwin Muir (London: Vintage, 2005), 3–4.
4. Jorge Luis Borges, "The Library of Babel," in *Labyrinths: Selected Stories and Other Writings*, ed. Donald A. Yates and James E. Irby (Harmondsworth: Penguin, 1970), 78–86.
5. Marc Augé, *Non-Places: An Introduction to the Anthropology of Supermodernity*, trans. John Howe (London: Verso, 1995).
6. Helmut Puff, "Waiting in the Antechamber," in *Timescapes of Waiting: Spaces of Stasis, Delay, and Deferral*, ed. Christoph Singer, Robert Wirth, and Olaf Berwald (Leiden: Brill, 2019), 17–34, 27. I am indebted to Helmut Puff for sharing his research on antechambers with me.
7. Baldassare Castiglione, *The Book of the Courtier*, ed. Daniel Javitch. Norton Critical Editions (New York: Norton, 2002).
8. Niccolò Machiavelli, *The Prince*, ed. Quentin Skinner (Cambridge: Cambridge University Press, 1988).
9. John Aubrey, "Thomas Hobbes, 1588–1679," in *"Brief Lives," Chiefly of Contemporaries, Set Down by John Aubrey, Between the Years 1669 & 1696*, ed. Andrew Clark (Oxford: Clarendon, 1898), 321–403, 331. In his early career as secretary to William Cavendish, Earl of Devonshire, Hobbes apparently made good use of the significant amount of time he spent waiting in antechambers: "By this way of life he had almost forgott his Latin; vide Latin verses. He therefore bought him bookes of an

Amsterdam print that he might carry in his pocket (particularly Caesar's Commentarys), which he did read in the lobby, or antechamber, whilest his lord was making his visits."
10. Friedrich Schiller, *Don Carlos and Mary Stuart*, trans. Hilary Collier Sy-Quia and Peter Oswald (Oxford: Oxford University Press, 2008). All further references will be given in the text by act, scene, and line number.
11. See Norbert Elias, *The Court Society*, trans. Edmund Jephcott (Oxford: Blackwell, 1983); Alain Grosrichard, *The Sultan's Court: European Fantasies of the East*, intr. Mladen Dolar, trans. Liz Heron (London: Verso, 1998); and Helmut Puff, *Waiting in the Antechamber: Towards a History of Waiting* (Stanford, Calif.: Stanford University Press, 2023) for a range of historical, cultural, and literary readings of royal and political courts, chambers and antechambers.
12. Puff, "Waiting in the Antechamber," 28.
13. Puff, 28.
14. Jean Bodin, *On Sovereignty: Four Chapters from "The Six Books of the Commonwealth,"* trans. Julian H. Franklin (Cambridge: Cambridge University Press, 1992).
15. Carl Schmitt, "Dialogue on Power and Access to the Holder of Power," in *Dialogues on Power and Space*, ed. Andreas Kalyvas and Federico Finchelstein, trans. Samuel Garret Zeitlin (London: Polity, 2015), 23–50.
16. See Reinhard Mehring's *Carl Schmitt: A Biography*, trans. Daniel Steuer (London: Polity, 2014) for the most authoritative account of Schmitt's relationship with the Nazis after 1933.
17. Carl Schmitt, *Political Theology: Four Chapters on the Concept of Sovereignty*, trans. George Schwab (Chicago: University of Chicago Press, 1985), 21.
18. Carl Schmitt, *Crisis of Parliamentary Democracy*, trans. Ellen Kennedy (Chicago: University of Chicago Press, 1988), 7.
19. Schmitt, "Dialogue on Power," 34.
20. Schmitt, 35.
21. Schmitt, 36.
22. Schmitt, 32; translation modified.
23. Schmitt, 34.

24. Schmitt, 34–35.
25. Schmitt, 35.
26. To be sure, Schmitt's political theory consistently distinguishes between "power" (which can be divided and multiplied) and "sovereignty" (which remains personal and decisionist) from *Political Theology* onward: it is precisely *because* power is so diffuse, in other words, that we need a sovereign to make a final decision. However, what interests me is the question of whether the divisibility of "power" itself begins to inhabit the alleged indivisibility of "sovereignty": the counsellor who decides in advance what is or is not a matter for the sovereign to decide is themselves a participant in that decision. In this sense, the sovereign decision is not simply the sovereign's "own" decision but what Derrida famously calls "the decision of the other in me." I am indebted to Antonio Cerella for his helpful comments on my interpretation of Schmitt.
27. Schmitt, "Dialogue on Power," 36.
28. Schmitt, 37.
29. Schmitt, 36.
30. See Schmitt's explicit and broadly contemporaneous reengagement with Benjamin's work on tragedy in his *Hamlet or Hecuba: The Intrusion of The Time into the Play*, trans. David Pan and Jennifer R. Rust (New York: Telos, 2009).
31. Jacques Derrida, *Rogues: Two Essays on Reason*, trans. Pascale-Anne Brault and Michael Naas (Stanford, Calif.: Stanford University Press, 2005), 100–101.
32. Derrida, *Rogues*, 101.
33. Schmitt, "Dialogue on Power," 34.
34. Schmitt, 36; translation modified.
35. Jacques Derrida, *The Politics of Friendship*, trans. George Collins (London: Verso, 1997). In this work, Derrida famously tracks the "becoming-enemy" of the sovereign himself in Schmitt's political theory as the figure of the enemy becomes progressively internalized from an external enemy, to an internal enemy, to a brother, and, finally, to the self itself: "The enemy had indeed to be there already, so near. He had to be waiting, lurking close by, in the familiarity of my own family, in my own home" (172).
36. Schmitt, "Dialogue on Power," 32.

37. Schmitt, 39.
38. See, for example, the recent UK revival of Schiller's tragedy in which the same actor, Tom Burke, played the roles of both the Marquis of Posa and the Grand Inquisitor (Ara Theatre Company, 2018).
39. Friedrich Schiller, *Briefe über Don Karlos*, in *Schillers Werke, Nationalausgabe*, ed. Julius Petersen, Gerhard Fricke, Lieselotte Blumenthal, and Benno von Wiese (Weimar: Hermann Böhlaus Nachfolge, 1943), 22:S.177.
40. Franz Kafka, letter to Oskar Pollak, November 9, 1903, in *Letters to Friends, Family, and Editors*, trans. Richard and Clara Winston (New York: Schocken, 1977), 9–11, 10; translation modified.
41. Walter Benjamin, "Franz Kafka: On the Tenth Anniversary of His Death," in *Selected Writings 2, 1927–1934*, ed. Michael. W. Jennings, Howard Eiland, and Gary Smith, trans. Rodney Livingstone and others (Cambridge, Mass.: Belknap Press of Harvard University Press, 1999), 794–818, 795.
42. See Roger Thiel, "Architecture," in *Franz Kafka in Context*, ed. Carolin Duttinger (Cambridge: Cambridge University Press, 2018), 137–45 for a recent study of Kafka's architectonics.
43. Jorge Luis Borges, "Kafka and His Precursors," in *Labyrinths: Selected Stories and Other Writings*, ed. Donald A. Yates and James E. Irby (Harmondsworth: Penguin, 1970), 234–36.
44. Franz Kafka, "The Great Wall of China," in *Complete Short Stories*, ed. Nahum Glatzer, trans. Tanya and James Stern (London: Vintage, 2005), 235–47.
45. Kafka, "Great Wall of China," 243.
46. Kafka, 243.
47. Kafka, 244.
48. Kafka, 245.
49. Franz Kafka, "The Cares of a Family Man," in *Complete Short Stories*, ed. Nahum Glatzer, trans. Willa and Edwin Muir (London: Vintage, 2005), 427–29, 428.
50. Benjamin, "Franz Kafka," 811.
51. Kafka, "Cares of a Family Man," 428.
52. Kafka, 429.
53. See Rodolphe Gasché, "Kafka's Law: In the Field of Forces Between Judaism and Hellenism," in "Comparative Literature Issue," *MLN* 117,

no. 5 (December 2002): 971–1002, for an excellent reading of Barnabas and other messengers in Benjaminian terms as "intermediary" figures who partially escape the master-slave relationship to the law in which everyone else in Kafka's fictional universe is ensnared.

54. Franz Kafka, *The Castle*, trans. Willa and Edwin Muir, with additional material trans. Eithne Wilkins and Ernst Kaiser (London: Secker and Warburg, 1922), 225.
55. Kafka, *Castle*, 219.
56. See Borges, "Kafka and His Precursors," 234. In conclusion, Borges asserts that "the form of this illustrious problem [Aristotle's formulation of the paradox of Zeno's arrow in the *Physics*] is, exactly, that of *The Castle*, and the moving object and the arrow and Achilles are the first Kafkian characters in literature."
57. Benjamin, "Franz Kafka," 794–95.
58. Benjamin, 795.
59. Geoffrey Bennington, *Scatter 1: The Politics of Politics in Foucault, Heidegger, and Derrida* (New York: Fordham University Press, 2016), 4; emphasis in original.

5. UNDER THE CLOTHES

1. Jean Genet, *Le Balcon* (Paris: Gallimard Folio, 2009). All further references are given in the text by scene number. In what follows, I am working from the last published version of Genet's much-revised text, which was published by Editions L'Arbalète in 1962; translation mine.
2. See Genet, *Balcon*, scene 5. In French, a "house of illusions [*maison d'illusions*]" is a colloquial name for a brothel.
3. Jean Genet, "Interview with Hubert Fichte," in *The Declared Enemy: Texts and Interviews*, ed. Albert Dichy, trans. Jeff Fort (Stanford, Calif.: Stanford University Press, 2004), 118–51, 131; quoted in Aaron Schuster, "Beyond Satire: The Political Comedy of the Present and the Paradoxes of Enjoyment," in *Sovereignty, Inc.: Three Enquiries in Politics and Enjoyment*, by William Mazzarella, Eric. L. Santner, and Aaron Schuster (Chicago: University of Chicago Press, 2020), 161–250, 166.
4. Alain Badiou, *Le Séminaire: Images du temps présent, 2001–2004* (Paris: Fayard, 2014). In Badiou's verdict, the "historical element" of the play

is somewhat "inert" because the saber and the brush no longer constituted real emblems of power by 1956.

5. See Percy Ernst Schramm, *Herrschaftszeichen und Staatssymbolik: Beiträge zu ihrer Geschichte vom dritten bis zum sechzehnten Jahrhundert*, 3 vols. (Stuttgart: Hiersemann Verlag, 1954–1956); Ernst Kantorowicz, *The King's Two Bodies: A Study in Medieval Political Theology* (Princeton, N.J.: Princeton University Press, 1957); and Norbert Elias, *The Court Society*, trans. Edmund Jephcott (Oxford: Blackwell, 1983).

6. Percy Ernst Schramm, "Die Geschichte des mittelalterlichen Herrschertums im Lichte der Herrschaftszeichen," *Historische Zeitschrift* 178 (1954): 3–24, 11.

7. Jean Jacques Rousseau, "Discourse on the Origin and Foundations of Inequality Amongst Men," in *The Discourses and other Early Political Writings*, ed. Victor Gourevitch (Cambridge: Cambridge University Press, 1997), 111–231, 134.

8. See here also Jean-Luc Nancy and Federico Ferrari's remarkable *Being Nude: The Skin of Images*, trans. Anne O'Byrne and Carlie Angelmire (New York: Fordham University Press, 2014).

9. Michel de Montaigne, "To the Reader," in *The Complete Essays*, trans. M. A. Screech (York: Penguin, 1993), lix. See also Emily Jo Strunks, "The Metaphors of Clothing and Nudity in the *Essais* of Montaigne," *Romance Notes* 19 (1978–1979): 83–89.

10. John O'Brien, "Fashion," in *Montaigne After Theory, Theory After Montaigne*, ed. Zahi Zalloua (Seattle: University of Washington Press, 2009), 55–74, 57.

11. See Nora Martin Peterson, "The Impossible Striptease: Nudity in Jean Calvin and Michel de Montaigne," *Renaissance and Reformation / Renaissance et Réforme* 37, no. 1 (Winter 2014): 65–85.

12. To be sure, Montaigne's reading of the figure of the "savage" belongs to a long philosophical, theological and political history of European constructions of the indigenous peoples of North America. See, for example, Giuliano Gliozzi, *Adam et le Nouveau Monde: La naissance de l'anthropologie comme idéologie coloniale: des généalogies bibliques aux théories raciales, 1500–1700*, trans. Arlette Estève and Pascal Gabellone (Lecques: Théétète, 2000); J. G. A. Pocock, *Barbarism and Religion, Vol. 4: Barbarians, Savages, and Empires* (Cambridge: Cambridge

University Press, 2005); and Tony C. Brown, *The Primitive, the Aesthetic, and the Savage: An Enlightenment Problematic* (Minneapolis: University of Minnesota Press, 2012).

13. Michel de Montaigne, "On the Custom of Wearing Clothing," in *The Complete Essays*, trans. M. A. Screech (New York: Penguin, 1993), 253–6, 253–4; translation modified.
14. Montaigne, "On the Custom of Wearing Clothing," 254.
15. Montaigne, 255.
16. Michel de Montaigne, "On the Inequality There Is Between Us," in *The Complete Essays*, trans. M. A. Screech (New York: Penguin, 1993), 288–99, 289; translation modified.
17. Hans Blumenberg, "Metaphorics of the 'Naked' Truth," in *Paradigms for a Metaphorology*, trans. Robert Savage (Ithaca, N.Y.: Cornell University Press, 2010), 40–51, 43–44. In what follows, I am greatly indebted to Blumenberg's classic reading of the Montaigne-Pascal exchange.
18. Blaise Pascal, "Raison des effets," in *Pensées,* ed. Philippe Selliers and Gérard Ferreyrolles (Paris: Librairie Générale Française, 2000), 6, 93–103, Fragment 123, 97; Selliers's numbering; translation mine.
19. Blaise Pascal, "Justice," in *Pensées*, ed. Philippe Selliers and Gérard Ferreyrolles (Paris: Librairie Générale Française, 2000), 4:85, Fragment 95, 85; translation mine.
20. Blaise Pascal, "Imagination," in *Pensées*, ed. Philippe Selliers and Gérard Ferreyrolles (Paris: Librairie Générale Française, 2000), 3, 66–73, Fragment 78, 70; translations mine.
21. Blaise Pascal, "Pensées Morales," in *Pensées [Éditions de 1670]* (Paris: Flammarion, 1913), chapter 29, 279.
22. Michael Moriarty, "Imaginary," *Paragraph* 17, no. 3 (1994): 236–43, 236–37.
23. Pascal, "Imagination," 66.
24. See Moriarty, "Imaginary," 237.
25. Pascal, "Imagination," 67. See also Moriarty, "Imaginary," 239–42.
26. Pascal, 69–70.
27. For a range of responses to Pascal and the Fall of Man, see Sara E. Melzer, *Discourses of the Fall: A Study of Pascal's* Pensées (Berkeley: University of California Press, 1986); Michael Moriarty, *Fallen Nature, Fallen Selves: Early Modern French Thought, Vol. 2* (Oxford:

Oxford University Press, 2006); and William Wood, *Blaise Pascal on Duplicity, Sin, and the Fall: The Secret Instinct* (Oxford: Oxford University Press, 2013).

28. Franz Kafka, entry for June 19, 1916, *Diaries, 1914–23*, ed. Max Brod, trans. Martin Greenberg and Hannah Arendt (New York: Schocken, 1965), 156.
29. Mark M. Anderson, *Kafka's Clothes: Ornamentation and Aestheticism in the Hapsburg Fin de Siècle* (Oxford: Clarendon, 1992). In what follows, I am indebted to Anderson's landmark study, notwithstanding any differences of emphasis or interpretation.
30. Anderson, *Kafka's Clothes*, 4.
31. Franz Kafka, *The Trial*, trans. Idris Parry (London: Penguin, 1994). In a further allusion to the Fall, Josef K. eats a "fine apple" (6) before being arrested.
32. Kafka, *Trial*, 178.
33. Franz Kafka, "Clothes," in *Complete Short Stories*, ed. Nahum Glatzer, trans. Willa and Edwin Muir (London: Vintage, 2005), 382–83.
34. Anderson, *Kafka's Clothes*, 31.
35. Kafka, *Trial*, 67.
36. Kafka, 67.
37. Kafka, 41.
38. See Marc Lucht and Donna Yarri, eds., *Kafka's Creatures: Animals, Hybrids, and Other Fantastic Beings* (New York: Lexington, 2010) for a range of recent responses to the figure of the animal in Kafka's fiction.
39. Kafka, *Trial*, 69.
40. Kafka, 151.
41. Kafka, 178.
42. Franz Kafka, "The Metamorphosis," in *Complete Short Stories*, ed. Nahum Glatzer, trans. Willa and Edwin Muir (London: Vintage, 2005), 89–139, 115.
43. Anderson, *Kafka's Clothes*, 131.
44. Jacques Derrida, *The Animal That Therefore I am*, ed. Marie-Louise Mallet, trans. David Wills (New York: Fordham University Press, 2008), 5.
45. Giorgio Agamben, "Nudity," in *Nudities*, trans. David Kishik and Stefan Pedatella (Stanford, Calif.: Stanford University Press, 2011), 55–90, 57.
46. Agamben, "Nudity," 58.

47. Agamben, 57.
48. Erik Peterson, "Theology of Clothes," in *Selection*, ed. C. Hasting and D. Nicholl (London: Sheed and Ward, 1954), 2:56–64, 57–58.
49. Agamben, "Nudity," 57.
50. Agamben, 74–77.
51. Agamben, 90.
52. Agamben, 64.
53. Henri de Lubac, *Surnaturel: Etudes historiques* (Paris: Lethielleux, 2010).
54. Agamben, "Nudity," 67.
55. Augustine of Hippo, *Confessions*, intr. and trans. R. S. Pine-Coffin (New York: Penguin, 1961), 21; see also Agamben, 70. In a commentary that is ironically very close to Lubac's position, Agamben appears to depart from the idea of an irreducible difference between nature and grace in Augustine and acknowledges that the latter actually saw man's prelapsarian nature as intrinsically graceful: "Adam was, in fact, created in grace, and therefore his nature, like his nudity, was cloaked with divine gifts right from the start."
56. Erik Peterson, "Monotheism as a Political Problem: A Contribution to the History of Political Theology in the Roman Empire," in *Theological Tractates*, ed. and trans. Michael J. Hollerich (Stanford, Calif.: Stanford University Press, 2013), 68–105.
57. Giorgio Agamben, *The Kingdom and the Glory: For A Theological Genealogy of Economy and Government (Homo Sacer II, 2)*, trans. Lorenzo Chiesa and Matteo Mandarini (Stanford, Calif.: Stanford University Press, 2011), 16.
58. Agamben, *Kingdom and the Glory*, 193. See Ernst Kantorowicz, *Laudes Regiae: A Study in Liturgical Acclamations and Mediaeval Ruler Worship* (Berkeley: University of California Press, 1946), 185n23. In Kantorowicz's analysis, we can draw a direct genealogy from Peterson's analysis of Christian acclamation—which itself drew on pagan Roman imperial sources—to the neo-paganism of National Socialism: "Heis Theos" is the precursor of "Ein Reich, ein Volk, ein Führer."
59. Hans Boersma, *Nouvelle Théologie and Sacramental Ontology: A Return to Mystery* (Oxford: Oxford University Press, 2009), 88–89.
60. Jean Genet, "Comment jouer *Le Balcon*," in *Le Balcon* (Paris: Gallimard Folio, 2009), 7–12, 12; emphasis in original.

61. See Lucien Goldmann, "Genet's *The Balcony*: A Realist Play," trans. Robert Sayre, *Praxis: A Journal of Radical Perspectives on the Arts* 4 (1978): 123–31; Jacques Lacan, *Le Séminaire, Livre V: Les formations de l'inconscient*, ed. Jacques-Alain Miller (Paris: Seuil, 1998); and Alain Badiou, *Pornographie du temps present* (Paris: Fayard, 2013).
62. Agamben, *Kingdom and the Glory*, 211.
63. Badiou, *Pornographie du temps present*, 45.
64. Blumenberg, "Metaphorics of the 'Naked' Truth," 43.
65. Hans Christian Andersen, "Kejserens nye klæder" [The Emperor's New Clothes], in *Eventyr, fortalt for Børn. Første Samling. Tredie Hefte* [Fairy tales, told to children, first collection, third booklet] (Copenhagen: C. A. Reitzel, 1837).
66. Jacques Derrida, *Glas*, trans. John P. Leavey Jr. and Richard Rand (Lincoln: University of Nebraska Press, 1986), 8b. In this text, we find what is (to my knowledge) the only sustained philosophical discussion of the theme of glory in Genet's work.
67. Badiou, *Pornographie du temps present*, 30. In Badiou's verdict, the Chief of Police "embodies the power of which images are the operators."
68. In reading this pivotal scene and the play more generally, I am indebted to Alenka Zupančič, "Power in the Closet (and Its Coming Out)," in *Lacan, Psychoanalysis, and Comedy*, ed. Patricia Gherovici and Manya Steinkoler (Cambridge: Cambridge University Press, 2016), 219–34; James Penney, "The Phallus Unveiled: Lacan, Badiou, and the Comedic Moment in Genet's *The Balcony*," *Paragraph* 42, no. 2 (2019): 170–87; and Aaron Schuster, "Beyond Satire: The Political Comedy of the Present and the Paradoxes of Enjoyment," in *Sovereignty, Inc.: Three Enquiries in Politics and Enjoyment*, by William Mazzarella, Eric. L. Santner, and Aaron Schuster (Chicago: University of Chicago Press, 2020), 161–250.
69. Zupančič, "Power in the Closet," 231.

6. INSIDE THE PUPPET THEATER

This epigraph is taken from Walter Benjamin, "Theses on the Philosophy of History," in *Illuminations*, trans. Harry Zohn (New York: Schocken, 1968), 253–64, 253.

1. Benjamin, "Theses on the Philosophy of History," 254.
2. Rebecca Comay, "Benjamin's Endgame," in *Walter Benjamin's Philosophy: Experience and Destruction*, ed. Andrew Benjamin and Peter Osborne (London: Routledge, 1994), 251–90, 260.
3. Comay, "Benjamin's Endgame," 260.
4. To be sure, Benjamin's theses are among the most overinterpreted texts in twentieth-century philosophy, but I refer the reader to the following recent commentaries: Ian Balfour, "Reversal, Quotation (Benjamin's History)," *MLN* 106 (1991): 622–47; Slavoj Žižek, *The Puppet and the Dwarf: The Perverse Core of Christianity* (Cambridge, Mass.: MIT Press 2003); and Samuel Weber, *Benjamin's-abilities* (Cambridge, Mass.: Harvard University Press, 2008).
5. Benjamin, "Theses on the Philosophy of History," 261.
6. Comay, "Benjamin's Endgame," 251–52.
7. Heinrich von Kleist, "The Puppet Theater," in *Selected Writings*, ed. and trans. David Constantine (Indianapolis: Hackett, 2004), 411–16.
8. See Jessica Lightfoot, *Wonders and the Marvellous from Homer to the Hellenistic World* (Cambridge: Cambridge University Press, 2021). In her opening chapter, Lightfoot recalls how both Plato and Aristotle declare that philosophy begins with wonder in *Theaetetus* 155d and *Metaphysics* 982b12–15.
9. Ernst Kantorowicz, *The King's Two Bodies: A Study in Medieval Political Theology* (Princeton, N.J.: Princeton University Press, 1957), 419–37.
10. Thomas Hobbes, *Leviathan: Or The Matter, Forme, and Power of a Common Wealth Ecclesiasticall and Civil*, ed. Richard Tuck (Cambridge: Cambridge University Press, 1996), 9.
11. Michel Foucault, *Discipline and Punish*, trans. Alan Sheridan (New York: Vintage, 1979), 136. In Foucault's words, "The celebrated automata [of the eighteenth century] were not only a way of illustrating an organism, they were also political puppets, small-scale models of power: Frederick II, the meticulous king of small machines, well-trained regiments and long exercises, was obsessed with them."
12. Miguel Cervantes, *Don Quixote*, trans. Edith Grossman (New York: HarperCollins, 2003), 632.

13. Cervantes, *Don Quixote*, 632.
14. Cervantes, 632–33.
15. Cervantes, 633.
16. See *Don Quixote*, part 2, chapter 62: "Which relates the adventure of the enchanted head, as well as other matters that have more truth in them than wit." In an intriguing divergence from Benjamin's own fable of the puppet of historical materialism and the dwarf of theology, however, Don Alonso destroys his enchanted head for fear it will attract the attention of the Spanish Inquisition: Cervantes's puppet evidently does not contain the wizened dwarf of theology—or, perhaps more insidiously, its very proximity to theology reveals that the latter may itself be a puppet show. I am indebted to Peter Boxall for drawing this episode to my attention.
17. Cervantes, 633.
18. Cervantes, 634.
19. For recent readings of Master Pedro's puppet show in *Don Quixote*, see Mary Malcolm Gaylord, "Pulling Strings with Master Peter's Puppets: Fiction and History in *Don Quixote*," *Cervantes: Bulletin of the Cervantes Society* 18, no. 2 (1998): 117–47; Dale Wasserman, "*Don Quixote* as Theater," *Cervantes: Bulletin of the Cervantes Society of America* 19, no. 1 (1999): 125–30; and Bruce R. Burningham, "Jongleuresque Dialogue, Radical Theatricality, and Maese Pedro's Puppet Show," *Cervantes: Bulletin of the Cervantes Society* 23, no. 1 (2003): 165–200.
20. Cervantes, *Don Quixote*, 632.
21. Cervantes, 634.
22. Cervantes, 634.
23. Walter Benjamin, "Franz Kafka: On the Tenth Anniversary of His Death," in *Selected Writings 2, 1927–1934*, ed. Michael. W. Jennings, Howard Eiland, and Gary Smith, trans. Rodney Livingstone and others (Cambridge, Mass.: Belknap Press of Harvard University Press, 1999), 794–818, 816.
24. Cervantes, *Don Quixote*, 633.
25. Hobbes, *Leviathan*, 9.
26. René Descartes, *Meditations on First Philosophy*, trans. John Cottingham (Cambridge: Cambridge University Press, 1986), 58.

27. Hobbes, *Leviathan*, 9.
28. Hobbes, 9.
29. Schmitt, *Political Theology*, 33.
30. Schmitt, 47.
31. Schmitt, *Leviathan in the State Theory*, 81.
32. Schmitt, 53–64.
33. Schmitt, 32.
34. Schmitt, 34.
35. Schmitt, 34.
36. See Carl Schmitt, *Ex Captivitate Salus: Erfahrungen der Zeit, 1945–47* (Cologne: Greven, 1950), 12. In 1945, when interned in an American military prison, Schmitt described his fate as "the bad, unworthy and yet authentic case of a Christian Epimetheus."
37. Schmitt, *Leviathan in the State Theory*, 57.
38. Carl Schmitt, "Dialogue on Power and Access to the Holder of Power," in *Dialogues on Power and Space*, ed. Andreas Kalyvas and Federico Finchelstein, trans. Samuel Garret Zeitlin (London: Polity, 2015), 23–50, 46.
39. Victoria Kahn, *The Future of Illusion: Political Theology and Early Modern Texts* (Chicago: University of Chicago Press, 2014), 6. In Kahn's ventriloquizing of Giambattista Vico, "We can know only what we have made or constructed ourselves: *verum et factum conventuntur* (truth and fact—in the sense of that which is done or made—are interchangeable)."
40. Humberto Maturana and Francisco Valera, *Autopoiesis and Cognition: The Realisation of the Living* (Dordrecht: D. Reidel, 1980).
41. Schmitt, "Dialogue on Power," 45. For an overview of Schmitt's postwar work on the cybernetic revolution, see Nicolas Guilhot, "Automatic Leviathan: Cybernetics and Politics in Carl Schmitt's Postwar Writings," *History of the Human Sciences* 33, no. 1 (2020): 128–46.
42. Jacques Derrida, *Learning to Live Finally: An Interview with Jean Birnbaum*, trans. Pascale-Anne Brault and Michael Naas (New York: Melville House 2007), 32.
43. Jacques Derrida, *The Beast and the Sovereign: Vol. 1*, trans. Geoffrey Bennington (Chicago: University of Chicago Press, 2009), 189.

44. Paul Valéry, "The Evening with Monsieur Teste," in *The Collected Works of Paul Valéry, Vol. 6: Monsieur Teste*, ed. and intr. Jackson Matthews (Princeton, N.J.: Princeton University Press, 1973), 8–21. In this early story, Valéry begins what has since become known by critics as the "Teste cycle": a collection of various fragments on this mysterious figure which he assembled throughout his career.
45. Valéry, "Evening with Monsieur Teste," 12.
46. Valéry, 12; translation modified.
47. Valéry, 10.
48. For readings of Valéry's novella, see Kathryn M. Grossman, "Monsieur Teste as Modern Parable," *Dalhousie French Studies* 1 (October 1979): 52–60; Ernest Bevan Jr., "Dialogue with the Self: Paul Valéry and Monsieur Teste," *Twentieth Century Literature* 26, no. 1 (Spring 1980): 15–26; and Jed Deppman, "Re-Presenting Paul Valery's Monsieur Teste," *symploke* 11, nos. 1–2 (2003): 197–211.
49. Derrida, *Beast and the Sovereign*, 191.
50. Valéry, "Evening with Monsieur Teste," 11.
51. Derrida, *Beast and the Sovereign*, 191–92.
52. Derrida, 189.
53. Arthur Bradley, *Originary Technicity: The Theory of Technology from Marx to Derrida* (London: Palgrave, 2011).
54. Derrida, *Beast and the Sovereign*, 28.
55. Derrida, 194.
56. Derrida, 189.
57. Maximilien Robespierre, *Oeuvres de Maximilien Robespierre* (Paris: Société des études Robespierristes, 1912–2007), 11:X, 173.
58. Peter Szondi, "Hope in the Past," in Walter Benjamin, *Berlin Childhood Around 1900*, trans. Howard Eiland (Cambridge, Mass.: Belknap Press of Harvard University Press, 2006), 1–36, 27. In Szondi's essay, he attributes this anecdote to a private interview with Theodor Adorno.
59. Walter Benjamin, letter to Gerhard Scholem, January 14, 1926, in *The Correspondence of Walter Benjamin, 1910–1940*, ed. Gershom Scholem and Theodor Adorno, trans. Manfred R. Jacobson and Evelyn M. Jacobson (Chicago: University of Chicago Press, 1994), 287–90, 288.

60. Walter Benjamin, "Berlin Puppet Theater," in *Radio Benjamin*, ed. Lecia Rosenthal, trans. Jonathan Lutes with Lisa Harries Schumann and Diana K. R. Reese (London: Verso, 2014), 17–23, 19.
61. Benjamin, "Berlin Puppet Theater," 19–20.
62. Walter Benjamin, *The Origin of German Tragic Drama*, trans. John Osborne (New York: Verso, 2009), 85. In Benjamin's famous verdict, the sovereign is "lord of creatures, but he remains a creature."
63. Walter Benjamin, "Old Toys," in *Selected Writings, Vol. 2: 1927–34*, ed. Michael W. Jennings, Howard Eiland, and Gary Smith, trans. Rodney Livingstone and others (Cambridge, Mass.: Belknap Press of Harvard University Press, 1999), 98–102.
64. Walter Benjamin, "The Cultural History of Toys," in *Selected Writings, Vol. 2: 1927–1934*, ed. Michael W. Jennings, Howard Eiland, and Gary Smith, trans. Rodney Livingstone and others (Cambridge, Mass.: Belknap Press of Harvard University Press, 1999), 113–16, 116.
65. Benjamin, "Old Toys," 100.
66. Giorgio Agamben, "In Praise of Profanation," trans. Kevin Attell, in *Profanations* (New York: Zone 2007), 73–92, 76. In Agamben's words, "Children, who play with whatever old thing falls into their hands, make toys out of things that also belong to the spheres of economics, war, law, and other activities that we are used to thinking of as serious."
67. Benjamin, "Cultural History of Toys," 115.
68. Benjamin, "Old Toys," 101.
69. Walter Benjamin, "Rastelli's Story," in *Selected Writings, Vol. 3: 1935–1938*, ed. Howard Eiland and Michael W. Jennings, trans. Howard Eiland and Michael W. Jennings (Cambridge, Mass.: Belknap Press of Harvard University Press, 2002), 96–98.
70. Benjamin, "Rastelli's Story," 96.
71. Benjamin, 96.
72. Benjamin, 97–98.
73. In a recent review article, Fenves reads "Rastelli's Story" as Benjamin's cryptic reply to Theodor Adorno's critique of the former's theory of the dialectical image in the *Arcades Project* as insufficiently dialectical. See Peter Fenves, "Benjamin Tells a Story," *Los Angeles Review of Books*,

September 29, 2016, https://lareviewofbooks.org/article/benjamin-tells-story/.

7. IN THE CROWD

1. Alfred Jarry, *Ubu roi*, ed. Noël Arnaud and Henri Bordillon (Paris: Gallimard, 1978). All further references will be given in the text by act and scene number; translation mine.
2. Claude Schumacher, "The First Night of *Ubu roi*," in *Alfred Jarry and Guillaume Apollinaire* (London: Macmillan, 1984), 68–81, 73.
3. William Butler Yeats, "The Tragic Generation," in *The Trembling of the Veil* (London: T. Werner Laurie, 1922), 157–224, 217.
4. Cory Clayton Browning, "'Terror, the Order of the Day,' The French Revolutionary Terror, and Its Restagings" (PhD diss., Cornell University, 2015), 70.
5. Alfred Jarry, *Oeuvres complètes*, ed. Michel Arrivé and Henri Bordillon (Paris: Gallimard, Pléiade, 1972), 1:417; translation mine.
6. See Schumacher, "First Night of *Ubu roi*," 74.
7. To be sure, Jarry's work is frequently seen as the beginning of the modernist theatrical gesture—principally associated with such movements as Brecht's Epic Theater and Artaud's Theatre of Cruelty—of transforming the audience from a passive group of spectators into a set of revolutionary actors or participants in the performance. In his essay "Réponses à un questionnaire sur l'art dramatique," Jarry revealingly defines theater as neither a Molière-style moral "lesson" (*leçon*) nor a Rousseauean "civic festival" (*fête civique*) but as an "*action*": "This other theater is neither public festival, nor lesson, nor relaxation [*délassement*] but action" (*Oeuvres complètes*, 412).
8. Gustave Le Bon, *The Crowd: A Study of the Popular Mind* (New York: Macmillan, 1896), 17. In fact, Le Bon's work of crowd psychology was itself a response to earlier work by Hippolyte Taine and Gabriel Tarde and would be succeeded by later work by William McDougall, Sigmund Freud, and José Ortega y Gasset.
9. Le Bon, *Crowd*, 118.
10. Jacques Rancière, *The Emancipated Spectator*, trans. Gregory Elliott (London: Verso, 2011).

11. Jeffrey T. Schnapp, *Staging Fascism: 18BL and the Theater of Masses for Masses* (Stanford, Calif.: Stanford University Press, 1996), 33. In 1934, Mussolini's call was answered by Alessandro Blasetti's famous production of *18 BL*, which featured a cast of three thousand actors performing in front of an audience of twenty thousand spectators.
12. Le Bon, *Crowd*, xv.
13. Le Bon, 2.
14. Kimberly Jannarone, "Audience, Mass, Crowd: Theatres of Cruelty in Interwar Europe," *Theatre Journal* 61, no. 2 (2009): 191–211, 194.
15. Le Bon, *Crowd*, 23–24; translation modified.
16. Le Bon, 49.
17. Le Bon, 61.
18. Le Bon, 57.
19. Le Bon, 57.
20. Le Bon, 57.
21. Le Bon, 57–58.
22. Le Bon, xix.
23. Le Bon, 153.
24. Le Bon, xx; translation modified.
25. José Ortega y Gasset, *The Revolt of the Masses*, 25th anniversary ed. (New York: Norton, 1957), 12.
26. Gasset, *Revolt of the Masses*, 19–20.
27. Sigmund Freud, Sigmund Freud Papers: Interviews and Recollections—1998; Set A—1998; Interviews and; Kelsen, Hans, 1953, Manuscript/Mixed Material, retrieved from the Library of Congress, www.loc.gov/item/mss3999001500/ (accessed June 2, 2024). To quickly sketch this brief intellectual encounter, Kelsen—who was at forty years old already a professor of law at the University of Vienna, a serving judge on the Austrian Supreme Constitutional Court, and the principal architect of the 1920 Austrian constitution—was invited by Freud to deliver a paper on the latter's recently published *Group Psychology and the Analysis of the Ego* (*Massenpsychologie und Ich-Analyse*, 1921) to his Vienna Psychological Society on November 30, 1921. In the following year, Kelsen published this paper, "Der Begriff die Staats und die Sozialpsychologie. Mit besonderer Berücksichtigung vons Freuds Theorie der Masse" (The Conception of the State and Social

Psychology, with Special Reference to Freud's Group Theory," 1922), in Freud's house journal *Imago* and would go on to make favorable allusions to Freudian psychoanalysis in subsequent work like "God and the State" ("Gott und Staat," 1922).

28. Freud, *Sigmund Freud Papers*, 4.
29. Freud, 4.
30. Freud, 4.
31. Hans Kelsen, "The Conception of the State and Social Psychology, with Special Reference to Freud's Group Theory," *International Journal of Psychoanalysis* 5, no. 1 (January 1924): 1–38.
32. Hans Vaihinger, *The Philosophy of "As If": A System of the Theoretical, Practical, and Religious Fictions of Mankind*, trans. C. K. Ogden (London: Routledge and Kegan Paul, 1924). In the appendix to the "Transcendental Dialectic" of the First Critique, Kant famously argues that ideas like the immaterial soul, the freedom of the will, and God do not refer to real objects but still contain a regulative function for reason. See Immanuel Kant, "On the Regulative Function of the Idea of Pure Reason," in *Critique of Pure Reason*, ed. and trans. Paul Guyer and Allen W. Wood (Cambridge: Cambridge University Press, 1998), 590–604.
33. Hans Kelsen, "Zur Theorie der juristischen Fiktionen. Mit besonderer Berücksichtigung von Vaihingers Philosophie des Als Ob," *Annalen der Philosophie* 1 (1919): 630–58. To summarize this essay, which is his first attempt to apply Vaihinger's philosophy of fiction to the sphere of law, Kelsen argues that legal fictions like personality play an important heuristic role as self-conscious anthropomorphisms that render intelligible the normative legal system for citizens. In very late works, Kelsen also returns to Vaihinger to redefine the *Grundnorm* or basic norm that underpins his entire legal system less as a Kantian necessary hypothesis or presupposition than as a Vaihingerian fiction. See Hans Kelsen, "The Function of a Constitution" (1964), trans. Iain Stewart, in *Essays on Kelsen*, ed. Richard Tur and William Twining (Oxford: Clarendon, 1986), 109–19.
34. Freud, *Sigmund Freud Papers*, 5.
35. Vaihinger, *Philosophy of "As If"*, 269.
36. Kelsen, "Conception of the State," 13.

37. Kelsen, 14. In Kelsen's verdict, Freud certainly escapes the worst excesses of Le Bon and other crowd theorists, but he nonetheless concludes that Freud's own crowd psychology contains a "conceptual error" (21) that leads him to repeat the former's gesture of hypostatization.
38. Kelsen, 35–36.
39. Kelsen, 38.
40. Carl Schmitt, "Juristische Fiktionen (Uber Vaihinger und die Philosophie des Als-Ob)," *Deutsche Juristen-Zeitung* 18 (1913): 804–6.
41. Carl Schmitt, *Political Theology: Four Chapters on the Concept of Sovereignty*, trans. George Schwab (Chicago: University of Chicago Press, 1985), 20.
42. Schmitt, *Political Theology*, 21. For an excellent reading of Schmitt's critique of Kelsen, see Miguel Vatter, *Divine Democracy: Political Theology After Schmitt* (New York: Oxford University Press, 2021), 28–30.
43. Sigmund Freud, "The Ego and the Id," in *The Standard Edition of the Complete Psychological Works of Sigmund Freud, Vol. 19 (1923–1925): The Ego and the Id and Other Works*, ed. James Strachey in collaboration with Anna Freud and assisted by Alix Strachey and Alan Tyson (London: Hogarth, 1961), 1–66.
44. Étienne Balibar, "The Invention of the Superego: Freud and Kelsen, 1922," in *Citizen Subject: Foundations for Philosophical Anthropology*, trans. Stephen Miller (New York: Fordham University Press, 2016), 227–55, 243. In what follows, I am indebted to Balibar's remarkable essay, notwithstanding differences of emphasis.
45. Balibar, "Invention of the Superego," 254–55.
46. See Arthur Bradley, "Political Theology of the As-If: Freud, Kelsen, Fiction," in *Political Theology and Its Discontents: Psychoanalysis, Religion, Politics*, ed. K. Daniel Cho and Boštjan Nedoh (London: Bloomsbury, forthcoming) for an extended discussion of the Freud-Kelsen debate. In this essay, I also read Freud's *The Future of An Illusion* [*Die Zukunft einer Illusion*] (1927)—where he decisively rejects Vaihinger's fictionalism as an apology for religious illusion—as an oblique response to, and critique of, Kelsen's attempt to construct a political theology of the as-if.
47. Michel Foucault, *Abnormal: Lectures at the Collège de France, 1974–1975*, ed. Valerio Marchetti and Antonella Salomoni, trans. Graham Burchell (London: Picador, 2003).

48. Foucault, *Abnormal*, 11.
49. Foucault, 12.
50. Foucault, 12.
51. Foucault, 13.
52. Foucault, 12.
53. Foucault, 12–13.
54. Michel Foucault, *Discipline and Punish: The Birth of the Prison*, trans. Alan Sheridan (New York: Vintage, 1977), 211.
55. Foucault, *Discipline and Punish*, 201; translation modified.
56. Foucault, 217.
57. Foucault, 200.
58. Foucault, *Abnormal*, 14.
59. Nicole Jerr, "Pretenders to the Throne: Sovereignty and Modern Drama" (PhD diss., Johns Hopkins University, 2014).
60. Jerr, "Pretenders to the Throne," 121.
61. Elettra Stimilli, *The Debt of the Living: Ascesis and Capitalism*, foreword by Roberto Esposito, trans. Arianna Bove (Albany: State University of New York Press, 2017). In Jarry's play, Ubu progressively imposes a tax on marriage, on remaining single and on death.
62. W. B. Yeats, "The Second Coming," in *Selected Poems*, ed. Timothy Webb (London: Penguin, 1991), 124.
63. See Michael Tratner, *Modernism and Mass Politics: Joyce, Woolf, Eliot, Yeats* (Stanford, Calif.: Stanford University Press, 1995).
64. Hal Foster, "Père Trump," in *What Comes After Farce? Art and Criticism at a Time of Debacle* (New York: Verso, 2020), 32–37. In what follows, I am indebted to Foster's essay, not least for bringing to my attention the photomontage by Mr. Fish with which this chapter concludes.
65. Hal Foster, "Preface," in *What Comes After Farce? Art and Criticism at a Time of Debacle* (New York: Verso, 2020), vii–x, viii.
66. Foster, "Père Trump," 35.
67. Schumacher, "First Night of *Ubu roi*," 68.
68. Rita Felski, *The Limits of Critique* (Chicago: University of Chicago Press, 2017).
69. In an August 15, 2017, news conference at Trump Tower, President Trump stated about the Charlottesville clashes: "You had some very

bad people in that group. But you also had people that were very fine people on both sides." "Full text: Trump's Comments on White Supremacists, 'Alt-Left' in Charlottesville," Politico., August 15, 2017, https://www.politico.com/story/2017/08/15/full-text-trump-comments-white-supremacists-alt-left-transcript-241662.

70. Jean Baudrillard, *Symbolic Exchange and Death*, intr. Mike Gane, trans. Ian Hamilton Grant (London: Sage, 1993), 4.

CONCLUSION

This epigraph is taken from Peter Brook, *The Empty Space* (New York: Touchstone, 1968), 9.

1. Brook, *Empty Space*, 9.
2. Brook, 174.
3. Claude Lefort, "The Permanence of the Theologico-Political?," in *Democracy and Political Theory*, trans. David Macey (Minneapolis: University of Minnesota Press, 1988), 213–55, 225.
4. Carl Schmitt, *The Leviathan in the State Theory of Thomas Hobbes: Meaning and Failure of a Political Symbol*, trans. George Schwab and Erna Hilfstein (Chicago: University of Chicago Press, 2008), 34.
5. Ngũgĩ wa Thiong'o, *Decolonising the Mind: The Politics of Language in African Literature* (London: James Currey, 1986), 37.
6. Ngũgĩ wa Thiong'o, *Decolonising the Mind*, 37–38.
7. Ngũgĩ wa Thiong'o, 42.
8. Ngũgĩ wa Thiong'o, 42.
9. Ngũgĩ wa Thiong'o, "Enactments of Power: The Politics of Performance Space," *TDR: The Drama Review* 41, no. 3 (Autumn 1997): 11–30, 12–13.
10. Peter Brook, "The Language of Stories: Peter Brook Interviewed by Georges Banu," in *Peter Brook and* The Mahabharata: *Critical Perspectives*, ed. David Williams (New York: Routledge, 1991), 45–51, 46.
11. Rustom Bharucha, "Peter Brook's *Mahabharata*: A View from India," *Theater* 19, no. 2 (1988): 5–20, 8.
12. Peter Brook, "Theatre, Popular and Special, and the Perils of Cultural Piracy: Peter Brook Interviewed by David Britton," in *Peter Brook and* The Mahabharata: *Critical Perspectives*, ed. David Williams (New York: Routledge, 1991), 52–58, 56; emphasis mine.

13. Bharucha, "Peter Brook's *Mahabharata*," 18.
14. Joseph A. Schumpeter, *Capitalism, Socialism, and Democracy* (London: Routledge, 1976), 82–83.
15. Bharucha, "Peter Brook's *Mahabharata*," 18.
16. See Antonin Artaud, *The Theatre and Its Double*, trans. Victor Corti (Richmond: Alma Classics, 2013).

BIBLIOGRAPHY

Agamben, Giorgio. *Homo Sacer: Sovereign Power and Bare Life.* Translated by Daniel Heller-Roazen. Stanford, Calif.: Stanford University Press, 1998.
———. "In Praise of Profanation." In *Profanations*, translated by Kevin Attell, 73–92. New York: Zone, 2007.
———. *The Kingdom and the Glory: For a Theological Genealogy of Economy and Government (Homo Sacer II, 2).* Translated by Lorenzo Chiesa and Matteo Mandarini. Stanford, Calif.: Stanford University Press, 2011.
———. "Nudity." In *Nudities*, translated by David Kishik and Stefan Pedatella, 55–90. Stanford, Calif.: Stanford University Press, 2011.
Andersen, Hans Christian. "Kejserens nye klæder" [The Emperor's New Clothes]. In *Eventyr, fortalt for Børn. Første Samling. Tredie Hefte* [Fairy tales, told to children, first collection. Third booklet]. Copenhagen: C. A. Reitzel, 1837.
Anderson, Mark M. *Kafka's Clothes: Ornamentation and Aestheticism in the Hapsburg Fin de Siècle.* Oxford: Clarendon, 1992.
Andrewes, Lancelot. "A Sermon Preached Before His Majestie, on Sunday the Fifth of August Last, at Holdenbie, ANNO DOM. 1610." In *Selected Sermons and Lectures*, edited by Peter McCullough, 178–206. Oxford: Oxford University Press, 2005.
Anglican Liturgical Library. *The Form and Order of the Service That Is to Be Performed and the Ceremonies That Are to Be Observed in the Coronation of Her Majesty Queen Elizabeth II in the Abbey Church of St. Peter Westminster on Tuesday the Second Day of June 1953.* London: Eyre and Spottiswoode, 1953.

Anidjar, Gil. *Blood: A Critique of Christianity.* New York: Columbia University Press, 2014.

Arendt, Hannah. *The Human Condition.* Chicago: University of Chicago Press, 1958.

Artaud, Antonin. *The Theatre and its Double.* Translated by Victor Corti. Richmond, Surrey: Alma Classics, 2013.

Aubrey, John. "Thomas Hobbes, 1588–1679." In *"Brief Lives," Chiefly of Contemporaries, Set Down by John Aubrey, Between the Years 1669 & 1696,* edited by Andrew Clark, 321–403. Oxford: Clarendon, 1898.

Augé, Marc. *Non-Places: An Introduction to the Anthropology of Supermodernity.* Translated by John Howe. London: Verso, 1995.

Augustine of Hippo. *Confessions.* Translated and introduced by R. S. Pine-Coffin. New York: Penguin, 1961.

Bacon, Francis. *Catalogue Raisonné.* 5 vols. Edited by Martin Harrison. London: Estate of Francis Bacon, 2016.

Badiou, Alain. "Gilles Deleuze, The Fold: Leibniz and the Baroque." In *Gilles Deleuze and the Theater of Philosophy,* edited by Constantin V. Boundas and Dorothea Olkowski, 51–69. London: Routledge, 1994.

——. *Pornographie du temps présent.* Paris: Fayard, 2013.

——. *Le Séminaire: Images du temps présent, 2001–2004.* Paris: Fayard, 2014.

Balfour, Ian. "Reversal, Quotation (Benjamin's History)." *MLN* 106 (1991): 622–47.

Balibar, Étienne. "The Invention of the Superego: Freud and Kelsen, 1922." In *Citizen Subject: Foundations for Philosophical Anthropology,* translated by Stephen Miller, 227–55. New York: Fordham University Press, 2016.

Balthasar, Hans Urs von. "Excursus on Brecht and Ionesco." In *Theo-Drama: Theological Dramatic Theory, Vol. 1: Prolegomena,* translated by Graham Harrison. San Francisco: Ignatius, 1988.

Banerjee, Amal. "Rousseau's Concept of Theatre." *British Journal of Aesthetics* 17, no. 2 (Spring 1977): 171–77.

Barish, Jonas. *The Anti-Theatrical Prejudice.* Berkeley: University of California Press, 1981.

Barthes, Roland. *On Racine.* Translated by Richard Howard. New York: Hill and Wang, 1964.

Baudrillard, Jean. *Symbolic Exchange and Death.* Translated by Ian Hamilton Grant and introduced by Mike Gane. London: Sage, 1993.

Bauman, Zygmunt. *Liquid Modernity.* London: Polity, 2000.

Benite, Zvi Ben-Dor Stefanos Geroulanos, and Nicole Jerr, eds. *The Scaffolding of Sovereignty: Global and Aesthetic Perspectives on the History of a Concept*. New York: Columbia University Press, 2017.

Benjamin, Walter. *Arcades Project*. Translated by Howard Eiland and Kevin McLaughlin. Cambridge, Mass.: Belknap Press of Harvard University Press, 1999.

——. *Berlin Childhood Around 1900*. Translated by Howard Eiland. Cambridge, Mass.: Belknap Press of Harvard University Press, 2006.

——. "Berlin Puppet Theater." In *Radio Benjamin*, edited by Lecia Rosenthal and translated by Jonathan Lutes with Lisa Harries Schumann and Diana K. R. Reese, 17–23. London: Verso, 2014.

——. "Crock Notes." In *On Hashish*, edited by Howard Eiland and translated by Howard Eiland and others, 81–85. Cambridge, Mass.: Belknap Press of Harvard University Press, 2006.

——. "The Cultural History of Toys." In *Selected Writings, Volume 2: 1927–1934*, edited by Michael W. Jennings, Howard Eiland, and Gary Smith and translated by Rodney Livingstone and others, 113–16. Cambridge, Mass.: Belknap Press of Harvard University Press, 1999.

——. "Franz Kafka: On the Tenth Anniversary of His Death." In *Selected Writings, Volume 2, 1927–1934*, edited by Michael. W. Jennings, Howard Eiland, and Gary Smith and translated by Rodney Livingstone and others, 794–818. Cambridge, Mass.: Belknap Press of Harvard University Press, 1999.

——. Letter to Gerhard Scholem, January 14, 1926. In *The Correspondence of Walter Benjamin, 1910–1940*, edited by Gershom Scholem and Theodor Adorno and translated by Manfred R. Jacobson and Evelyn M. Jacobson, 287–90. Chicago: University of Chicago Press, 1994.

——. Letter to Gerhard Scholem, September 16, 1924. In *The Correspondence of Walter Benjamin, 1910–1940*, edited by Gershom Scholem and Theodor Adorno and translated by Manfred R. Jacobson and Evelyn M. Jacobson, 246–51. Chicago: University of Chicago Press, 1994.

——. Letter to Greta Karplus, ca. May 26, 1933. In *Gesammelte Briefe*, 6 vols., edited by Christophe Gödde and Henri Lonitz, 4:216–20. Frankfurt: Suhrkamp, 1995–2000.

——. "Main Features of my Second Impression of Hashish." In *On Hashish*, edited by Howard Eiland and translated by Howard Eiland and others, 23–30. Cambridge, Mass.: Belknap Press of Harvard University Press, 2006.

———. "Old Toys." In *Selected Writings, Volume 2: 1927–1934*, edited by Michael W. Jennings, Howard Eiland, and Gary Smith and translated by Rodney Livingstone and others, 98–102. Cambridge, Mass.: Belknap Press of Harvard University Press, 1999.

———. *The Origins of German Tragic Drama*. Translated by John Osborne. New York: Verso, 2009.

———. "Rastelli's Story." In *Selected Writings, Volume 3: 1935–1938*, edited by Howard Eiland and Michael W. Jennings and translated by Howard Eiland and Michael W. Jennings, 96–98. Cambridge, Mass.: Belknap Press of Harvard University Press, 2002.

———. "Surrealism: The Last Snapshot of the European Intelligentsia." In *Reflections: Essays, Aphorisms, Autobiographical Writings*, edited and introduced by Peter Demetz and translated by Edmund Jephcott, 177–92. New York: Harcourt Brace, 1978.

———. "Theses on the Philosophy of History." In *Illuminations*, translated by Harry Zohn, 253–64. New York: Schocken, 1968.

Bennett, Jane. *Vibrant Matter: A Political Ecology of Things*. Durham, N.C.: Duke University Press, 2010.

Bennington, Geoffrey. *Scatter 1: The Politics of Politics in Foucault, Heidegger, and Derrida*. New York: Fordham University Press, 2016.

Bertelli, Sergio. *The King's Body: Sacred Rituals of Power in Medieval and Early Modern Europe*. Translated by R. Burr Litchfield. University Park: Penn State University Press, 2001.

Bevan, Ernest, Jr. "Dialogue with the Self: Paul Valéry and Monsieur Teste." *Twentieth Century Literature* 26, no. 1 (Spring 1980): 15–26.

Bharucha, Rustom. "Peter Brook's *Mahabharata*: A View from India." *Theater* 19, no. 2 (1988): 5–20.

Bloch, Marc. *The Royal Touch: Sacred Monarchy and Scrofula in England and France*. Translated by J. E. Anderson. London: Routledge and Kegan Paul, 1973.

Blumenberg, Hans. "Metaphorics of the 'Naked' Truth." In *Paradigms for a Metaphorology*, translated by Robert Savage, 40–51. Ithaca, N.Y.: Cornell University Press, 2010.

Bodin, Jean. *On Sovereignty: Four Chapters from* The Six Books of the Commonwealth. Translated by Julian H. Franklin. Cambridge: Cambridge University Press, 1992.

Boersma, Hans. *Nouvelle Théologie and Sacramental Ontology: A Return to Mystery.* Oxford: Oxford University Press, 2009.

Borges, Jorge Luis. "Kafka's Precursors." In *Labyrinths: Selected Stories and Other Writings*, edited by Donald A. Yates and James E. Irby, 234–36. Harmondsworth: Penguin, 1970.

——. "The Library of Babel." In *Labyrinths: Selected Stories and Other Writings*, edited by Donald A. Yates and James E. Irby, 78–86. Harmondsworth: Penguin, 1970.

Bourg, Julian. "Translator's Foreword." In Claude Lefort, *Complications: Communism and the Dilemmas of Democracy*, translated and introduced by Julian Bourg, 1–20. New York: Columbia University Press, 2007.

Bradley, Arthur. *Negative Theology and Modern French Philosophy.* London: Routledge, 2004.

——. *Originary Technicity: The Theory of Technology from Marx to Derrida.* London: Palgrave Macmillan, 2011.

——. "Political Theology of the As-If: Freud, Kelsen, Fiction." In *Political Theology and its Discontents: Psychoanalysis, Religion, Politics*, edited by K. Daniel Cho and Boštjan Nedoh. London: Bloomsbury, forthcoming.

——. *Unbearable Life: A Genealogy of Political Erasure.* New York: Columbia University Press, 2019.

Brandt, Reinhard. "Zum 'Streit der Fakultäten.'" In *Kant Forschungen.* Vol. 1. *Neue Autographen und Dokumente zu Kants Leben, Schriften und Vorlesungen*, edited by R. Brandt and Werner Stark, 31–72. Hamburg: Felix Meiner, 1987.

Bredekamp, Horst. *Leviathan: Body Politic as Visual Strategy in the Work of Thomas Hobbes.* Edited and translated by Elizabeth Clegg. Berlin: De Gruyter, 2020.

Brook, Peter. *The Empty Space.* New York: Touchstone, 1968.

——. "The Language of Stories: Peter Brook Interviewed by Georges Banu." In *Peter Brook and* The Mahabharata: *Critical Perspectives*, edited by David Williams, 45–51. New York: Routledge, 1991.

——. "Theatre, Popular and Special, and the Perils of Cultural Piracy: Peter Brook Interviewed by David Britton." In *Peter Brook and* The Mahabharata: *Critical Perspectives*, edited by David Williams, 52–58. New York: Routledge, 1991.

Brown, Tony C. *The Primitive, the Aesthetic and the Savage: An Enlightenment Problematic.* Minneapolis: University of Minnesota Press, 2012.

Browning, Cory Clayton. "'Terror, the Order of the Day': The French Revolutionary Terror and Its Restagings." PhD diss., Cornell University, 2015.

Burke, Peter. *The Fabrication of Louis XIV.* New Haven, Conn.: Yale University Press, 1992.

Burningham, Bruce R. "Jongleuresque Dialogue, Radical Theatricality, and Maese Pedro's Puppet Show." *Cervantes: Bulletin of the Cervantes Society* 23, no. 1 (2003): 165–200.

Canning, Joseph. *A History of Medieval Political Thought, 300–1450.* London: Routledge, 1996.

Cappelletto, Chiara. "The Puppet's Paradox: An Organic Prosthesis." *RES* 59–60 (Spring–Autumn 2011): 325–36.

Castiglione, Baldassare. *The Book of the Courtier.* Edited by Daniel Javitch. Norton Critical Editions. New York: Norton, 2002.

Caygill, Howard. *Walter Benjamin: The Colour of Experience.* London: Routledge, 1995.

Cervantes, Miguel. *Don Quixote.* Translated by Edith Grossman. New York: HarperCollins, 2003.

Cixous, Hélène, and Jacques Derrida. *Veils.* Translated by Geoffrey Bennington. Stanford, Calif.: Stanford University Press, 2001.

Comay, Rebecca. "Benjamin's Endgame." In *Walter Benjamin's Philosophy: Experience and Destruction*, edited by Andrew Benjamin and Peter Osborne, 251–90. London: Routledge, 1994.

Coole, Diana and Samantha Frost eds. *New Materialisms: Ontology, Agency, and Politics.* Durham, N.C.: Duke University Press, 2010.

The Coronation of Their Majesties King Charles III and Queen Camilla. London: Barnard and Westwood, 2023.

Coughlan, Sean. "Sacred coronation Oil Will Be Animal-Cruelty Free." BBC News, March 3, 2023. https://www.bbc.co.uk/news/uk-64836101.

Cowdray, H. E. J. *Pope Gregory VII, 1073–1085.* Oxford: Oxford University Press, 1988.

Cranmer, Thomas. "The Archbishop's Speech at the Coronation of King Edward V, February 20th, 1547." In *Miscellaneous Writings and Letters*, edited by John Edmund Cox, 126–27. Cambridge: Cambridge University Press, 1846.

Critchley, Simon. *The Faith of the Faithless: Experiments in Political Theology.* London: Verso, 2012.

———. *Tragedy, the Greeks, and Us*. New York: Profile, 2019.

Daems, Jim, and Holly Faith Nelson, eds. *Eikon Basilike with Selections from John Milton's* Eikonoklastes. Calgary: Broadview, 2005.

Dante Alighieri. *Inferno*. In *The Divine Comedy*, translated and introduced by Allen Mandelbaum. Berkeley: University of California Press, 1980.

Deleuze, Gilles. *The Fold: Leibniz and the Baroque*. Translated by Tom Conley. New York: Athlone, 1993.

———. *Foucault*. Translated by Sean Hand. London: Continuum, 1999.

———. *Francis Bacon: The Logic of Sensation*. Translated by Daniel W. Smith. London: Continuum, 2003.

———. *Negotiations, 1972–90*. Translated by Martin Joughin. New York: Columbia University Press, 1990.

Deppman, Jed. "Re-Presenting Paul Valery's Monsieur Teste." *symploke* 11, nos. 1–2 (2003): 197–211.

Derrida, Jacques. *The Animal That Therefore I am*. Edited by Marie-Louise Mallet. Translated by David Wills. New York: Fordham University Press, 2008.

———. *The Beast and the Sovereign: Volume 1*. Translated by Geoffrey Bennington. Chicago: University of Chicago Press, 2009.

———. *Glas*. Translated by John P. Leavey Jr. and Richard Rand. Lincoln: University of Nebraska Press, 1986.

———. *Learning to Live Finally: An Interview with Jean Birnbaum*. Translated by Pascale-Anne Brault and Michael Naas. New York: Melville House, 2007.

———. *Politics of Friendship*. Translated by George Collins. London: Verso, 1997.

———. *Rogues: Two Essays on Reason*. Translated by Pascale-Anne Brault and Michael Naas. Stanford, Calif.: Stanford University Press, 2005.

———. "A Silkworm of One's Own (Points of View Stitched on the Other Veil)." In *Acts of Religion*, edited by Gil Anidjar and translated by Geoffrey Bennington, 309–55. New York: Routledge, 2002.

———. "The Theorem and the Theater." In *Of Grammatology*, translated and introduced by Gayatri Chakravorty Spivak, 302–13. Baltimore, Md.: Johns Hopkins University Press, 1976.

———. "Vacant Chair: Censorship, Mastery, Magisteriality." Translated by Jan Plug. In *Eyes of the University: Right to Philosophy* 2, 43–63. Stanford, Calif.: Stanford University Press, 2004.

Descartes, René. *Meditations on First Philosophy*. Translated by John Cottingham. Cambridge: Cambridge University Press, 1986.

de Vries, Hent. *Religion and Violence: Philosophical Perspectives from Kant to Derrida*. Baltimore, Md.: Johns Hopkins University Press, 2001.

Donne, John. "Number 13: Preached at St Paul's, upon Christmas Day. 1628. Lord, Who Hath Beleeved Our Report? *Domine, quis credidit auditui nostro?*" In *The Sermons of John Donne*, vol. 8, edited by Evelyn M. Simpson and George R. Potter, 292–311. Berkeley: University of California Press, 1962.

Dyson, J. P. "The Structural Function of the Banquet Scene in *Macbeth*." *Shakespeare Quarterly* 14, no. 4 (Autumn 1963): 369–78.

Egginton, William. *How the World Became a Stage: Presence, Theatricality, and the Question of Modernity*. Albany: State University of New York Press, 2002.

Elias, Norbert. *The Court Society*. Translated by Edmund Jephcott. Oxford: Blackwell, 1983.

Euben, J., Peter. *The Tragedy of Political Theory: The Road Not Taken*. Princeton, N.J.: Princeton University Press, 1990.

Felski, Rita. *The Limits of Critique*. Chicago: University of Chicago Press, 2017.

Fenves, Peter. "Benjamin Tells a Story." *Los Angeles Review of Books*, September 29, 2016. https://lareviewofbooks.org/article/benjamin-tells-story/.

Flynn, Bernard. *The Philosophy of Claude Lefort: Interpreting the Political*. Evanston, Ill.: Northwestern University Press, 2005.

Forman, Simon. *The Bocke of Plaies and Notes Therof p Formans for Common Pollicie*. Quoted in William Shakespeare, *Macbeth*, edited by Kenneth Muir, xvi. London: Methuen, 1972.

Foster, Hal. "Père Trump." In *What Comes After Farce? Art and Criticism at a Time of Debacle*, 32–37. New York: Verso, 2020.

———. "Preface." In *What Comes After Farce? Art and Criticism at a Time of Debacle*, vii–x. New York: Verso, 2020.

Foucault, Michel. *Abnormal: Lectures at the Collège de France, 1974–1975*. Edited by Valerio Marchetti and Antonella Salomoni. Translated by Graham Burchell. London: Picador, 2003.

———. *Discipline and Punish: The Birth of the Prison*. Translated by Alan Sheridan. New York: Vintage, 1977.

Frank, Jason. *The Democratic Sublime: On Aesthetics and Popular Assembly*. Cambridge: Cambridge University Press, 2021.

———. "Pathologies of Freedom in Melville's America." In *Radical Future Pasts: Untimely Political Theory*, edited by Roman Coles, Mark Reinhardt, and George Shulmanm, 435–58. Lexington: University of Kentucky Press, 2014.

Freud, Sigmund. *Group Psychology and the Analysis of the Ego* in *The Standard Edition of the Complete Psychological Works, Vol. 18 (1920–1922)*. Translated from the German under the general editorship of James Strachey; in collaboration with Anna Freud; assisted by Alix Strachey and Alan Tyson. London: Hogarth, 1955.

———. "The Ego and the Id." In *The Standard Edition of the Complete Psychological Works of Sigmund Freud, Vol. 19 (1923–1925): The Ego and the Id and Other Works*. Translated from the German under the general editorship of James Strachey; in collaboration with Anna Freud; assisted by Alix Strachey and Alan Tyson, 1–66. London: Hogarth, 1961.

———. *Sigmund Freud Papers: Interviews and Recollections, 1998; Set A, 1998; Interviews and; Kelsen, Hans, 1953*. Manuscript/mixed material. Retrieved from the Library of Congress. www.loc.gov/item/mss39990o1500/ (accessed June 4, 2024).

Friedland, Paul. *Political Actors: Representative Bodies and Theatricality in the French Revolution*. Ithaca, N.Y.: Cornell University Press, 2002.

"Full Text: Trump's Comments on White Supremacists, 'Alt-Left' in Charlottesville." Politico, August 15, 2017. https://www.politico.com/story/2017/08/15/full-text-trump-comments-white-supremacists-alt-left-transcript-241662.

Gasché, Rodolphe. "Kafka's Law: In the Field of Forces between Judaism and Hellenism." In "Comparative Literature Issue," *MLN* 117, no. 5 (December 2002): 971–1002.

Gasset, José Ortega y. *The Revolt of the Masses*. 25th anniversary ed. New York: Norton, 1957.

Gaylord, Mary Malcolm. "Pulling Strings with Master Peter's Puppets: Fiction and History in *Don Quixote*." *Cervantes: Bulletin of the Cervantes Society* 18, no. 2 (1998): 117–47.

Genet, Jean. *Le Balcon*. Paris: Gallimard Folio, 2009.

———. "Comment jouer *Le Balcon*." In *Le Balcon*, 7–12. Paris: Gallimard Folio, 2009.

———. "Interview with Hubert Fichte." In *The Declared Enemy: Texts and Interviews*, edited by Albert Dichy and translated by Jeff Fort, 118–51. Stanford, Calif.: Stanford University Press, 2004.

Gliozzi, Giuliano. *Adam et le Nouveau Monde: La naissance de l'anthropologie comme idéologie coloniale: des généalogies bibliques aux théories raciales, 1500–1700*. Translated by Arlette Estève and Pascal Gabellone. Lecques: Théétète, 2000.

Gocer, Asli. "The Puppet Theater in Plato's Parable of the Cave." *Classical Journal* 95, no. 2 (December–January 1999–2000): 119–29.

Goldmann, Lucien. "Genet's *The Balcony*: A Realist Play." Translated by Robert Sayre. *Praxis: A Journal of Radical Perspectives on the Arts* 4 (1978): 123–31.

Gourgouris, Stathis. "The Void Occupied Unconcealed." In *Lessons in Secular Criticism*, 120–44. New York: Fordham University Press, 2013.

Grosrichard, Alain. *The Sultan's Court: European Fantasies of the East*. Introduced by Mladen Dolar. Translated by Liz Heron. London: Verso, 1998.

Grossman, Kathryn M. "Monsieur Teste as Modern Parable." *Dalhousie French Studies* 1 (October 1979): 52–60.

Greenblatt, Stephen. *Renaissance Self-Fashioning: From More to Shakespeare*. Chicago: University of Chicago Press, 1980.

Guilhot, Nicolas. "Automatic Leviathan: Cybernetics and Politics in Carl Schmitt's Postwar Writings." *History of the Human Sciences* 33, no. 1 (2020): 128–46.

Hadot, Pierre. *The Veil of Isis: An Essay on the History of the Idea of Nature*. Translated by Michael Chase. Cambridge, Mass.: Belknap Press of Harvard University Press, 2006.

Hegel, G. W. F. *Phenomenology of Spirit*. Translated by A. V. Miller. Oxford: Oxford University Press, 1977.

———. "The Spirit of Christianity and Its Fate." In *Early Theological Writings*, translated by T. M. Knox, 182–301. Chicago: University of Chicago Press, 1948.

Heidegger, Martin. *The Essence of Truth: On Plato's Cave Allegory and Theaetetus*. Translated by Ted Sadler. London: Bloomsbury, 2013.

Hobbes, Thomas. *The Citizen* in *Man and Citizen (De Homine* and *De Cive)*. Edited by Bernard Gert. Indianapolis: Hackett, 1991.

———. *Leviathan: Or The Matter, Forme, and Power of a Common Wealth Ecclesiasticall and Civil*. Edited by Richard Tuck. Cambridge: Cambridge University Press, 1996.

Honig, Bonnie. "Charged: Debt, Power, and the Politics of the Flesh in Shakespeare's *Merchant*, Melville's *Moby-Dick* and Santner's *The Weight of all Flesh*." In Eric Santner, *The Weight of all Flesh: On the Subject-Matter of Political Economy*, 131–82. New York: Oxford University Press, 2016.

Ionesco, Eugène. *Les Chaises*. Edited by Michel Lioure. Paris: Gallimard, 1996.

———. "'Le Coeur n'est pas sur la main." In *Notes et contre-notes*, 152–61. Paris: Gallimard, 1966.

———. "Lettre à un metteur en scène" (Janvier 1952). In *Notes et contre-notes*, 262–63. Paris: Gallimard, 1966.

———. *Macbett*. Paris: Gallimard, 1972.

———. "Propos sur mon théâtre et sur les propos des autres." In *Notes et contre-notes*, 101–28. Paris: Gallimard, 1966.

———. "Sur la crise du théâtre." In *Notes et contre-notes*, 308. Paris: Gallimard, 1966.

———. "Sur '*Les Chaises*': Lettre au premier metteur en scène." In *Notes et contre-notes*, 257–62. Paris: Gallimard, 1966.

James VI and I. *Basilicon Doron*. In *Political Writings*, edited by Johann P. Sommerville, 1–61. Cambridge: Cambridge University Press, 1994.

Jannarone, Kimberly. "Audience, Mass, Crowd: Theatres of Cruelty in Interwar Europe." *Theatre Journal* 61, no. 2 (2009): 191–211.

Jarry, Alfred. *Oeuvres complètes*. Vol. 1. Edited by Michel Arrivé and Henri Bordillon. Paris: Gallimard, Pléiade, 1972.

———. *Ubu roi*. Edited by Noël Arnaud and Henri Bordillon. Paris: Gallimard, 1978.

Jerr, Nicole. "Exit the King? Modern Theater and the Revolution." In *The Scaffolding of Sovereignty: Global and Aesthetic Perspectives on the History of a Concept*, edited by Zvi Ben-Dor Benite, Stefanos Geroulanos and Nicole Jerr, 340–63. New York: Columbia University Press, 2017.

———. "Pretenders to the Throne: Sovereignty and Modern Drama." PhD diss., Johns Hopkins University, 2014.

Johnson, Samuel. "Miscellaneous Observations on the Tragedy of *Macbeth*" (1745). In *Selections from Johnson on Shakespeare*, vol. 1, edited by

Bertrand H. Bronson with Jean M. O'Meara, 259–60. New Haven, Conn.: Yale University Press, 1986.

Jünger, Ernst. Letter to Carl Schmitt, August 28, 1941. In Ernst Jünger and Carl Schmitt, *Briefe, 1930–83*, edited by Helmuth Kiesel, 127. Stuttgart: Klett-Cotta, 2012.

Kafka, Franz. "Before the Law." In *Complete Short Stories*, edited by Nahum Glatzer and translated by Willa and Edwin Muir, 3–4. London: Vintage, 2005.

———. "The Cares of a Family Man." In *Complete Short Stories*, edited by Nahum Glatzer and translated by Willa and Edwin Muir, 427–29. London: Vintage, 2005.

———. *The Castle*. Translated by Willa and Edwin Muir, with additional material translated by Eithne Wilkins and Ernst Kaiser. London: Secker and Warburg, 1922.

———. "Clothes." In *Complete Short Stories*, edited by Nahum Glatzer and translated by Willa and Edwin Muir, 382–83. London: Vintage, 2005.

———. Entry for June 19, 1916. In *Diaries, 1914–1923*, edited by Max Brod and translated by Martin Greenberg and Hannah Arendt, 156. New York: Schocken, 1965.

———. "The Great Wall of China." In *Complete Short Stories*, edited by Nahum Glatzer and translated by Tanya and James Stern, 235–47. London: Vintage, 2005.

———. Letter to Oskar Pollak, November 9, 1903. In *Letters to Friends, Family, and Editors*, translated by Richard and Clara Winston, 9–11. New York: Schocken, 1977.

———. "The Metamorphosis." In *Complete Short Stories*, edited by Nahum Glatzer and translated by Willa and Edwin Muir, 89–139. London: Vintage, 2005.

———. *The Trial*. Translated by Idris Parry. London: Penguin, 1994.

Kahn, Victoria. *The Future of Illusion: Political Theology and Early Modern Texts*. Chicago: University of Chicago Press, 2014.

Kant, Immanuel. *The Conflict of the Faculties*. Translated by Mary J. Gregor. New York: Abaris, 1979.

———. *Critique of Judgment*. Edited and translated by Werner S. Pluhar. Indianapolis: Hackett, 1987.

———. *Critique of Pure Reason*. Edited and translated by Paul Guyer and Allen W. Wood. Cambridge: Cambridge University Press, 1998.

Kantorowicz, Ernst. *The King's Two Bodies: A Study in Medieval Political Theology*. Princeton, N.J.: Princeton University Press, 1957.

———. *Laudes Regiae: A Study in Liturgical Acclamations and Mediaeval Ruler Worship*. Berkeley: University of California Press, 1946.

Kelsen, Hans. "The Conception of the State and Social Psychology, with Special Reference to Freud's Group Theory." *International Journal of Psychoanalysis* 5, no. 1 (January 1924): 1–38.

———. "The Function of a Constitution" (1964). In *Essays on Kelsen*, edited by Richard Tur and William Twining and translated by Iain Stewart, 109–19. Oxford: Clarendon, 1986.

———. "God and the State" (1922). In *Essays in Legal and Moral Philosophy*, introduced by Ota Weinberger and translated by Peter Heath, 61–82. Boston: D. Reidel, 1973.

———. "Zur Theorie der juristischen Fiktionen. Mit besonderer Berücksichtigung von Vaihingers Philosophie des Als Ob." *Annalen der Philosophie* (1919): 630–58.

Kleist, Heinrich von. "The Puppet Theater." In *Selected Writings*, edited and translated by David Constantine, 411–16. Indianapolis: Hackett, 2004.

Kottman, Paul A. *A Politics of the Scene*. Stanford, Calif.: Stanford University Press, 2008.

Lacan, Jacques. *Le Séminaire. Livre V: Les formations de l'inconscient*. Edited by Jacques-Alain Miller. Paris: Seuil, 1998.

Lacoue-Labarthe, Philippe. "Typography." Translated by Eduardo Cadava. In *Typography: Mimesis, Philosophy, Politics*, edited by Christopher Fynsk and introduced by Jacques Derrida, 43–138. Stanford, Calif.: Stanford University Press, 1998.

Latour, Bruno. "From *Realpolitik* to *Dingpolitik*, or How to Make Things Public." In *Making Things Public: Atmospheres of Democracy*, edited by Bruno Latour and Peter Weibel, 14–41. Cambridge, Mass.: MIT Press, 2005.

Laoutaris, Chris. *Shakespearean Maternities: Crises of Conception in Early Modern England*. Edinburgh: Edinburgh University Press, 2008.

Le Bon, Gustave. *The Crowd: A Study of the Popular Mind*. New York: Macmillan, 1896.

Lefort, Claude. "The Permanence of the Theologico-Political?" In *Democracy and Political Theory*, translated by David Macey, 213–55. Minneapolis: University of Minnesota Press, 1988.

Le Goff, Jacques. "A Coronation Program for the Age of Saint Louis: The Ordo of 1250." In *Coronations: Medieval and Early Modern Monarchic Ritual*, edited by János M. Bak, 46–57. Berkeley: University of California Press, 1990.

Leibniz, Gottfried. "A New System of the Nature and Communication of Substances, and also of the Union that Exists Between the Soul and the Body." Translated by Jonathan Bennett. https:// www.earlymoderntexts .com/assets/pdfs/leibniz1695c.pdf (accessed June 4, 2024).

Lightfoot, Jessica. *Wonders and the Marvellous from Homer to the Hellenistic World* Cambridge: Cambridge University Press, 2021.

Lorenz, Philip. *Tears of Sovereignty: Perspectives of Power in Renaissance Drama*. New York: Fordham University Press, 2013.

Lubac, Henri de. *Surnaturel: Etudes historiques*. Paris: Lethielleux, 2010.

Lucht, Marc, and Donna Yarri, eds. *Kafka's Creatures: Animals, Hybrids, and Other Fantastic Beings*. New York: Lexington, 2010.

Lupton, Julia Reinhard. "The Renaissance *Res Publica* of Furniture." In *Animal, Vegetable, Mineral: Ethics and Objects*, edited by Jeffrey Jerome Cohen, 211–36. New York: Punctum, 2011.

Machiavelli, Niccolò. *The Prince*. Edited by Quentin Skinner. Cambridge: Cambridge University Press, 1988.

Marin, Louis. *Portrait of the King*. Translated by Martha M. Houle, with a foreword by Tom Conley. London: Macmillan, 1988.

Marshall, David. "Rousseau and the State of Theater." *Representations* 13 (Winter 1986): 84–114.

Maturana, Humberto, and Francisco Valera. *Autopoiesis and Cognition: The Realisation of the Living*. Dordrecht: D. Reidel, 1980.

Mazzarella, William, Eric. L. Santner, and Aaron Schuster. *Sovereignty, Inc.: Three Enquiries in Politics and Enjoyment*. Chicago: University of Chicago Press, 2020.

Mehring, Reinhard. *Carl Schmitt: A Biography*. Translated by Daniel Steuer. London: Polity, 2014.

Meier, Christian. *The Greek Discovery of Politics*. Translated by David McLintock. Cambridge, Mass.: Harvard University Press, 1990.

Melville, Herman. *Moby-Dick*. Edited by Hershel Parker. Norton Critical Edition. New York: Norton, 2018.

Melzer, Sara E. *Discourses of the Fall: A Study of Pascal's Pensées*. Berkeley: University of California Press, 1986.

Milton, John. *A Defence of the People of England* [*Defensio pro Populo Anglicano*]. In *Political Writings*, edited by Martin Dzelzainis and translated by Claire Gruzelier, 51–254. Cambridge: Cambridge University Press, 1991.

———. *Eikonoklastes*. In *Complete Prose Works of John Milton, Vol. 3, 1648–1649*, edited by Merrit Y. Hughes. New Haven, Conn.: Yale University Press, 1962.

———. *Second Defence of the English People* [*Defensio Secunda*]. In *Complete Poems and Major Prose*, edited by Meritt Y. Hughes, 817–38. Indianapolis: Hackett, 2003.

———. "The Tenure of Kings and Magistrates." In *Political Writings*, edited by Martin Dzelzainis and translated by Claire Gruzelier, 3–50. Cambridge: Cambridge University Press, 1991.

Montaigne, Michel de. "On the Custom of Wearing Clothing." In *The Complete* Essays, translated by M. A. Screech, 253–56. New York: Penguin, 1993.

———. "On the Inequality There Is Between Us." In *The Complete* Essays, translated by M.A. Screech, 288–99. New York: Penguin, 1993.

———. "To the Reader." In *The Complete* Essays, translated by M. A. Screech, lix. New York: Penguin, 1993.

Moriarty, Michael. *Fallen Nature, Fallen Selves: Early Modern French Thought II*. Oxford: Oxford University Press, 2006.

———. "Imaginary." *Paragraph* 17, no. 3 (1994): 236–43.

Murphy, Kathryn. "Drawing the Curtain." *Apollo* 15 (August 2015). https://www.apollo-magazine.com/drawing-the-curtain/ (accessed June 4, 2024).

Nancy, Jean-Luc, and Federico Ferrari. *Being Nude: The Skin of Images*. Translated by Anne O'Byrne and Carlie Angelmire. New York: Fordham University Press, 2014.

O'Brien, John. "Fashion." In *Montaigne After Theory, Theory After Montaigne*, edited by Zahi Zalloua, 55–74. Seattle: University of Washington Press, 2009.

Ozouf, Mona. *Festivals and the French Revolution*. Cambridge, Mass.: Harvard University Press, 1988.

Pascal, Blaise. "Imagination." In *Pensées*, edited by Philippe Selliers and Gérard Ferreyrolles, 66–73. Paris: Librairie Générale Française, 2000.

———. "Justice." In *Pensées*, edited by Philippe Selliers and Gérard Ferreyrolles. 85. Paris: Librairie Générale Française, 2000.

———. "Pensées Morales." In *Pensées (Éditions de 1670)*, 279. Paris: Flammarion, 1913.
Pascal, Blaise. "Raison des effets." In *Pensées*, edited by Philippe Selliers and Gérard Ferreyrolles, 93–103. Paris: Librairie Générale Française, 2000.
Penney, James. "The Phallus Unveiled: Lacan, Badiou and the Comedic Moment in Genet's *The Balcony*." *Paragraph* 42, no. 2 (2019): 170–87.
Peterson, Erik. "Monotheism as a Political Problem: A Contribution to the History of Political Theology in the Roman Empire." In *Theological Tractates*, edited and translated by Michael J. Hollerich, 68–105. Stanford, Calif.: Stanford University Press, 2013.
———. "Theology of Clothes." In *Selection*, vol. 2, edited by C. Hasting and D. Nicholl, 56–64. London: Sheed and Ward, 1954.
Peterson, Nora Martin. "The Impossible Striptease: Nudity in Jean Calvin and Michel de Montaigne." *Renaissance and Reformation / Renaissance et Réforme* 37, no. 1 (Winter 2014): 65–85.
Picard, Charles. "Le Trône vide d'Alexandre dans la Cérémonie de Cyinda et le culte du Trône vide à travers le monde Gréco-Romain." *Cahiers Archéologiques Fin de l'Antiquité et Moyen Age* 7 (1954): 1–17.
Plato. *Laws*. In *The Collected Dialogues*, edited by Edith Hamilton and Huntington Cairns and translated by A. E. Taylor, 1225–1516. Princeton, N.J.: Princeton University Press, 1961.
———. *The Republic*. In *The Collected Dialogues*, edited by Edith Hamilton and Huntington Cairns and translated by Paul Shorey, 575–844. Princeton, N.J.: Princeton University Press, 1961.
———. *Theaetetus*. In *The Collected Dialogues*, edited by Edith Hamilton and Huntington Cairns and translated by F. M. Cornford, 845–919. Princeton, N.J.: Princeton University Press, 1961.
Pliny. *Natural History Books XXXIII–XXXV*. Translated by H. Rackham. London: William Heinemann, 1952.
Pocock, J. G. A. *Barbarism and Religion, Vol. 4: Barbarians, Savages, and Empires*. Cambridge: Cambridge University Press, 2005.
Przyluski, Jean. "Le Théâtre d'Ombres et la Caverne de Platon." *Byzantion: Revue Internationale des Études Byzantines* 13 (1938): 595–603.
Puff, Helmut. "Waiting in the Antechamber." In *Timescapes of Waiting: Spaces of Stasis, Delay, and Deferral*, edited by Christoph Singer, Robert Wirth, and Olaf Berwald, 17–34. Leiden: Brill Rodopi, 2019.

———. *Waiting in the Antechamber: Towards a History of Waiting*. Stanford, Calif.: Stanford University Press, 2023.

Pye, Christopher. "The Sovereign, the Theater, and the Kingdome of Darknesse: Hobbes and the Spectacle of Power." *Representations* 8 (1984): 84–106.

Rancière, Jacques. *The Emancipated Spectator*. Translated by Gregory Elliott. London: Verso, 2011.

———. "From Archipolitics to Metapolitics." In *Disagreement: Politics and Philosophy*, translated by Julie Rose, 61–94. Minneapolis: University of Minnesota Press, 1998.

———. "The Paradoxes of Political Art." In *Dissensus: On Politics and Aesthetics*, introduced and translated by Steven Corcoran, 142–59. London: Bloomsbury, 2010.

Robespierre, Maximilien. *Œuvres de Maximilien Robespierre*. 11 vols. Paris: Société des études Robespierristes, 1912–2007.

Rousseau, Jean-Jacques. "Discourse on the Origin and Foundations of Inequality Amongst Men." In *The Discourses and Other Early Political Writings*, edited by Victor Gourevitch, 111–231. Cambridge: Cambridge University Press, 1997.

———. *Letter to Monsieur D'Alembert on the Theater*. Introduced and translated by Allan Bloom. Ithaca, N.Y.: Cornell University Press, 1968.

Runciman, David. *Pluralism and the Personality of the State*. Cambridge: Cambridge University Press, 1997.

Santner, Eric L. *The Royal Remains: The People's Two Bodies and the Endgames of Sovereignty*. Chicago: University of Chicago Press, 2011.

Schiller, Friedrich. *Briefe über Don Karlos* in *Schillers Werke, Nationalausgabe*. 43 vols. Edited by Julius Petersen, Gerhard Fricke, Lieselotte Blumenthal, and Benno von Wiese. Weimar: Hermann Böhlaus Nachfolge, 1943.

———. *Don Carlos and Mary Stuart*. Translated by Hilary Collier Sy-Quia and Peter Oswald. Oxford: Oxford University Press, 2008.

Schmitt, Carl. *Crisis of Parliamentary Democracy*. Translated by Ellen Kennedy. Chicago: University of Chicago Press, 1988.

———. "Dialogue on Power and Access to the Holder of Power." In *Dialogues on Power and Space*, edited by Andreas Kalyvas and Federico Finchelstein and translated by Samuel Garret Zeitlin, 23–50. London: Polity, 2015.

———. Entry for November 12, 1947. In *Glossarium: Aufzeichnungen aus den Jahren 1957–51*, edited by Eberhard Freiherr von Medem, 39–40. Berlin: Duncker and Humblot, 1991.

———. *Ex Captivitate Salus: Erfahrungen der Zeit, 1945–1947*. Cologne: Greven, 1950.

———. *Hamlet or Hecuba: The Intrusion of the Time into the Play*. Translated by David Pan and Jennifer R. Rust. New York: Telos, 2009.

———. "Juristische Fiktionen (Uber Vaihinger und die Philosophie des Als-Ob)," *Deutsche Juristen-Zeitung* 18 (1913): 804–6.

———. Letter to Ernst Jünger, July 4, 1941. In Ernst Jünger and Carl Schmitt, *Briefe, 1930–83*, edited by Helmuth Kiesel, 121. Stuttgart: Klett-Cotta, 2012.

———. *The Leviathan in the State Theory of Thomas Hobbes: Meaning and Failure of a Political Symbol*. Translated by George Schwab and Erna Hilfstein. Chicago: University of Chicago Press, 2008.

———. *Political Theology: Four Chapters on the Concept of Sovereignty*. Translated by George Schwab. Chicago: University of Chicago Press, 1985.

———. *Romanticism and Political Form*. Translated by Gary L. Ulman. Westport, Conn.: Greenwood, 1996.

Schnapp, Jeffrey T. *Staging Fascism: 18BL and the Theater of Masses for Masses*. Stanford, Calif.: Stanford University Press, 1996.

Schramm, Percy Ernst. "Die Geschichte des mittelalterlichen Herrschertums im Lichte der Herrschaftszeichen." *Historische Zeitschrift* 178 (1954): 3–24.

———. *Herrschaftszeichen und Staatssymbolik: Beiträge zu ihrer Geschichte vom dritten bis zum sechzehnten Jahrhundert*. 3 vols. Stuttgart: Hiersemann Verlag, 1954–1956.

———. *A History of the English Coronation*. Translated by Leopold G. Wickham Legg. New York: Oxford University Press, 1937.

Schumacher, Claude. "The First Night of *Ubu roi*." In *Alfred Jarry and Guillaume Apollinaire*, 68–81. London: Macmillan, 1984.

Schuster, Aaron. "Beyond Satire: The Political Comedy of the Present and the Paradoxes of Enjoyment." In *Sovereignty, Inc.: Three Enquiries in Politics and Enjoyment*, by William Mazzarella, Eric. L. Santner, and Aaron Schuster, 161–250. Chicago: University of Chicago Press, 2020.

Schumpeter, Joseph A. *Capitalism, Socialism, and Democracy*. London: Routledge, 1976.

Scott, Heidi. "Whale Oil Culture, Consumerism, and Modern Conservation." In *Oil Culture*, edited by Ross Barrett and Daniel Worden, 3–18. Minneapolis: University of Minnesota Press, 2014.

Seltz, Jean. "An Experiment by Walter Benjamin." In *On Hashish*, by Walter Benjamin, edited by Howard Eiland and translated by Maria Louise Ascher, 147–55. Cambridge, Mass.: Belknap Press of Harvard University Press, 2006.

"September 1642: Order for Stage-Plays to Cease." In *Acts and Ordinances of the Interregnum, 1642–1660*, edited by C. H. Firth and R. S. Rait (London, 1911), 26–27. British History Online. http://www.british-history.ac.uk/no-series/acts-ordinances-interregnum/.

Shakespeare, William. *Hamlet*. The Arden Shakespeare. Edited by Anne Thompson and Neil Taylor. London: Bloomsbury, 2016.

———. *King Henry IV, Part 1*. The Arden Shakespeare. Edited by David Scott Kastan. London: Thomson, 2002.

———. *King Henry VI, Part 3*. The Arden Shakespeare. Edited by John D. Cox and Eric Rasmussen. London: Thomson, 2001.

———. *King Lear*. The Arden Shakespeare. Edited by R. A. Foakes. London: Thomson, 1997.

———. *King Richard II*. The Arden Shakespeare. Edited by James R. Siemon. London: Bloomsbury, 2009.

———. *Macbeth*. The Arden Shakespeare. Edited by Sandra Clark and Pamela Mason. London: Bloomsbury, 2015.

———. *Richard III*. The Arden Shakespeare. Edited by James R. Siemon. London: Bloomsbury, 2009.

Shannon, Claude. *The Mathematical Theory of Communication*. Evanston: University of Illinois Press, 1949.

Skinner, Quentin. "Hobbes on Representation." *European Journal of Philosophy* 13, no. 2 (2005): 155–84.

Sloterdijk, Peter. *In the World Interior of Capital*. London: Polity, 2013.

Sofer, Andrew. *The Stage Life of Props*. Ann Arbor: University of Michigan Press, 2010.

Starobinski, Jean. *Jean-Jacques Rousseau: La transparence et l'obstacle*. Paris: Gallimard, 1971.

Steinmetz-Jenkins, Daniel. "Claude Lefort and the Illegitimacy of Modernity." *Journal for Cultural and Religious Theory* 10, no. 1 (Winter 2009): 102–17.

Stimilli, Elettra. *The Debt of the Living: Ascesis and Capitalism.* Foreword by Roberto Esposito. Translated by Arianna Bove. Albany: State University of New York Press, 2017.

Strunks, Emily Jo. "The Metaphors of Clothing and Nudity in the *Essais* of Montaigne." *Romance Notes* 19 (1978–1979): 83–89.

Sylvester, David. *Interviews with Francis Bacon: The Brutality of Fact.* London: Thames and Hudson, 2008.

———. *Looking Back at Francis Bacon.* London: Thames and Hudson, 2022.

Szondi, Peter. "Hope in the Past." In *Berlin Childhood Around 1900*, by Walter Benjamin. Translated by Howard Eiland, 1–36. Cambridge, Mass.: Belknap Press of Harvard University Press, 2006.

Taminiaux, Jacques. *Le Théâtre des philosophes: La tragédie, l'être, l'action.* Grenoble: Jérôme Millon, 1995.

Thiel, Roger. "Architecture." In *Franz Kafka in Context*, edited by Carolin Duttinger, 137–45. Cambridge: Cambridge University Press, 2018.

Thiong'o, Ngũgĩ wa. *Decolonising the Mind: The Politics of Language in African Literature.* London: James Currey, 1986.

———. "Enactments of Power: The Politics of Performance Space," *TDR: The Drama Review* 41, no. 3 (Autumn 1997): 11–30.

Tratner, Michaell. *Modernism and Mass Politics: Joyce, Woolf, Eliot, Yeats.* Stanford, Calif.: Stanford University Press, 1995.

Turner, Victor. *From Ritual to Theater: The Human Seriousness of Play.* New York: PAJ, 1982.

Tynan, Kenneth. *Curtains.* New York: Athenaeum, 1961.

———. "Ionesco, Man of Destiny?" *Observer*, June 22, 1958.

Yeats, W. B. "The Second Coming." In *Selected Poems*, edited by Timothy Webb, 124. London: Penguin, 1991.

———. "The Tragic Generation." In *The Trembling of the Veil*, 157–224. London: T. Werner Laurie, 1922.

Vaihinger, Hans. *The Philosophy of "As If:" A System of the Theoretical, Practical, and Religious Fictions of Mankind.* Translated by C. K. Ogden. London: Routledge and Kegan Paul, 1924.

Valéry, Paul. "The Evening with Monsieur Teste." In *The Collected Works of Paul Valéry, Vol. 6: Monsieur Teste*, edited and introduced by Jackson Matthews, 8–21. Princeton, N.J.: Princeton University Press, 1972.

Vatter, Miguel. *Divine Democracy: Political Theology After Schmitt.* New York: Oxford University Press, 2021.

Vernant, Jean-Pierre, and Pierre Vidal-Naquet. *Myth and Tragedy in Ancient Greece*. Translated by Janet Lloyd. New York: Zone, 1990.

Vieira, Mónica Brito. *The Elements of Representation in Hobbes: Aesthetics, Theatre, Law, and Theology in the Construction of Hobbes's Theory of the State*. Leiden: Brill, 2009.

Wasserman, Dale. "*Don Quixote* as Theater." *Cervantes: Bulletin of the Cervantes Society of America* 19, no. 1 (1999): 125–30.

Weber, Samuel. *Benjamin's-abilities*. Cambridge, Mass.: Harvard University Press, 2008.

———. *Theatricality as Medium*. New York: Fordham University Press, 2004.

Wood, William. *Blaise Pascal on Duplicity, Sin, and the Fall: The Secret Instinct*. Oxford: Oxford University Press, 2013.

Žižek, Slavoj. *For They Know Not What They Do*. London: Verso, 2008.

———. *The Puppet and the Dwarf: The Perverse Core of Christianity*. Cambridge, Mass.: MIT Press, 2003.

Zupančič, Alenka. "Power in the Closet (and Its Coming Out)." In *Lacan, Psychoanalysis, and Comedy*, edited by Patricia Gherovici and Manya Steinkoler, 219–34. Cambridge: Cambridge University Press, 2016.

INDEX

ablution, 60, 64, 66
"Account of Paintings and Colours, An" (Pliny the Elder), 108
Act of Consecration, 57–58, 59, 78, 80
actors, 176, 195, 204, 259n38; political, 8, 10, 25, 164, 199, 203; spectators and, 13–14, 16, 217, 271n7
Adam (biblical figure), 142, 144, 150–51, 154, 156, 158–59, 264n55
Adorno, Theodor, 269n58, 270n73
Agamben, Giorgio, 30, 143, 162, 243n3, 264n58; on children with toys, 191–92, 270n66; glory and, 163, 164; nudity and, 156–57, 264n55; on state of nature, 111, 240n21; theology of clothes and, 156–61
Album of Theatre Programs, The, 196
Alembert, Jean d', 5–6, 11–12, 15
aletheia (unconcealment), 87, 102, 238n9

Alexander the Great, 29, 145
"Altar of the Nation," 241n40
ambergris, whales, 58, 72, 78
Andersen, Hans Christian, 164, 166
Anderson, Mark M., 150, 152, 155
Andrewes, Lancelot, 68
Anglican Liturgical Library, 57
Anidjar, Gil, 70
animals, 48–49, 78, 150, 154–55, 158–59. *See also* whales
Animal That Therefore I Am, The (Derrida), 155
anointment: God and, 68, 71; of Jesus, 65; liquid modernity and, 251n58; in *Macbeth*, 62, 63; machinery, 78–82; in *Moby Dick*, 72–74, 76, 81; of people, 70–71; reverse, 65; royal, 23, 57–72, 76, 78–82, 247n2, 249n18; royal touch and, 63, 249n18; with tears, 65–66; witches and, 249n19. *See also* oil, holy

antechamber: chamber and, 5, 124, 131, 133–34; of Hell, 114; Marquis of Posa and, 123–28, 135; Shuvalkin and, 134–37; unknown, 129–34; waiting in, 115–16, 132–34, 256n9
antechamber of power (*Vorraum der macht*), 5, 115–23, 128, 136
anterooms, 117, 131, 134–35
antespaces, 114, 116
anticamera, 116, 117
anti-Semitism, 160, 180–81
"anti-theater," absurd or nihilist, 28
antitheater of sovereignty: cave allegory and, 1–4; with Commonwealth as dissolved, 9–11; empty space and, 16–22; "Nothing, if you please" and, 11–16; political antitheater and, 10, 12, 16–18, 20; state of nature and, 8–10, 15, 18; theater of sovereignty and, 227, 228; theatricality and, 5–8, 12, 21; with theory, theater and thaumaturgy, 22–25
"Apprendre à vivre enfin." *See* "Learning to Live Finally"
Arcades Project (Benjamin), 90–91, 270n73
arche-writing (*arche-écriture*), 184
Arendt, Hannah, 7–8
Aristotle, 23, 172, 173, 266n8
art, 2, 30, 95, 221, 255n57; Bacon and, 44–46; Baroque, 110, 110–11; of governing, 203; Ionesco and, 28–29; "Réponses à un questionnaire sur l'art dramatique," 271n7; theater as political, 7
Artaud, Antonin, 14, 199, 228, 234, 271n7
art de les gouverner, l' (art of governing), 203
Artificiall Man, 173, 179–84
"Artists Who Painted with the Pencil" (Pliny the Elder), 108–9
as-if, political theology of the, 206–13, 274n46
assujettissement. See subjectivation
Aubrey, John, 116, 256n9
audience, 12, 57, 78, 116, 190, 229; *The Balcony*, 139–40, 166; *The Chairs*, 27–28, 50; critic and, 205–6, 222; spectators, 2–4, 13–14, 16, 45, 50, 62, 133, 140, 196, 199–206, 217, 222–24, 271n7, 272n11; theatrical, 201, 203–4, 220, 233; with *Ubu roi*, 195–97, 199. *See also* crowds
Aufklärung, 38, 87
Augé, Marc, 115–16
Augustine of Hippo, 149, 156, 158–59, 161, 264n55
autodecoronation, 65
automata, 173, 179, 266n11
automate couronné, l'. See "crowned automaton"
automaton, 81, 169, 171, 172, 179, 189
autopoiesis, theory of, 184

Bacon, Francis, 7, 23, 52; empty chair and, 30–31, 51; with

Screaming Popes series, 43–46, *47*, 48–49, 246n49
Badiou, Alain, 95, 141, 163, 260n4
Balcony, The (*Balcon, Le*) (Genet), 139–42, 162–66, 260n1
Balibar, Étienne, 212, 213
Balthasar, Hans Urs von, 52
Banu, Georges, 231
Barish, Jonas, 6
Baroque, 101, 109, 136, 153, 233; allegory, 152; art, *110*, 110–11; façade, 85–87
"Baroque House, The" (Deleuze), 94–99, *96*
Barthes, Roland, 115
basic norm. *See Grundnorm*
Baudrillard, Jean, 224
Bauman, Zygmunt, 60, 78, 251n58
Beast and the Sovereign, The (Derrida), 184, 185–88
Beckett, Samuel, 225, 228
"becoming-audience," of the crowd, 217, 220
"becoming-crowd," of the audience, 204, 206, 220
"becoming-enemy" of the sovereign, 258n35
"becoming-master" of the puppet, 173, 188, 189–90
"Before the Law" ("Vor dem Gesetz") (Kafka), 115, 130–31
"Begriff die Staats und die Sozialpsychologie, Der." *See* "Conception of the State and Social Psychology, The"
behind the curtain. *See derrière le rideau*
"Beim Bau der Chinesischen Mauer." *See* "Great Wall of China, The"
Benite, Zvi Ben-Dor, 20
Benjamin, Walter, 80, 98, 109, 175, 259n53, 266n4, 270n73; antechamber and, 134–37; curtainology and, 87–94, 101, 107, 111, 112; drugs and, 90–94, 112, 253n14, 253n17; historical materialism and, 93, 169–72, 193, 267n16; on Kafka, 129, 134–37, 177; Karplus with letter from, 89, 90, 93, 111–12; on Mussolini and holy oil, 60; Odradek and, 131–32; *Puppenphilosophie* and, 185; puppet theater and, 189–93; Scholem with letter from, 253n14; sovereignty and, 118, 173, 191, 270n62
Bennington, Geoffrey, 136–37
Bentham, Jeremy, 216–17
Bentley, Richard, 72, 80
Berlin Childhood Around 1900 (Benjamin), 89, 90
"Berlin Puppet Theater" (Benjamin), 190
Bertelli, Sergio, 247n2, 249n18
Bharucha, Rustom, 231–32
Birnbaum, Jean, 184
Blair, Tony, 36, 244n22
Blasetti, Alessandro, 272n11
Bloch, Ernst, 93

Bloch, Marc, 59, 249n18
blood, 35–36, 60, 179, 219, 234, 250n29; holy oil and, 66–74; of Jesus, 85
Blueshirts, 219
Blumenberg, Hans, 87, 146
bodies, 8, 46, 48, 51, 123, 182; animal, 49, 158–159; Bacon with, 44–45; castration, 166–67, 235; *The King's Two Bodies*, 30, 62, 141, 248n12; mechanical, 179, 181, 188; naked, 140, 142, 149, 152–53, 157–58, 163, 233; phallus, 106, 165–67, 184; politic, 21, 62, 179, 188, 255n59; royal, 58, 62, 64, 79; solid, 62, 73, 77–79; soul and, 97, 98, 99–101. *See also* nudity
Bodin, Jean, 118
Boersma, Hans, 161
Bonaparte, Napoleon, 203
Book of Proverbs, 83
Book of the Courtier, The (Castiglione), 116
Borges, Jorge Luis, 115, 129–30, 134, 260n56
Bosse, Abraham, 83, *84*, 85–86, 111–12
"bothsidesism," media and, 224
"bourgeois modernity," 177
brand name, 79–81, 252n60
"bread and circus" (*panem et circenses*) spectacles, 203
Brecht, Bertolt, 14, 28, 199, 271n7
Bredekamp, Horst, 85, 255n59
Briefe über Don Karlos (Schiller), 127–28

Brief Lives (Aubrey), 116, 256n9
British Parliament, 38–40, 245n27
Britton, David, 232
Brook, Peter, 14, 23, 225–33
brothels ("house of illusions"), 139–40, 142, 165–67, 260n2
Burke, Tom, 259n38

Caesar, 145
Cage, John, 225
Calvin, John, 144
Capital (Marx), 185
"Cares of a Family Man, The" ("Sorge des Hausvaters, Die") (Kafka), 131–32
Carl Schmitt (Mehring), 257n16
Castiglione, Baldassare, 116
Castle, The (*Schloss, Das*) (Kafka), 132–34, 260n56
castration, 166–67, 235
Catalogue Raisonné (Bacon), 44
cathedral, 28, 29–30, 52
cave, allegorical: Plato with, 1–4, 9, 13, 15, 22–23, 226, 234, 238n9; as theater, 1–4
Cavendish, William, 256n9
Caygill, Howard, 92, 254n19
Celestine V (Pope), 114
Cervantes, Miguel de, 173–78, 190, 267n16, 267n19
chairs, 23, 153; empty, 27–34, 37, 49–55; stools, 30, 33–37, 44, 46, 244n19; vacant, 37–43, 245n31, 245n37. *See also* thrones
Chairs, The (Ionesco), 27–29, 32, 43–44, 50–55, 243n3

chambers, of power, 118, 121, 123, 125, 131, 134, 233. *See also* antechamber
Charles I (King of England), 66–71
Charles III (King of England), 61, 78, 80–81
Charlottesville, 224, 275n69
Chateaubriand, François-René de, 30
Chavannes, Puvis de, 197
children, 132; primal sons, 207–9; with puppet theaters, 189–190; with toys, 190–92, 270n66
Christianity, 86–87, 102–6, 160–61
Chronicles, 68, 70–71
church, 59, 70, 127, 141, 158, 160–61, 229
Civil War (1642), England, 6, 60
Clastres, Pierre, 214
"Clothes" ("Kleider") (Kafka), 151–52
clothing: of Adam and Eve, 144, 150, 154, 156, 158–59; in *The Balcony*, 139; cosplay, 5, 139–42, 163, 167; "The Emperor's New Clothes," 164, 166; as force, 143–50; garments of skin, 150–56; glory and, 162–67; of kings, 145–48; "On the Custom of Wearing Clothing," 143–45; robes, 24, 71, 139, 144, 149, 170, 171; theology of, 156–61
"Coeur n'est pas sur la main, Le" (Ionesco), 28
Coleridge, Samuel Taylor, 204
Comay, Rebecca, 170

"Comment jouer *Le Balcon*" (How to perform *The Balcony*) (Genet), 162
Commonwealth, 9–11, 83, 86, 111, 179–80, 240n21
"Conception of the State and Social Psychology, The" ("Begriff die Staats und die Sozialpsychologie, Der") (Kelsen), 207, 210–11, 272n27
Confessions (Augustine of Hippo), 159, 264n55
Conflict of the Faculties, The (*Streit der Fakultäten, Der*) (Kant), 37, 39–43, 245n31, 245n37
"Conflict of the Philosophy Faculty with the Theology Faculty, The" (Kant), 38–39
consciousness, 93, 105–6, 108, 155, 185
consecration, 57–59, 64–65, 71, 74, 78, 80, 248n12
coronations, 29, 51, 64, 65, 71; in *Macbeth*, 32, 34, 63; royal, 57–59, 61, 72, 76, 78, 80–81, 247n2
cosplay, 5, 139–42, 163, 167
"Country Doctor, The" (Kafka), 152–53
Court Society, The (*höfische Gesellschaft, Die*) (Elias), 141
Cranmer, Thomas, 59–60
creative destruction (*schöpferische Zerstörung*), 228, 232, 235
creaturely sovereignty, 189–93
Crisis of Parliamentary Democracy (Schmitt), 119

Critchley, Simon, 4
critics, 200, 239n11; theater, 177–178, 197, 205–6, 220, 222, 224; Trump and, 220–24
Critique of Judgment (Kant), 42, 245n37
Critique of Pure Reason (Kant), 208–210
"Critique of Teleological Reason" (Kant), 42, 245n37
"crock." *See* opium
Cromwell, Oliver, 66, 116
Crowd, The (*Psychologie des foules*) (Le Bon), 198–206, 271n8
crowds: angry, 195–97, 199, 204, 219, 221–22; audience and, 200–4, 206, 217, 220; "becoming-audience" of, 217, 220; Massentheater and, 199, 203–5, 213, 216, 224; onstage, 197–98, 199; with political theology of the as-if, 206–13, 274n46; psychology, 198–202, 271n8, 274n37; rioting, 195–97, 199, 204, 222; theory, 198–200, 205–6, 210, 216, 220–21, 274n37; Trump(ed), 219–224; with trumped critic, 200, 224; Ubu-esque, 213–19, 221–23
"crowned automaton" (*automate couronné, l'*), 189
cruelty, 45–46, 48, 78, 212, 218, 234, 271n7
cry of the royal blood to heaven, The. *See Regii sanguinis clamor ad coelum*

curtain (*Vorhänge*), 23, 27, 48, 50, 90–91, *110*; *derrière le rideau*, 101–8; fold and, 94–101, 109–12; inexplicability of, 88–89, 94–102, 107, 109–11, 233; on *Leviathan* frontispiece, 83, *84*, 85; political rideaulogy, 88, 108–12; prayer shawl and, 88, 94, 102, 107–9; of sovereignty, 87–89, 109
curtainology (*rideaulogie*), 87–94, 98–99, 101, 107, 109, 111–12
Curtains (Tynan), 243n3
Cyrus the Great (King of Persia), 58

Dadaism, 195
Damian, Peter, 59
Damiens, Robert-François, 213
Dante Alighieri, 113–14, *115*, 116–17, 124
David, Jacques-Louis, 241n40
death, of God, 28
Death Penalty (Derrida), 188–89
debt crisis, 218
Debt of the Living, The (Stimilli), 218, 275n61
De Cive (Hobbes), 9, 83, 240n21
De Civitate Dei contra Paganos (Augustine of Hippo), 158–59
Declaration of Right (1689), 40
Decolonising the Mind (Thiong'o), 229, 241n33
deconsecration, 65, 71
decoronation, 64, 65, 71

Defensio pro Populo Anglicano (*Defence of the People of England*) (Milton), 66–68, 70–71
Defensio Secunda. *See Second Defence of the English People*
Deleuze, Gilles, 23, 49, 88, 101, 109; on Bacon, 44–46, 48; Baroque house and, 94–99, *96*
"De l'inégalité qui est entre nous." *See* "On the Inequality There Is Between Us"
"De l'usage de se vestir." *See* "On the Custom of Wearing Clothing"
democracy, 21, 25, 35, 55, 119, 121, 234; as empty space, 6, 31, 51, 52, 54; liberal, 17, 19, 37, 205, 209, 226; representative, 6, 12–13, 20, 220
Demogorgon ("people-monster"), 52, 217
Derrida, Jacques, 23, 87, 118, 155, 173, 189, 258n26; enemy and, 258n35; *Glas*, 101–6, 164, 265n66; prayer shawl and, 88, 107–9; puppet theater and, 184–88; on Rousseau, 12, 14, 15; on sovereignty, 122–23; vacant chairs and, 41–42, 245n31, 245n37
derrière le rideau (behind the curtain), 101–8
"Des Cannibales." *See* "On the Cannibals"
Descartes, René, 173, 179, 181–82

"Des coustumes anciennes." *See* "On Ancient Customs"
"Dialogue on Power and Access to the Holder of Power" ("Gespräch über die Macht und den Zugang zum Machthaber") (Schmitt), 118–19, 121, 124, 183
Discipline and Punish (Foucault), 213, 216, 266n11
Discourse on the Origin and Foundations of Inequality Among Men (Rousseau), 143
disrobing, 149
Divina Commedia (Dante Alighieri), 114
divisibility, of power, 122, 134
Domine, quis credidit auditui nostro?. *See* "Lord, Who Hath Beleeved Our Report?"
Don Carlos (Schiller), 116–17, 123–29, 135, 259n38
Donne, John, 68–69, 73–74
Don Quixote (Cervantes), 174–78, 190, 267n16, 267n19
Doré, Gustave, *115*
"Double Session The" (Derrida), 102
drape, 83, 94, 96, 97, 99
dream interpretation, 207–8, 209
drugs, 90–94, 112, 253n14, 253n17
dualist theory, 181
Durkheim, Emile, 210
dwarf, 170, 172, 176, 180, 190, 192–93, 267n16
Dyer, George, 44
Dyson, J. P., 32, 34, 35–36, 244n19

economy, 11, 21–22, 48, 226, 233, 234; political, 73, 78, 218; symbolic, 55, 165
Editions L'Arbalète, 260n1
Edward I (King of England), 57
Edward IV (King of England), 62–63
Edward the Confessor (King of England), 63
Edward VI (King of England), 59
Ego and the Id, The (*Ich und das Es, Das*) (Freud), 212
18BL (mass theater event), 272n11
Eikon Basilike (Portrait of the king), 67, 69–70
Eikonoklastes (Iconoclast) (Milton), 67, 71
Elias, Norbert, 141
Elizabeth II (Queen of England), 57–58, 59, 60–61, 80–82
"Emperor's New Clothes, The" (Andersen), 164, 166
empty chairs, 27–34, 37, 49–55
empty place (*lieu vide*), 17, 31, 52, 103, 226, 231
empty space, 10, 40, 55, 235; antitheater of sovereignty and, 16–22; democracy as, 6, 31, 51, 52, 54; theater and, 23, 25, 225–34
Empty Space, The (Brook), 225–27
empty throne, 29–31, 41, 43, 51–53, 233, 243n10
emulsification, 60, 62, 63, 64
"Enactments of Power" (Thiong'o), 230

enchanted head, in *Don Quixote*, 175, 267n16
Endangered Species Act, 81
enemy, 69, 90, 148, 166, 174–75, 258n35
English Reformation, 59–60, 68, 79, 144
Epic (*episches*) Theater, 28, 271n7
Essays (Montaigne), 143
Essence of Truth, The (Heidegger), 238n9
Eve (biblical figure), 142, 144, 150, 154, 156, 158–59
"Evening with Monsieur Teste, The" ("soirée avec Monsieur Teste, La") (Valéry), 185–89, 190, 269n44
Ex Captivitate Salus (Schmitt), 268n36
ex cathedra, 43–49
executions, 66–71, 130, 188–89, 213, 234
Exodus, 85, 102
"Experiment by Walter Benjamin, An" (Selz), 112
Ezekiel 1:1–2, 29

fabrication, 91, 183
façade, 5, 85–87, 97–98
"Faith and Knowledge" (Derrida), 184
Fall of Man, 142, 149, 150, 156–57, 159, 167
Fascism, 60, 161, 219, 224, 272n11
fathers: primal, 208, 222; sons killed by, 207–9

Fenves, Peter, 270n73
Festival of the Supreme Being, 241n40
First Council of Constantinople, 29
Fisher, Geoffrey (Archbishop of Canterbury), 57–58
fold (*pli, le*), 91, 94–101, 109–12, 151
Fold, The (Deleuze), 94–99, *96*
Forman, Simon, 34, 244n18
Form and Order of the Service That Is to Be Performed, The, 57
formations de l'inconscient, Les (Lacan), 163
"form at rest," 45
Foster, Hal, 200–23
Foucault (Deleuze), 95
Foucault, Michel, 95, 117, 173, 199, 213–18, 221, 266n11
fourth wall, 140
France, 53, 141, 145, 161, 178, 195
Francis Bacon (Deleuze), 44–45
François I (King of France), 53
Frank, Jason, 73, 74, 76
Frankfurter Zeitung (newspaper), 191
"Franz Kafka" (Benjamin), 129, 134–37, 177
Frederick the Great (Friedrich der Große) (King of Prussia), 37, 122–23, 173, 266n11
free market, 232
French Revolution, 53, 185, 241n40
French Terror, 126, 201
French theater, 12
Freud, Sigmund, 102, 173, 212–13, 271n8, 274n37, 274n46; group psychology and, 207–10, 216, 220, 222, 272n27; Library of Congress Freud archive, 206
Friedrich Wilhelm II (King of Prussia), 37
frontispieces: *De Cive*, 83; *Leviathan*, 83, *84*, 85–86, 88, 110–12
furniture, 51, 53, 244nn18–19. *See also* chairs
Future of An Illusion, The (*Zukunft einer Illusion, Die*) (Freud), 274n46
Future of Illusion, The (Kahn), 64, 268n39

garments of skin, 150–56
Gasset, José, Ortega y, 206, 271n8
"Geist des Christentums und sein Shicksal, Der." *See* "Spirit of Christianity and Its Fate, The"
Genesis, 70, 142, 144, 150, 154–56, 227
Genet, Jean, 101, 139–42, 162–66, 260n1, 265n66
Geroulanos, Stefanos, 20
"Gespräch über die Macht und den Zugang zum Machthaber." *See* "Dialogue on Power and Access to the Holder of Power"
"Ghost, A" (Benjamin), 89
Glas (Derrida), 101–6, 164, 265n66
Glaucon, 2–3, 9
glory (*gloire, la*), 30, 160, 162–67, 264n58
Glossarium (Schmitt), 86, 98

God, 28, 67, 80, 108, 159–60, 182, 211, 227; with Adam and Eve, 150, 156; anointment and, 68, 71; *hetoimasia tou thronou* and, 29–31; Kant on, 273n32; man and, 85–86, 103–4; "Savage," 197–99, 219–20; soul and, 97, 208–10; throne of, 142, 233
"God and the State" ("Gott und Staat") (Kelsen), 211
Goff, Jacques Le, 29
"Gott und Staat." *See* "God and the State"
grace, 142, 151–52, 157–61, 264n55
"Great Wall of China, The" ("Beim Bau der Chinesischen Mauer") (Kafka), 130
Gregory VII (Pope), 59
group mind, 201, 210, 217
group psychology (*Massenpsychologie*), 207–10, 216, 220, 222, 272n27
Group Psychology and the Analysis of the Ego (*Massenpsychologie und Ich-Analyse*) (Freud), 208, 210, 220, 272n27
Grundnorm (basic norm), 273n33

Hadot, Pierre, 87
Hamlet (Shakespeare), 115
Hapsburg Empire, 124, 129
hashish, 90–91, 93, 253n14, 253n17
Hausmann-era building, 90, 98
Hebrew Bible, 58–59, 69, 142, 181
Hegel, G. W. F., 101, 102–3, 105, 106, 254n19

Heidegger, Martin, 7, 102, 106, 238n9, 240n23
Hell, 113, 114, *115*, 116–17
Henry IV (King of England), 59, 66, 67
Henry IV, Part I (Shakespeare), 62
Henry VI (King of England), 62
Henry VI, Part 3 (Shakespeare), 62–63
Henry VIII (King of England), 68, 116
Herrschaftsarchitektur, of political modernity, 98, 117
Herrschaftszeichen und Staatssymbolik. See Signs of Power and Symbols of the State, The
hetoimasia tou thronou (throne of preparation, empty throne), 29–31
"Hiding Places" (Benjamin), 89
"His Majesty's Most Gracious Speech," 39
historical materialism, 93, 169–172, 193, 267n16
Hobbes, Thomas, 5, 23, 75–76, 87, 234, 239n14, 240n26; in antechambers, 256n9; Artificiall Man and, 173, 179–84; Commonwealth, 111, 179, 180, 240n21; empty space and, 18–22; façade and, 86; influence of, 19; with person as sovereign, 10–11; with political antitheater, 10, 12, 226; political theory and, 6, 8; state of nature and, 8–10, 15, 18, 83, 85, 88, 111, 239n20, 240n21;

theater of sovereignty and, 11,
  185; theatricality and, 7–8.
  See also Leviathan
höfische Gesellschaft, Die. *See Court
  Society, The*
Holbein, Hans, 116
"holder" of power (*Machthaber*),
  120, 125, 135–36
Homer, 2, 13, 266n8
homo artificialis, 11, 182
Homo Sacer (Agamben), 111
Honig, Bonnie, 73, 75, 76
"Hope in the Past" (Szondi), 189,
  269n58
"house of illusions." *See* brothels
How to perform *The Balcony*. *See*
  "Comment jouer *Le Balcon*"
Human Condition, The (Arendt), 7
hypostasis, 209–10, 211, 213, 220

Ich und das Es, Das. *See Ego and the
  Id, The*
Iconoclast. *See Eikonoklastes*
imagination, of crowds, 202–3
"Imagination" (Pascal), 148
Imago (journal), 272n27
"Imperial Message, An"
  ("kaiserliche Botschaft, Eine")
  (Kafka), 130–32
impotence, power and, 116, 119, 121,
  124
"Im Vorraum der Macht" (In the
  antechamber of power)
  (Schmitt), 118
inexplicability: of curtain, 88–89,
  94–102, 107, 109–11, 233; of

empty chair, 54; life of
  furniture, 51; unfolding and, 91,
  94, 95, 109–10
Inferno (Dante Alighieri), 113–14
"In Praise of Profanation"
  (Agamben), 191–92, 270n66
"intellectual aristocracy," 205, 206
Interpretation of Dreams, The
  (*Traumdeutung, Die*) (Freud),
  207–8
In the antechamber of power. *See*
  "Im Vorraum der Macht"
Ionesco, Eugène, 23, 35, 228; *The
  Chairs*, 27–29, 32, 43–44, 50–55,
  243n3; empty chair and, 30–31,
  51
Iron Guard, Romania, 28
Isaiah 6:1–4, 29
Israel, 58
Italian Renaissance, 117
I Will Marry When I Want
  (*Ngaahika Ndeenda*) (Thiong'o
  and Mirii), 229, 230, 241n33

James I (King of England), 10, 34,
  35, 68
James II (King of England), 40
Jannarone, Kimberly, 201–2
Jarry, Alfred, 213, 221, 224, 271n7;
  with rioting crowds, 195–97, 199,
  204, 222; *Ubu roi*, 195–200, *196*,
  204, 214–20, 222, 275n61
Jerr, Nicole, 20–21, 53, 217–18
Jesus Christ, 29, 58, 65, 85–86
Jews, 87, 103, 142, 160–61, 180–81
Johnson, Samuel, 63, 249n19

Judaism, 88–89, 102–4, 106, 160
Jünger, Ernst, 75, 76

Kafka, Franz, 41, 115, 118, 143, 260n56, 263n31, 263n38; antechambers and, 129–34; Benjamin on, 129, 134–37, 177; clothes and, 150, 151–52; garments of skin and, 150–56; Odradek and, 130–32, 136
"Kafka and His Precursors" (Borges), 129–30, 134, 260n56
Kafka's Clothes (Anderson), 150
Kahn, Victoria, 64, 268n39
"kaiserliche Botschaft, Eine." *See* "Imperial Message, An"
Kamīrī īthū Community Education and Cultural Centre, Kenya, 229, 230
Kant, Immanuel, 41, 43, 92, 200, 211, 245n31, 254n19; British Parliament and, 38–40; *Critique of Judgment*, 42, 245n37; democracy and, 52; empty chair and, 30–31, 37, 51; on God, 273n32; with pure reason, 208, 209–10
Kantorowicz, Ernst, 30, 62, 64–66, 141, 161, 173, 248n12, 264n58
Karplus, Greta, 89, 90, 93, 111–12
katapetasma. *See* veils
Kelsen, Hans, 200, 220, 272n27, 273n33, 274n37; legal formalism and, 216; legal normativism and, 119, 121; political theology of the as-if and, 206–13; theater of sovereignty and, 209

Kempelen, Wolfgang von, 171, 172
Kenya, popular theater in, 229–30, 241n33
Kingdom and the Glory (Agamben), 30, 160, 162, 264n58
King Lear (Shakespeare), 62, 228
kings, 53, 173, 228, 245n27; clothing, 145–148; coronations, 59, 61, 72, 76, 78, 80–81, 247n2; in *Don Quixote*, 174–76; execution of, 66–71, 189, 234; holy oil and anointment of, 61–72, 78–81, 247n2, 249n18; philosopher-king, 40, 43, 51; puppet, 189–90, 192; *The Tenure of Kings and Magistrates*, 67, 71–72; thrones and, 31–41, 64, 218. *See also specific kings*
King's Two Bodies, The (Kantorowicz), 30, 62, 141, 248n12
King Ubu. *See Ubu roi*
"kitchen sink" social realism, 28
"Kleider." *See* "Clothes"
Kleist, Heinrich von, 173, 190
Kottman, Paul, 6, 8–9, 239n14, 239n20, 240n26
Krafft-Ebing, Richard von, 141

Lacan, Jacques, 163
Laclau, Ernesto, 40
Laws (Plato), 3
"Learning to Live Finally" ("Apprendre à vivre enfin") (Derrida), 184
Le Bon, Gustave, 198–206, 210, 217, 220, 271n8, 274n37

Lefort, Claude, 16, 18–19, 30, 234; democracy and, 6, 17, 20–21, 31, 37, 52, 55; "empty place" and, 22, 31, 40, 226–27
legal formalism, 200, 216
legal normativism, 119, 121
Leibniz, Gottfried, 94–101, *96*, 109
Letter to Monsieur d'Alembert on the Theater (*Lettre à M. D'Alembert sur les spectacles*) (Rousseau), 5–6, 11–12, 14–15
Leviathan (Hobbes), 5, 7, 185, 190; frontispiece to, 83, *84*, 85–86, 88, 110–12; "Of Persons, Authors, and Things Personated," 8, 240n26
Leviathan: Body Politic as Visual Strategy in the Work of Thomas Hobbes (Bredekamp), 85, 255n59
Leviathan in the State Theory of Thomas Hobbes, The (Schmitt), 10–11, 87, 180
"Library of Babel, The" (Borges), 115
Library of Congress Freud archive, 206
lieu vide. *See* empty place
Lightfoot, Jessica, 172–73, 266n8
liquefaction, 60, 75, 77
liquid modernity, 60, 73, 78, 251n58
littérature engagée, 28
London, theaters closed in, 6, 9
"Lord, Who Hath Beleeved Our Report?" (*Domine, quis credidit auditui nostro?*) (Donne), 68–69
Lorenz, Philip, 65

Louis-Philippe (King of France), 90
Louis XVI (King of France), 189
Lubac, Henri de, 158, 159, 161, 264n55
Lucretius, 145
Luke, 58, 65
Lupton, Julia Reinhard, 30, 34–35, 244nn18–19

Macbeth (Shakespeare), 51–52, 244n16, 244n19, 249n19; anointment in, 62, 63; with king and throne, 31–37; staging of, 34; *Ubu roi* and, 195; Weird Sisters in, 34, 63
Macbett (Ionesco), 31, 35, 53
Machiavelli, Niccolò, 7, 62, 116
machina machinarum (machine of machines), 182–83
machinery, holy oil and, 78–82
machines, 24, 99, 153, 162–63, 184, 214–15; automata, 173, 179, 266n11; automaton, 81, 169, 171, 172, 179, 189; mechanical bodies, 179, 181, 188; mechanization, 11, 182; Schachtürke, 169–72, *171*, 175, 191; state as, 9, 11, 21
Machthaber. *See* "holder" of power
magic-lantern spectacles, 203
magistrates, 67, 72, 149
Mahabharata, 228, 231–32
"Main Features of my Second Impression of Hashish" (Benjamin), 90
Majestic Theater, Brooklyn, 232

Mallarmé, Stephane, 102, 196–97
Maltheus, Jean, 83
marionettentheater, 3, 172, 177–78, 185, 191, 193
marionettes. *See* puppets
marketplace, theater in, 232
Märkisches Museum, Berlin, 191
Marquis of Posa (fictional character), 116, 123–28, 135, 259n38
Marx, Karl, 28, 80, 162, 184–85, 252n60
Massenpsychologie. See group psychology
Massenpsychologie und Ich-Analyse. See Group Psychology and the Analysis of the Ego
Massentheater, 199, 203–5, 213, 216, 224
"mass theater" (*teatro di masse*), 199
master: puppet, 173, 183–84, 188–90, 193, 234; slaves and, 172, 173, 177, 178, 259n53
Master Pedro (fictional character), 174–78, 267n19
Maturana, Humberto, 184
Mazzarella, William, 61, 79
McDougall, William, 271n8
McLuhan, Marshall, 54
mechanical bodies, 179, 181, 188
mechanical Turk. *See* Schachtürke
mechanization, process of, 11, 182
media, Trump and, 222–224
Meditations (Descartes), 179, 181
Mehring, Reinhard, 257n16
Melville, Herman, 60, 72–78, 81–82

Mendès, Catulle, 196
Merleau-Ponty, Maurice, 18
Metamorphosis, The (*Verwandlung, Die*) (Kafka), 155–56
Metaphysics (Aristotle), 266n8
metatheater, of sovereignty, 10, 20, 226
Michelet, Jules, 30
Midsummer Night's Dream, A (Shakespeare), 228
Mieris the Elder, Frans van (1635–1681), *110*, 110–11
Milton, John, 60, 66–72, 250n29
Mirii, Ngũgĩ wa, 229, 241n33
Misanthrope, Le (Molière), 12–13
"Miscellaneous Observations on the Tragedy of *Macbeth*" (Johnson), 63, 249n19
mise en scène. *See* staging
Moby-Dick (Melville), 72–78, 81–82
modernity: "bourgeois," 177; liquid, 60, 73, 78, 251n58; political, 6–7, 19, 51, 98, 117, 142–43, 163, 176–77, 181, 234; theater and, 10, 22–23, 25, 226
Mohammed Ali Bey, 192
Molière, 12–13, 271n7
monad, 96–101, 109
"Monotheism as a Political Problem" (Peterson), 160
Monsieur Teste (fictional character). *See* "Evening with Monsieur Teste, The"
Montaigne, Michel de, 143–50, 261n12
Moreau, Gustave, 197

more than one, no more one. *See* "plus d'un"
Moriarty, Michael, 148
Moses (biblical figure), 85, 142
Moulin, Pierre du, 69–70, 250n29
"movement 'in-place'" (*mouvement sur place*), 46
Mr. Fish, *223*
Munch, Edvard, 46
Muslims, 174, 175
Mussolini, Benito, 60, 198, 199, 219, 272n11
Muybridge, Eadweard, 45

National Socialism, 160–61, 264n58
Natura et Gratia, De (Augustine of Hippo), 159
Naturalis Historiae (Pliny the Elder), 108–9
natura pura. *See* "pure nature"
nature, 97, 143; grace and, 157–61, 264n55; Hobbes and state of, 8–10, 15, 18, 83, 85, 88, 111, 239n20, 240n21; nudity and, 144
Nazis, 48, 118, 160, 161, 257n16
"New System of the Nature and "Communication of Substances and also of the Union that Exists Between the Soul and the Body, A" (Leibniz), 97
New Testament, 58, 142
Ngaahika Ndeenda. *See I Will Marry When I Want*
nihilism, 90–91
Non-Places (Augé), 116
Norman Anonymous, 59

"Nothing, if you please" (*Rien, si l'on veut*), 11–16
nudity: of Adam, 144, 150–51, 154, 156, 264n55; garments of skin, 150–56; Montaigne and, 143–46; naked bodies, 140, 142, 149, 152–53, 157–58, 163, 233; original sin and, 144, 149, 150–51; theology of, 156, 159, 161. *See also* clothing
"Nudity" (Agamben), 143, 156–58

Obolensky, Chloe, 232
O'Brien, John, 144
Observer (newspaper), 28
Odradek, 130–32, 136
offices, 23, 30, 39, 54, 163, 166; bureaucratic, 119; divine, 59, 62, 68, 69; *ex cathedra*, 43–49; Kafka and, 129; Trump unfit for, 223; Ubu-esque, 215
Of Grammatology (Derrida), 12, 14, 15
"Of Persons, Authors, and Things Personated" (Hobbes), 8, 240n26
"Of Simulation and Dissimulation" (Bacon), 7
oil: bodies and, 77; as liquid modernity, 73; war, 58, 79; water and, 64, 66; whale, 73–78, 81
oil, holy, 233; ambergris and, 58, 72, 78; "animal cruelty-free," 78; blood and, 66–74; consecration, 57–59, 64–65, 71, 74, 78, 80; coronations, 72, 76, 78, 80;

oil, holy (*continued*)
  machinery and, 78–82; ritual of royal anointment with, 23, 57–72, 76, 78–82, 247n2, 249n18; water washing away, 63, 72
Old Testament, 85, 180
"On Ancient Customs" ("Des coustumes anciennes") (Montaigne), 144
On Hashish (Benjamin), 253n17
On Racine (Barthes), 115
onstage, crowds, 197–98, 199
"On the Cannibals" ("Des Cannibales") (Montaigne), 144
"On the Custom of Wearing Clothing" ("De l'usage de se vestir") (Montaigne), 143–145
"On the Inequality There Is Between Us" ("De l'inégalité qui est entre nous") (Montaigne), 144, 145–46
opium ("crock"), 90–94, 112, 253n17
original sin, 142, 144, 149, 150–51
"originary technicity," 188
Origin of German Tragic Drama, The (Benjamin), 189–90, 270n62

panem et circenses. See "bread and circus" spectacles
panopticon, 216–17
papal chairs, 30, 44, 46
Paper Machine (Derrida), 184
"Paris, the Capital of the Nineteenth Century" (Benjamin), 89–90
Paris Commune, 201, 205

parliament, 38–40, 119, 121, 245n27
Parrhasius, 108–9, 110, 111
Pascal, Blaise, 144, 146–150
passivity, of crowds, 198
Paul (Apostle), 85–86
Pelagius, 158
"Penal Colony, The" (Kafka), 153
Pensées (Pascal), 144, 146–49
people, blood of, 70, 71
"people-monster." See Demogorgon
"Père Trump" (Foster), 200, 221, 275n64
performance space, 230
"Permanence of the Theologico-Political?, The" ("Permanence du théologico-politique?") (Lefort), 16–17, 30, 55
person: actors and, 8; sovereign, 10–11, 21, 180, 182–83, 207, 226, 240n26
persona, 8, 10, 93, 177–78, 220
personalism, sovereign, 25, 118, 122, 180–81
persona mixta, 59
Peterson, Erik, 156, 160, 161
petite aristocratie intellectuelle, un. See "small intellectual aristocracy"
phallus, 106, 165–67, 184
Philip II (fictional character), 116, 123–28
philosopher-king, 40, 43, 51
Philosophy of "As If," The (Vaihinger), 208, 273n32
Picard, Charles, 29
picture-thinking. See *Vortsellung*

Pius XII (Pope), 160
Plato, 102, 106, 173, 266n8; with cave allegory, 1–4, 9, 13, 15, 22–23, 226, 234, 238n9; with theory and theater, 6, 7
play space, in theater, 225
pleasure, 6, 77, 186
pli, le. See fold
Pliny the Elder, 108–9, 255n57
"plus d'un" (more than one, no more one), 118
political antitheater, 10, 12, 16–18, 20, 226
political art, theater as, 7
political modernity, 19, 51, 181, 234; antitheatrical prejudice and, 6–7; denudification and, 142–43, 163; *Don Quixote* and, 176–77; Herrschaftsarchitektur of, 98, 117
political theater, 22, 31, 55, 125
"political-theological-libidinal economy," 48
political theology, 46, 242n47; as-if, 206–213, 274n46; emulsion of oil and water, 66; Lefort on, 18–19
Political Theology (Schmitt), 118, 119, 160, 180, 211–12, 253n8, 258n26
political theory, 5, 8, 18, 20, 22, 25, 111; antechamber and, 118, 119; "becoming-enemy" of sovereign and, 258n35; detheatricalization of, 19; modern, 4, 6–7, 10, 16, 21, 179, 226, 234; with power and sovereignty, 258n26
political veil, 109, 233

politics: actors, 8, 10, 25, 164, 199, 203; art, 7; economy and, 73, 78, 218; politics of, 136–137; power, 4, 8, 23, 132, 146, 166, 205, 214; puppet show, 23, 173; rideaulogy, 88, 108–12; sanctum sanctorum, 85, 133, 233; thaumaturgy, 5, 22–25, 234; theater and, 12–13
Politics of Friendship, The (Derrida), 122, 258n35
Politics of the Scene (Kottman), 6, 239n14, 239n20, 240n26
Pollak, Oskar, 129
Pompey the Great, 102–3, 105
Pope, body of, 48, 49
pornography, 142, 153, 155, 157, 163
Portrait of Pope Innocent X, 43
Portrait of the king. *See Eikon Basilike*
Potemkin, Grigory (Prince), 134–35, 137
power: anachronistic figures of, 141; antechamber of, 5, 115–23, 128, 136; chamber of, 118, 121, 123, 125, 131, 134, 233; of crowds, 201; "Dialogue on Power and Access to the Holder of Power," 118–19, 121, 124, 183; divisibility of, 122, 134; "Enactments of Power," 230; without glory, 165; "holder" of, 120, 125, 135–36; impotence and, 116, 119, 121, 124; "Im Vorraum der Macht," 118; political, 4, 8, 23, 132, 146, 166, 205, 214; pure core of, 87; sadomasochistic rituals of, 139,

power (*continued*)
141; sanctum sanctorum of, 124; seat of, 5, 23, 51, 52, 121, 124; *The Signs of Power and Symbols of the State*, 141; sovereign, 17, 24, 31, 118, 120, 123, 129, 131, 136, 185, 188, 227, 258n26; speaking truth to, 41, 126, 222
prayer shawl (tallith), 88, 94, 102, 107–9
primal father (*Urvater*), 208, 222
Prince, The (Machiavelli), 7, 116
prison, panopticon as theoretical, 216–17
prisoners, 1–4, 234, 268n36
"prison of the parallelepiped," 48, 49
Proceß, Der. See Trial, The
program, for *Ubu roi, 196*
property, 90, 93–94, 99–101
"Propos sur mon théâtre et les propos des autres" (Ionesco), 28–29
props, 23, 228, 233; robes, 24, 71, 139, 144, 149, 170, 171; toilet brush, 24, 195, 215. *See also* chairs; puppets
Protestants, 68, 93, 104
Proudhon, Pierre-Joseph, 100
psyche, collective, 210
Psychologie des foules. See Crowd, The
psychology: crowd, 198–202, 271n8, 274n37; group, 207–10, 216, 220, 222, 272n27
Psychopathia Sexualis (Krafft-Ebing), 141
Puff, Helmut, 116, 117

Puppenphilosophie, 185
puppet kings, 189–90, 192
puppet master, 173, 183–84, 188–90, 193, 234
puppet show (*thaumata*), 171, 267n16; Benjamin with, 189; cave allegory and, 1–2; of Master Pedro, 174–178, 267n19; political, 23, 173
puppet theater: Artificiall Man, 179–84; "Berlin Puppet Theater," 190; (un)creaturely sovereignty, 189–93; Derrida and, 184–88; Monsieur Teste kills puppet, 185–89; Schachtürke, 169–72, *171*, 175, 191
pure core of power (*reinen Machtskernes*), 87
"pure nature" (*natura pura*), 158–59, 161
Puritans, 6, 9, 68
Pushkin, Alexander, 134

"Question of Dictatorship" (Valéry), 185
"Questions de théâtre" (Jarry), 197

Racknitz, Joseph Friedrich von, *171*
raison des effets, la. See "reason of effects"
Rancière, Jacques, 7, 13, 199, 201
Rastelli, Enrico, 192
"Rastelli's Story" (Benjamin), 192–93, 270n73
realism, 21, 28, 44

"reason of effects" (*raison des effets, la*), 146–47
rebelión de las masa, La. See *Revolt of the Masses, The*
Regii sanguinis clamor ad coelum (cry of the royal blood to heaven, The) (Moulin), 69–70
"Reign of Idiots," *223*
reinen Machtskernes. See pure core of power
religion, 19, 102–4, 106
Religion Within the Limits of Reason Alone (Kant), 38
Rémond, Georges, 197
Renaissance, 116, 117, 124, 144, 158
"Renaissance *Res Publica* of Furniture, The" (Lupton), 244nn18–19
"Réponses à un questionnaire sur l'art dramatique" (Jarry), 271n7
representability, 5, 10, 18, 25, 227; democracy, 6, 12–13, 20, 220; economy of, 11, 21–22, 226, 233, 234
Republic, The (Plato): "antitheatrical prejudice" and, 6; cave allegory in, 1–4, 9, 13, 15, 22–23, 226, 234, 238n9
Revelation, 29, 142
Revolt of the Masses, The (*rebelión de las masa, La*) (Gasset), 206
Rhinocéros (Ionesco), 32, 53
Richard II (King of England), 248n12
Richard II (Shakespeare), 61–67, 71–72

rideaulogie. See curtainology
Rien, si l'on veut. See "Nothing, if you please"
riots, crowds, 195–97, 199, 204, 222
robes, 24, 71, 139, 144, 149, 170, 171
Robespierre, Maximilien de, 189
Rogues (Derrida), 122
Roi se meurt, Le (Ionesco), 53
Roman Catholics, 48, 52, 59, 68, 70, 146; National Socialism and, 160–161; theology, 156, 158, 247n6
Roman Empire, 29, 59, 102–3, 117, 203, 214–15, 264n58
Romeo and Juliet (Shakespeare), 228
Rothko, Mark, 225
Rousseau, Jean-Jacques, 5–6, 11, 17, 75, 143, 239n20; Derrida on, 12, 14, 15; empty space and, 18–21; with political antitheater, 12, 16; republican spectacle and, 14–16, 18, 21, 241n40; with theater and spectacle, 13–14, 15–16, 21
royal coronations, 57–59, 61, 72, 76, 78, 80–81, 247n2
Royal Remains (Santner), 46
royal touch, anointment, 63, 249n18
Royal Touch, The (Bloch), 59, 249n18

sadomasochism, 139, 141, 153, 157
Salmasius, Claudius, 66–67
sanctum sanctorum, 23, 124; Judaic, 88, 89; political, 85, 133, 233; of whale, 75, 77
Santner, Eric, 46, 61, 73, 79, 252n60
"Savage God," 197–99, 219–20

"savages," nudity of, 144, 149
Schachtürke (mechanical Turk), 169–72, *171*, 175, 191
Schiller, Friedrich, 116–17, 123–29, 135, 259n38
Schloss, Das. See *Castle, The*
Schmitt, Carl, 10–11, 75–76, 86–87, 98, 117, 160, 253n8; antechamber of power and, 118–23; anti-Semitism and, 180–81; enemy and, 258n35; on Hobbes and Artificiall Man, 180–84; *Machthaber* and, 120, 125; in military prison, 268n36; Nazis and, 257n16; with political theology of the as-if, 211–12; on power and impotence, 124; *Puppenphilosophie* and, 185; sovereign power and, 118, 129, 258n26
Schnapp, Jeffrey T., 272n11
Scholem, Gershom, 60, 253n14
schöpferische Zerstörung. See creative destruction
Schramm, Percy Ernst, 141
Schumpeter, Joseph, 232
Schuster, Aaron, 61, 79
Scott, Heidi, 76–77
Scream, The, 46
Screaming Popes series, Bacon with, 43–46, *47*, 48–49, 246n49
screams, 51, 52, 154, 195
Seated Figure, 44
seat of power, 5, 23, 51, 52, 121, 124. See also throne
seawater, 60, 64, 65

"Second Coming, The" (Yeats), 219
Second Defence of the English People (Defensio Secunda) (Milton), 250n29
Security, Territory, Population (Foucault), 213
seeing. See *thea*
self-hypostatization, 211, 213
Selz, Jean, 90–94, 112
Shakespeare, William, 23, 52, 115; empty chair and, 30–31, 51; *Henry IV, Part I*, 62; *Henry VI, Part 3*, 62–63; *King Lear*, 62, 228; *Richard II*, 61–67, 71–72. See also *Macbeth*
Shannon, Claude, 54
Shuvalkin (fictional character), 134–37
Signs of Power and Symbols of the State, The (*Herrschaftszeichen und Staatssymbolik*) (Schramm), 141
"Silkworm of One's Own, A (Points of View Stitched on the Other Veil)" (Derrida), 88, 102, 106–7
Six livres de la République (Bodin), 118
slaves, 73, 172, 173, 177, 178, 259n53
"small intellectual aristocracy" (*un petite aristocratie intellectuelle*), 205
social contract, 75–76, 183
Social Contract, The (Rousseau), 12–13, 16
social media, 200

social realism, "kitchen sink," 28
Society Must Be Defended (Foucault), 214
Socrates, 2–3
"sofa government," 244n22
sofas, 44, 153
Sofer, Andrew, 24
"soirée avec Monsieur Teste, La." *See* "Evening with Monsieur Teste, The"
Solomon (King of Israel), 58, 65
sons, fathers killed by, 207–9
"Sorge des Hausvaters, Die." *See* "Cares of a Family Man, The"
soul: body and, 97, 98, 99–101; God and, 97, 208–10; Leibnizian, 96–97; state with body and, 181–82
sovereign, "becoming-enemy" of, 258n35
sovereignty: *The Beast and the Sovereign*, 184, 185–188; Benjamin and, 270n62; with chamber and antechamber, 124; creaturely, 189–193; curtain of, 87–89, 109; defined, 4–5; grotesque, 214, 217–19, 221; marionettentheater of, 172, 191; metatheater of, 10, 20, 226; mise-en-scène of, 22; person, 10–11, 21, 180, 182–83, 207, 226, 240n26; personalism, 25, 118, 122, 180–81; power and, 17, 24, 31, 118, 120, 123, 129, 131, 136, 185, 188, 227, 258n26; "screaming," 52; tears of, 65; of theater, 5, 23, 232–35; theatricality and, 238n11; Ubu-esque, 213, 215. *See also* antitheater of sovereignty; theater of sovereignty
Sovereignty, Inc. (Schuster), 79
"Sovereignty, Inc.," 61
"sovereignty ink," 61
"sovereignty of the audience." *See* theatrocracy
spectacles, 13, 162, 203, 213; *Letter to Monsieur d'Alembert on the Theater*, 5–6, 11–12, 15; "of pleasure," 6; republican and, 14–16, 18, 21, 241n40
spectators (*theorioi*), 45, 50, 62, 133, 272n11; actors and, 13–14, 16, 217, 271n7; *The Balcony*, 140; in cave allegory, 2, 4; in *Laws*, 3; *Ubu roi*, 196; unemancipated, 199, 200–6, 222–24. *See also* audience
Specters of Marx (Derrida), 184
Spelt, Adriaen van der, *110*, 110–11
Spinoza, Baruch, 87, 180–81
"Spirit of Christianity and Its Fate, The" ("Geist des Christentums und sein Shicksal, Der") (Hegel), 102, 106
staging (*mise en scène*), 18–20, 75, 197, 208, 227, 229; Brook with Shakespeare plays, 228; Foucault with, 213; of *Macbeth*, 34; of modern political power, 23; political puppet theater, 192; of sovereignty, 22
Staging Fascism (Schnapp), 272n11
Starobinski, Jean, 16

state, 203; body and soul of, 181–82; church and, 59, 127, 160–61; "The Conception of the State and Social Psychology," 207, 210–11, 272n27; dualist theory of, 181; God and, 209, 211; *The Leviathan in the State Theory of Thomas Hobbes*, 10–11, 87, 180; as machine, 9, 11, 21; parliament, 38–40, 119, 121, 245n27; *The Signs of Power and Symbols of the State*, 141; "sofa government," 244n22

state of nature, Hobbes and, 8–10, 15, 18, 83, 85, 88, 111, 239n20, 240n21

Stimilli, Elettra, 218, 275n61

stools, 30, 33–37, 44, 46, 244n19

Streit der Fakultäten, Der. See Conflict of the Faculties, The

Study After Velázquez's Portrait of Pope Innocent X, 45, 47, 48–49

subjectivation (*assujettissement*), 95, 220

superego (*Über-Ich, das*), 212

Super-Human (*Über-Mensch*), 183

"Sur la crise du théâtre" (Ionesco), 31

Surnaturel (Lubac), 161

"Surrealism" (Benjamin), 92–93

Sylvester, David, 44

Symons, Arthur, 196

Szondi, Peter, 189, 269n58

tabernacle, 58, 85, 86

Taine, Hippolyte, 271n8

tallith. *See* prayer shawl

Tarde, Gabriel, 271n8

tears, 60, 62, 65–66, 69, 105

teatro di masse. See "mass theater"

temple, 58, 85, 87, 88, 102, 104–6

Tenure of Kings and Magistrates, The (Milton), 67, 71–72

"Teste cycle," 269n44

thauma ("wonder"), 3, 172

thaumata. See puppet show

thea (seeing), 1, 4, 6

Theaetetus (Plato), 3, 266n8

theater (*theatron*): "anti-theater," 28; cave as, 1–4; critic, 52, 177–78, 197, 205–6, 220, 222, 224; of cruelty, 46, 48; curtains in, 27; empty space and, 23, 25, 225–34; Epic, 28, 271n7; fourth wall, 140; French, 12; Kenya and popular, 229–30, 241n33; *Letter to Monsieur d'Alembert on the Theater*, 5–6, 11–12, 14–15; London with closing of, 6, 9; marionette, 23; in marketplace, 232; "mass," 199; Massentheater, 199, 203–5, 213, 216, 224; modern, 22–23, 25, 226; performance space, 230; play space in, 225; political, 22, 31, 55, 125; as political art, 7; political theory and, 4, 5; politics and, 12–13; premodern, 10; "Questions de théâtre," 197; sovereignty of, 5, 23, 232–35; spectacle and, 13–14, 15–16, 21; "Sur la crise du théâtre," 31; theory, thaumaturgy and, 22–25; theory and, 3–6, 7;

truth in, 226. *See also* antitheater of sovereignty; puppet theater

theater of sovereignty: antitheater and, 227, 228; Benjamin and, 173, 191; defined, 4; Foucault and, 216; Hobbes and, 11, 185; Kelsen and, 209; minimalist, 3, 15; modern, 15, 18, 22–23, 25, 226; political theory and, 6, 10, 22, 234; Shakespeare and, 62; sovereignty of theater and, 5, 23, 232–35

Theater of the Absurd, 27–28, 32, 195, 243n3

Théâtre de l'Oeuvre, Paris, 195, 197

Theatre of Cruelty, 234, 271n7

theatricality, 140, 213, 214, 240n23; antitheater of sovereignty and, 5–8, 12, 21; sovereignty and, 238n11

theatricalize, 18, 200, 201

theatrocracy (*theatrokratia*, "sovereignty of the audience"), 2–3, 201

theatrokratia. *See* theatrocracy

theatron. *See* theater

theology: of clothes, 156–61; "The Conflict of the Philosophy Faculty with the Theology Faculty," 38–39; dwarf of, 180, 267n16; "The Permanence of the Theologico-Political," 16–17, 30, 55; political, 18–19, 46, 66, 242n47; "political-theological-libidinal" economy, 48; *Political Theology*, 118–19, 253n8, 253n26; Roman Catholic, 156, 158, 247n6

"Theology of Clothes" (Peterson), 156

theōria. *See* theory

theorioi. *See* spectators

theory (*theōria*), 2; *Leviathan and the State Theory of Thomas Hobbes*, 10–11, 87, 180; theater, thaumaturgy and, 22–25; theater and, 3–6, 7. *See also* political theory

"Theses on the Philosophy of History" (Benjamin), 169–70, 172, 175, 177, 190, 192–93

Thiong'o, Ngũgĩ wa, 14, 229–31, 241n33

throne of preparation. *See hetoimasia tou thronou*

thrones, 24, 49, 57, 75; empty, 29–31, 41, 43, 51–53, 233, 243n10; of God, 142, 233; kings and, 31–41, 64, 218; papal, 46; royal, 23, 30, 31, 34, 35, 37; seat of power, 5, 23, 51, 52, 121, 124

"time machine," 24

Tocqueville, Alexis de, 30

toilet brush, 24, 195, 215

"To Speculate—on Freud" (Derrida), 102

Totem and Taboo (Freud), 208

"To the Reader" (Montaigne), 143

toys, children with, 190–92, 270n66

"Transcendental Dialectic" (Kant), 273n32

Trauerspiel, 135, 173, 189, 191

Traumdeutung, Die. See
    Interpretation of Dreams, The
Tree of Liberty, 241n40
Trembling of the Veil, The (Yeats),
    196–97, 219
Trial, The (*Proceß, Der*) (Kafka),
    143, 150–55, 263n31
Trompe-l'oeil Still Life with a Flower
    Garland and a Curtain, 110–11
Trump, Donald, 140, 198, 223; on
    Charlottesville, 224, 275n69;
    "Père Trump," 200, 221, 224,
    275n64; popularity of, 221–22;
    "Reign of Idiots," 223;
    Trump(ed) crowds, 219–24;
    "Ubu Trump" meme, 221
trumped critic, 200, 224
truth, 226, 268n39; *aletheia*, 87, 102,
    238n9; to power, 41, 126, 222;
    theory of, 87, 104, 240n23
Tynan, Kenneth, 28, 54, 243n3

Über-Ich, das. See superego
Über-Mensch. See Super-Human
Ubu-esque, 213–19, 221–23
Ubu roi (*King Ubu*) (Jarry),
    195–200, *196*, 204, 214–20, 222,
    275n61
"Ubu Trump" meme, 221
Ueber Den Schachspieler Des
    Herrn Von Kempelen Und
    Dessen Nachbildung, 171
unconcealment. *See aletheia*
unfolding, 91, 94, 95, 109–10
universalism, 231
university: chair, 30, 37; Kant on,
    38, 39

unveiling, 87, 102, 106–7, 153
Urvater. See primal father

"Vacant Chair" (Derrida), 41–42,
    245n31, 245n37
Vaihinger, Hans, 208, 212,
    273nn32–33, 274n46
Valéry, Paul, 185–91, 269n44
Varela, Francisco, 184
veils (*katapetasma*), 23, 108, 163, 210;
    Christianity, 86, 87, 102, 103,
    105; Judaism, 105, 106; political,
    109, 233; of tabernacle, 85, 86; of
    Temple, 85, 87, 88, 102, 104; *The*
    Trembling of the Veil, 196–97,
    219; unveiling, 87, 102, 106–7,
    153. *See also* curtains
Velázquez, Diego, 43, 45, *47*, 48–49
Verlaine, Paul, 197
Verwandlung, Die. See
    Metamorphosis, The
vestibules, 114, 116–17, 129
victory, 170, 175
Virgil, 114, *115*
visibility, 10, 87
volonté de tous. See "will of all, the"
Vor dem Gesetz". See "Before the
    Law"
Vorhänge. See curtain
Vorraum der macht. See
    antechamber of power
Vortsellung (picture-thinking), 202–3
Vries, Hent de, 40, 42–43

waiting, in antechambers, 115–16,
    132–34, 256n9
Walter Benjamin (Caygill), 254n19

Wamba (Visigothic king), 59, 60
water: blood and, 73; holy oil washing away, 63, 72; oil and, 64, 66; seawater, 60, 64, 65; tears, 60, 62, 65–66, 69, 105
Weird Sisters (fictional characters), 34, 63
Weltbildes. See "world-picture"
whales: ambergris, 58, 72, 78; oil, 73–78, 81; sanctum sanctorum of, 75, 77; sperm, 61, 72, 76, 81. See also *Moby-Dick*
What Comes After Farce? (Foster), 221
William III (King of England), 40
"willing suspension of disbelief," 204
"will of all, the" (*volonté de tous*), 16
witchcraft, 63
witches, 34, 63, 249n19
"woke capitalism," 78

Wöllner, Johann Christoph von, 37–38
"wonder." See *thauma*
Wonders and the Marvellous from Homer to the Hellenistic World (Lightfoot), 266n8
"world-picture" (*Weltbildes*), 240n23

Yeats, W. B., 196–200, 219–21
Yuran, Noam, 252n60

Zadok (priest), 57, 58, 65
Zeit, Die (newspaper), 118
Zeno's arrow, 134, 260n56
Zeuxis, 108–9
Žižek, Slavoj, 52
Zukunft einer Illusion, Die. See *Future of An Illusion, The*
Zupančič, Alenka, 166
"Zur Theorie der juristischen Fiktionen" (Kelsen), 273n33

Printed in the USA
CPSIA information can be obtained
at www.ICGtesting.com
JSHW020330270924
70503JS00001B/2